The construction of public opinion in a digital age

Manchester University Press

The construction of public opinion in a digital age

Catherine Happer

MANCHESTER UNIVERSITY PRESS

Copyright © Catherine Happer 2024

The right of Catherine Happer to be identified as the author of this work has been asserted in accordance with the Copyright, Designs and Patents Act 1988.

Published by Manchester University Press
Oxford Road, Manchester, M13 9PL

www.manchesteruniversitypress.co.uk

British Library Cataloguing-in-Publication Data
A catalogue record for this book is available from the British Library

ISBN 978 1 5261 8022 3 hardback

First published 2024

The publisher has no responsibility for the persistence or accuracy of URLs for any external or third-party internet websites referred to in this book, and does not guarantee that any content on such websites is, or will remain, accurate or appropriate.

Typeset
by New Best-set Typesetters Ltd

Contents

Acknowledgements	*page* vi
Introduction	1
1 The disconnect: mis-managing public trust	23
2 Filtering for opinion: a new conceptual model	49
3 Class, education and media cultures: 'them' versus 'us'	73
4 The new gatekeepers of digital content and opinion	96
5 Climate, COVID-19 and the cost of living: getting up close to global crises	120
Conclusion	143
Appendix: empirical studies and datasets, 2011–2020	159
Bibliography	166
Index	192

Acknowledgements

This book draws on over a decade of research and scholarship and, as I most often work in collaboration with other researchers, there is a very long list of people to whom I owe a debt of gratitude. I'll start with an apology to all those I've forgotten!

I first owe thanks to all those involved in the Glasgow University Media Group, my intellectual home and also a place where many friendships have been fostered over the years. Most importantly this includes the previous director, the late Greg Philo. As much as I learned from Greg formally as he guided me though the early studies documented in this book, I learned a good deal more from our endless discussions about the state of the world in the GUMG office. At varying times, we'd be joined by Alan MacLeod, Emma Briant, Alison Eldridge, Giuliana Tiripelli and Cairsti Russell. Particular debt is owed to the late Professor John Eldridge, who, like Greg, possessed a very casual way of imparting great wisdom over coffee. Both are sorely missed. More recently, the GUMG has been made up of a new collection of colleagues and friends – Beth Pearson, Hayes Mabweazara, Catriona Forrest, Dominic Hinde, Ana Langer, Isaac Hoff, Paul Reilly, Lluis deNadal, Yu Sun and Betty Ferrari – and more recent debates on, for example, the cost-of-living crisis have also made their way into the pages of this book.

Other collaborations have been invaluable too, in the practicalities of collecting data as well as formulating ideas – and thanks particularly to Andy Hoskins and William Merrin, and Antony Froggatt and Laura Wellesley and colleagues at Chatham House. Tim Storer always provides a very welcome interdisciplinary perspective. Thanks also to Fergus McNeill and Paul McGuinness for their work on the crime and media study, and to all of those people who helped with the organisation of the focus groups, with special mention to Daniela Latina, Martin Brocklebank and John Mark Philo. Richard Black and James Painter have also been very generous with sharing their expertise on climate change and media.

I'm also very grateful to colleagues in Sociology at Glasgow, who are not only a very nice bunch of people but very supportive of any intellectual endeavour. Special thanks to Teresa Piacentini, Les Back, who cleared space in my workload for me to write, and Andy Smith for the many years of encouragement and support.

I further want to thank all the staff at Manchester University Press and particularly Shannon Kneis, who have made publishing this book a very pleasant experience, as well as Kate Wright and Giuliana Tiripelli (again), who read drafts of this book and offered detailed and constructive comments. Thanks too to the various research funders which made the research possible: the UK Energy Research Centre (UKERC), Glasgow City Council, the Avatar Alliance Foundation and the Engineering and Physical Sciences Research Council (EPSRC).

Finally to the most important people of all: Aidan and Roddy, my mum and dad and all my family and close friends. And especially Matt – everything I do is better because he is there for me. Thanks so much.

Introduction

In a digital media world in which propaganda, misinformation and conspiracy theories thrive and it's increasingly difficult to assert what is true and what is false, what is credible and what is not, on 23 March 2020 the UK government gave an order, and almost everyone got the message: the country was in lockdown. This was in part because consistent information spread across diverse and multiple sources, but also because people looked out of their windows, the streets were empty, the shops were shut, and there were very few cars on the road. Lived experience and repeated observation are an enduring approach to formulating our beliefs and understanding.

But the further we move away from lived experience, as is increasingly the case through our immersion in digital media environments, the more we're forced to draw on alternative methods. So while most didn't dispute that the country was in lockdown, some people believed that COVID-19, the reason for the lockdown, was a hoax, and others believed that it was an attack on human rights, while others stayed in their homes in fear and didn't even take the daily walk in spite of not being in a risk category. But how do people come to hold such different positions, and what is the role of media and information in the shaping of public opinion and belief? More crucially, what might be the societal impacts of the opinions and beliefs that people come to hold, and, as a consequence, what can these tell us about the power of contemporary media?

If this once was a question of different interpretations of the same information in a narrow media landscape – where traditional news broadcasts were watched by a majority of households live across a nation – it's much more complex now with the motivations for and practices of seeking out information a key element of consideration. It must also be looked at in a context in which questions of 'truth' and 'trust' and their relation to belief and our broader value systems are being reworked, and the technological infrastructure is changing how we come to know about things, assess expertise and share knowledge.

In exploring these questions, this book draws on a series of qualitative research studies conducted over ten years in the UK, with supplements in the US, which explore the formation and development of public opinion across topics which are the subject of political, social, scientific and other public discourses and which interact to construct contested spaces. Taken together, these studies represent a significant body of data across many hours of discussion with participants from a diversity of socio-economic and geographical backgrounds. It examines the ways in which information is negotiated and assessed as trusted and credible, and how this is absorbed into existing value and belief systems to shape thought and opinion. The conditions under which people select, negotiate or reject media messages when there are a range of alternatives to choose from are, then, a key focus. From this body of evidence, the book presents a new model for understanding the processes by which media interact with a range of other filters to produce patterns of opinion which can be mapped across demographics, social contexts, identities and modes of engagement.

The contextualisation of these processes in systems of media, communications and political decision-making in which public opinion is intricately and centrally implicated in social change is, however, of equal importance here. So this empirical model of public opinion formation, and its exploration of why people may come to hold particular positions, must be understood within its socio-historical location. Beginning in 2011, the period of research is one of significant social and political change and covers Brexit, the election of Donald Trump as US president, Covid and increasingly evidenced climate impacts. A central argument is that, in this time, we have seen the emergence of a 'disconnect' between mainstream media, as the primary mechanism for promoting the promises and solutions of neoliberalism, and people's real-world experiences of the outcomes that the system actually produces. This is experienced to different degrees by different groups in society – which relate to questions of class, education, age and so on, though not in simple ways as I will show – and the extent to which people seek out the alternative sources of information now made available by digital technologies also varies a great deal. Those who experience the feelings of disaffection and powerlessness produced by this gap between promise and reality most intensely are likely to be pushed furthest away from mainstream media which no longer speak *to* them or *for* them, while some will avoid news altogether (Edgerly, 2022; Newmann et al., 2023).

In this period we've witnessed the social contract between professional journalists and the public which broadly functioned in the twentieth century increasingly severed. This contract was founded on trust in the former to produce an 'objective' – or at least superior – version of events, and this allowed for a leap of faith in respect of information on those things that the public themselves would not directly experience or fully understand. While journalism arguably *managed* public opinion more than it *represented* it, and certainly was not in the business of simply reporting 'truth', news media played an important role in facilitating a shared orientation point around a broadly consensual understanding of what was going on in the world and how we would expect it to be. The collapse in trust and the turn to digital alternatives, primarily social media, lead to an atomisation of thought and belief and a set of newly constructed and fast-moving opinion communities, which, as I will argue, enable new, less directly visible agents to exert control in respect of what people think and the ideas they hold. While the argument here is that trust in journalism was squandered rather than stolen away, this erosion of journalism, what Daniel Kreiss (2017: 445) describes as the 'core communicative institution of democracy', signals a loss of something that has significant societal value.

Here I use the term 'management of public opinion' in respect of the aim to direct (or dominate) the circulation of ideas which hold influence in the culture, and to steer that influence to particular ends. But I offer a nuanced perspective on the management of opinion – in that, yes, it should be seen as a central weapon in the exercise of power, but it can also be a valuable tool for those who wish to drive positive outcomes. In fact, I would argue that such a positive managing role is essential in a functioning democracy in order to produce some sort of collective sense of what should be done for the public good. This is particularly the case in what have become increasingly crisis-prone societies – a good illustration of this crucial role in managing public understanding being the media's promotion of public health guidance during the pandemic. More generally, I would argue, as an event which accelerated and intensified all the existing communicative processes in democratic societies – almost a test case in a highly controlled environment, if you like – this unique period in public life offers a lot for media scholars to learn from.

In this focus, I engage with a long-standing debate within media scholarship on the way we should conceptualise the role and nature of 'public opinion' within capitalist democracies. A fundamental question here is the degree to which 'public opinion' is a product of persuasive communications or propaganda, or might in any way represent organic or independent thought. In response to this question, Herman and Chomsky (1988), for example, present a structural argument in which the manufacture of consent is largely achieved by corporate media whose design purpose is to keep the public ignorant of what is actually going on and to minimise public resistance. Much earlier, in 1922, Walter Lippmann (2010) offered a similar if more nuanced analysis in which public opinion is formed through 'the triangular relationship' between social experience, forms of communication, and 'the stored up images, the preconceptions, and prejudices which interpret, fill them out, and in their turn powerfully direct [...] vision itself' (2010: 21). For the most part, people are reliant upon the elites who control the communications environment, because they themselves are limited in experience, in expertise and in imagination.

Lippmann offered this as a critique of representative democracies which orientate decision-making around this highly managed form of 'public opinion'. Stuart Hall (1973), writing decades later, developed a model in which media become powerful through a process of decoding – a largely subconscious recognition of reference points, symbols and cultural ideas – which legitimises the messages communicated. These arguments are supported by a historical body of evidence which shows that the media broadly set the parameters within which issues are considered (or marginalised) and how much public importance is attributed to them.

Both of these analyses however, while focused on the power of media and communications to steer public attention and belief, crucially leave space for thought and opinion-forming independent of what circulates in the public sphere. Hall talked about negotiation and resistance to media ideology on the basis of access to alternative forms of knowledge, while Lippmann referred to 'blind spots' which emerge when the narratives promoted have no anchor in the non-media experience of life. At these points, other influences – such as the communities of knowledge and belief we physically exist in – interact with experience to help people make sense of things. As articulated by the Russian literary critic Mikhail Bakhtin, our words and our framings are always 'half-ours and half-someone else's' (quoted in Strauss, 2014: 15). As our opinions and ideas are constructed through the interaction of a range of different influences, of which media are one (albeit an important one), I have chosen the term 'management' rather than terms such as 'manufacture' which may embed the assumption that there is nothing there to begin with (although 'public opinion' also operates as a discursive mechanism in journalism and political communications, and I will discuss this later in this Introduction).

I use the term 'mis-management' to refer to points where attempts to control opinion or public thought have produced unpredictable or unwanted outcomes. These may be rooted in moments where any anchor in the non-media experience of life has been lost, where trust has evaporated or where there is a conflict with value systems or collective understandings of experience. It is in these moments of (dis)connection that media messaging can give life to unexpected beliefs and ideas – and as I will chart, where this is widely experienced, this 'disconnect' can itself become a force in political and societal change. This can work to expose abuses of power and the injustices of the system, and in some cases it may pose a real threat to stability and public well-being. In either instance it can remove people from a more centred culture, including the conventional politics of policy and action.

I extend the term 'management' to the parallel process taking place in social media cultures in which users endlessly manage public opinion about themselves and in their interests. The capacity of individual or a collective of ordinary users to manage their own reputations and/or the dissemination of their opinions is determined by their profile, their reach and the access of others to alternative knowledge and experience with which to form their views. In some cases, these processes can and do have significant implications for which ideas and sources are seen as credible and hold currency. However, they take place in broader social media cultures which are themselves heavily managed by platform ownership and design, algorithms, content moderation, state legislation and other forms of power, also in their own – and much better resourced – interests.

This terminology and approach opens up the question of how much and at which moments opinion is managed by our media culture. Those with the greatest access to media and resources still tend to manage public thought in their favour – this is what Antonio Gramsci (1971) described as cultural hegemony – though what individuals do with information can be unpredictable in a fragmented digital media environment. Ultimately any real threat to the existing order will always be met with attempts to accommodate resistance into systems of power as hegemony is reworked. But failures to manage public opinion open up opportunities for social change. Identifying where those opportunities might emerge is an important aim of the empirical work documented in these chapters.

Systems of media, communications and power

The foundation of this book and the arguments within it then lie in the understanding that media and communications sit within a system of capitalist power. As deeply embedded in this complex system, media should not be seen as independently powerful. But nor would it be true to simply say the media exist only to serve powerful interests. Certainly the media tend to consolidate around capitalist hegemony, legitimising powerful interests organised around the ownership of the means to generate wealth. But the media's unique position in the interface between economics and culture, between interests and values, means that analysis of the former cannot always answer questions about the intended and unintended consequences of the driving tendencies of the system. Patterns in media content (as well as social outcomes) can vary, and the wider media representation of issues is not always consensual. If that weren't the case, we might never have seen conflicts in the reporting of the science of tobacco's damaging impacts on public health (Oresekes and Conway, 2010). Instead the media should be understood as a site of conflict within which various agents compete for space and legitimacy. An important point is that media and communications do not simply reflect the world and how it is organised but can be productive in themselves.

If the role of media and communications in the exercise of power has always been complex, the advent of digital technologies raises new challenges for media scholars. The circuit of communications previously involved the flow of information from, between and through social and political institutions, media organisations, the public and decision-makers at all levels (Philo et al., 2015). Ultimately, though, it was organised around the production of content by journalists and media professionals. As Shoshana Zuboff explains in her seminal text, 'surveillance capitalism', rooted in behavioural future markets, should now be seen as the 'fountainhead of capitalist wealth and power in the twenty first century' (Zuboff, 2019: 11). As the driving force of this digital infrastructure is unquestionably the appropriation of users' personal data, this may suggest that a focus on the flow of information which is less directly marketised becomes less significant.

But that seems a bit like saying that the press have always been mainly concerned with selling papers. It's correct in as much as to say that the press wouldn't exist *unless* they sell papers, or even that the press mainly preserve the wealth and status of media owners by, for example, supporting governments which allow for media expansion (or withdrawing it from those who promote pluralism). Yes, the press do those things to sustain their business. But they are also agents of influence in all sorts of other ways. The information which flows through the press represents a fragile balance between the priorities and values of markets and of the state, and of owners – and then of readers, who are positioned both as audiences to be entertained and as the object of 'the public interest'. Similarly, platform cultures are the product of sometimes contradictory forces that can produce new ideas and ways of thinking which must be accommodated into systems of power, while often simultaneously being implicated in opening 'new frontiers of power' such as the one Zuboff documents.

These systems of power *have* changed in nature, though – and they shift the field of analysis for those focused on information flows and their impacts. The circuit expands to include tech companies, AI and platform ownership, and sees new global players emerge. These include, for example, social media moderators, who, in approach and influence in respect of information flows, can in some ways share characteristics with journalists. Further, while content produced by journalists continues to travel through the new dimensions of the circuit, this type of production is not necessarily its key organising principle. It is the case that the range of powerful groups producing and managing content in some form in order to legitimate ideas has expanded. But the key transformative element in relation to questions of public opinion and belief is that these are now articulated in public and exist as content themselves – facilitated, shaped and captured often by conventional means, but produced largely by and for collectives through new practices, motivations and meanings which demand an entirely new conceptual lens for analysis.

Public opinion as the engine of social change

A second founding assumption of this book is that public opinion has a clear if complex relationship to outcomes in society and that to understand how opinions are formed is fundamental for understanding the exercise of power. This offers a counter to the argument that political decision-making happens regardless of what ordinary people say or do. It's evidentially the case that this is the view of the increasing numbers who abstain from voting and the many academics and commentators who critique the hollowing-out of politics in the West. And indeed this has been a feature of neoliberal politics, during which time political party membership, union activity and more active forms of mass political participation are all in decline (Trentini, 2022), and the distance between the public and those in power, including their supporters in the media, has grown.

But while politicians may not be perfectly responsive to the democratic will, public opinion and collective response continue to – and most importantly still have the capacity to – input into decision-making in a range of ways. At the most basic level, governments rely on electoral support, and in the most extreme cases, public resistance to policy action can bring governments down: the example most often offered in British living memory is Thatcher's government and the poll tax, a policy which played a central role in her resignation as Prime Minister after eleven years in 1990. But what is more illustrative of the complex interplay of communications, media, power and the public in producing outcomes is the Brexit referendum of 2016. Much documented here has been the media construction of salience around issues such as immigration (bolstered by mainstream political rhetoric) and growing EU powers, combined with new and coordinated propaganda techniques, which minority parties capitalised on and which forced a divided government led by David Cameron to respond to (Philo et al., 2013; Briant, 2018; Sobolewska and Ford, 2020). But as I will argue in Chapter 1, the foundation was a growing public frustration with the current manifestation of politics, a lack of trust in public life and a desire for change, which research had evidenced much earlier. In these moments, to use the terminology of Stuart Hall (1973), power becomes 'articulated in practice' in that (dis)connections which are produced under specific conditions can have real effects.

With Brexit, the line between political action, media reporting and public opinion is blurred and difficult to define. But the information the public has access to and the interpretations and beliefs they form play a role in social change and can redirect the plans of powerful groups. That change is not simply a *direct* response to public opinion – as one influence among a range of factors – does not negate the fact that what happens in society is in part dependent on people's thinking and action (or lack of it). What recent political events in the West, including the election of Trump in the US and Brexit in the UK, have underlined is that when people *lose* their investment in trust and belief, politics has to change course. In these scenarios, spaces open up for very real abuses of power that rest on distortions of information and evidence. The converse, however, is that the only real engine for positive change, one which can disrupt power, is significant public concern and action which demands a response. Climate change, as the greatest political challenge of our age, is the test case, and the relation between evidence, communications and public response is addressed in depth in Chapter 5.

At the more moderate level, what the public think is also factored into decision-making. For example, politicians prepare press releases on policy action which are formulated in ways which take account of how the media might report them and how they will be received by the public (even if that's based on a sometimes skewed sense of their reception). A key change in recent decades is the obsessive monitoring of social media that the communications departments of political parties engage in (something I was told of directly by a then communications director for No. 10 Downing Street in 2016). With a particular though not exclusive focus on the platform previously known as Twitter (now X), these departments aim to assess the salience of particular issues, as well as the approval or disapproval (shown through likes, upvoting, etc.) of particular forms of action. In 2021, for example, we saw the UK government respond to the language and concerns of what is sometimes referred to as 'the culture wars', and in particular 'cancel culture', with policy action such as the Higher Education (Freedom of Speech) Bill, which proposes fines for institutions limiting freedom of expression (Clarence-Smith, 2022). The currently ubiquitous 'culture wars' are the product of a range of often competing discourses across different media, underpinned by shifting political and social groupings, which play out intensely and demand attention most stridently on publicly accessible social media – all watched by our political class.

The popular campaign by the Manchester United striker Marcus Rashford to reverse a parliament vote against the extension of school meals over the summer of 2021 similarly is an example of how social media collectives can demand a political response. In this environment high-profile individuals have the potential to reach and influence collective viewpoints in unprecedented ways, though the balance is towards elite voices who most often don't challenge power as Rashford did. It may once have been imagined that the opportunities that social media offer in respect of the democratisation of political speech, and in particular the inclusion of a diversity of voices, would somehow compensate for the loss of unionisation and other forms of organised mass politics. But the absence of alternatives to the very narrow range of voices and perspectives promoted across both professional and social media remains (Jackson and Moloney, 2016; Yang et al., 2017).

If this is most obvious in the public-facing social media and less so in the more private platforms such as WhatsApp, it is worth thinking about who owns what. As power is reconfigured in the social media environment, control of content, and the ideas contained within, remains an important objective, which I discuss with reference to Meta (previously Facebook) in Chapter 4. Why would any of this matter if public opinion wasn't important? In fact, a key finding from the research documented in this book is that audiences are most open to new ideas when they do not tap into a body of beliefs and perspectives that have been established over time, usually through repeated media engagement. If the aim is to preserve the status quo or legitimacy of 'common sense' assumptions, it makes sense for those in power to limit any challenge to them.

Finally, a few words on the media's role in influencing behaviours and its wider relationship to societal change. Most relevant research refutes a simple causal link between information and changes in behaviour. But my own research indicates that in the midst of the varied range of factors which drive people to make changes, media and information can play a role (Philo and Happer, 2013; Happer and Philo, 2016), for example, when media connect with existing positions – sympathetic attitudes and unmet commitments which may need a final push – or when information is combined with structural support in the form of government policy, or council initiatives such as bike lanes to encourage cycling. The reinforcement of ideas through and across media environments forces people to regard them as important, and over time, where beliefs and experiences align, commitments can alter. But the media can operate to limit action too, by marginalising or limiting perspectives which offer new ways of doing things. Where people feel, for example, that change is pointless and/or evidence is consistently produced to counter arguments for change, then this can be a powerful propaganda tool. We saw this play out in the mainstream media coverage of political alternatives such as Jeremy Corbyn's Labour election campaign in the UK in 2019, which received largely negative attention, and Bernie Sanders's presidential campaign in the US, which struggled to be heard at all in spite of speaking to public sentiment in both rhetoric and policy (Patterson, 2016; Mills, 2017).

In recent years, researchers have explored the motivations of Covid 'anti-vaxxers'. Much has been made of the influencing role of 'fake news' circulating on digital platforms, but again we can see the way in which media interact with existing beliefs and contexts to produce different effects. In October 2020 the *Lancet* predicted that at least one in six people in the UK would refuse the vaccination when it was offered and lambasted online platforms for allowing misinformation to circulate (Burki, 2020). In the event, take-up of the vaccination was much higher than predicted and in one age group was over 90 per cent (BBC News Online, 2022).

In the US, vaccination refusal was much higher (Solis Arce et al., 2021) but vaccination scepticism in all its forms reached a population which already included a fairly established community of 'anti-vaxxers'. This group is founded on a complex mix of ethical, religious and political concerns (Hussain et al., 2018) and in a highly polarised political and media environment, which correlates with falling levels of trust in government and authority, which have intensified in the last five years (Edelman, 2018; Edelman, 2020). The information environment was already aligned along Democrat/Republican lines, to a degree not replicated along political alignments in the UK (Jurkowitz et al., 2020). This also affects the communications that the public access and invest trust in; for example, high-profile politicians in the UK rarely express vaccine scepticism, unlike some members of the US Republican party (until an abrupt about-turn when panic about outcomes set in (Stacey and Politi, 2021)). The media here play a significant influencing role but are absorbed into existing belief structures and socio-political contexts in ways which shape particular outcomes.

The individualism inherent to neoliberalism which is enabled by and manifested through social media has tended towards social action that is protective of 'individual freedoms' (which David Harvey describes as 'a mode of opposition as a mirror image to itself' (2016: unpaginated)). We might make the argument that the main freedom demonstrated in this case is the freedom to choose which information to invest in, however adrift from evidence and dangerous it might be. But the question of vaccination resistance does offer a counter to the argument that individual action doesn't make a difference. Unfortunately, switching your light bulbs doesn't solve climate change. However, individual choice can be decisive in a situation where there is the possibility of collectives being mobilised around such action – in this context, causing very real threats to public health, which again see politicians responding. From this perspective, the individual and the collective cannot be separated as they are both integrated into the system of decision-making, and often it is media and communications and the communities they construct which facilitate these processes.

Understanding 'public opinion'

Having laid out briefly the way in which public opinion might be implicated in social change, we must consider what we're actually talking about and how this can be distorted as an instrument of change. There is a need to distinguish between, on the one hand, 'public opinion' as a discursive mechanism which is utilised by interest groups to achieve particular ends and which in some cases demands a response from those in power, and, on the other hand, what the public actually believes, which is *related to* the former and often highly managed, but not exactly the same.

In the title of an essay from 1972, Bourdieu famously claimed that 'public opinion does not exist'. In fact, he wasn't really claiming that. Instead in the essay he explores the social conditions under which ideas of 'public opinion' are produced – arguments which tap into the now widespread critiques of attempts to conceive 'the public' and 'the public sphere' more generally. In his historical analysis, Habermas rooted the emergence of the latter in the development of the early bourgeoisie as they aimed to extend the influence of their private deliberations to a wider audience; in large part to manage public opinion in favour of their own interests (Habermas, 1992). Through these practices, he argued, we could begin to see an identifiable 'public' in the sense of a collective coming together around questions and priorities (if not always agreeing).

While this is a very useful way of looking at how ideas emerge and consolidate, critics have noted that this sense of 'publicness' is highly exclusive and is articulated by and representative of those who are already positioned to have a platform, with some arguing it may make more sense to talk of a series of 'publics' organised around differentiated communities and priorities (for example, see Fraser, 1990). In addition to its lack of inclusivity, any notion of a singular 'public' or even 'publics' in relation to opinion, trust or anything else is necessarily one of crude simplicity. As Lippmann (2010) noted, in these understandings, the best we can aim for is a sense of 'superficial harmony' achieved only by taking the complexity of the world out of public discourse.

This point is emphasised by Bourdieu when he examines the way in which polling questions are formulated, and their tendency to focus on the political preoccupations of the interest groups which they represent (and who pay for them). In the essay, he illustrates the way in which polls demand responses to questions that people may never have thought about before, to which they simply choose positions which seem appropriate (e.g. I am working class, therefore I should choose the first option). Consequently, a key purpose is to 'impose the illusion' that 'public opinion' actually exists and to 'disguise the fact that the state of opinion at any given moment is a system of forces, of tensions, and that there is nothing more inadequate than a percentage to represent the state of opinion' (Bourdieu, 1993a: 150).

How then could we ever hope to capture something which is constantly in motion, often incoherent and produced as different positions at different times and in different circumstances – with the moves between the positionings that individuals take up happening at ever faster pace across digital platforms, not to mention the fact that 'the public' is stratified by class, gender, race, age and so on? The bottom line is that democracy by its very nature requires some knowledge of public attitudes, and so it is important to assess critically the mechanisms for collecting this knowledge, how this knowledge is used and what its limitations are. In this, even Bourdieu notes that polls 'can make a useful contribution' if they are seen as a snapshot of thought processes in time (Bourdieu, 1972: 128), and are used as one of a number of methods to aid understanding (and in this sense, the advent of social media offers real alternatives, though they are not problem-free, as I will go on to discuss).

What we see, however, is that these snapshots of 'public opinion' are held as representative of a more static vision of what the public thinks or where the public mood sits in public discourse, and are then used to demand or defend social action. Journalists often justify their probing of politicians by reference to the results of polls as representative of public opinion – for example, demanding that politicians say how they will act on an issue such as immigration following public polling indicating that people see it as a priority. The most rigorous of journalists may draw on academic research as evidence of public sentiment or expectation. But often journalists simply draw on what they assume the public believe on the basis of their own observation or 'common sense'. Here *what other journalists say* privately and in print or broadcast plays a significant influencing role, as most journalists, for logistical and other less defensible reasons, rarely move beyond those circles in their news-gathering (Lewis et al., 2004). Because of the distinctiveness of the backgrounds, experience and influences of journalists, particularly those operating at the highest levels, this can create a real mismatch between 'public opinion' as presented by journalists (to politicians and their audiences) and what the public think, even with the crudest measure we have in the form of surveys and polls.

This phenomenon – the mismatch – was very clearly on display throughout the pandemic in the UK, when for many months the Westminster government broadcast live daily press briefings, at which representatives of the most high-profile news outlets were invited to ask questions after short updates from politicians and scientists. This was a time when the stakes couldn't be higher in respect of journalists demanding effective decision-making from those in government. In the early months of the virus, and in the context of growing daily death tolls, one question was omnipresent across not only the briefings but also in press headlines, broadcast news and news programmes, and that was: *when will the lockdown end?* (Happer, 2020). In fact, on 24 March 2020, the day after the lockdown was called, YouGov reported that 93 per cent of the public supported the measures (Stone, 2020). That support continued for the first six months of the pandemic, and indeed in September 2020 the majority felt that restrictions were being lifted too quickly (McDonnell, 2020). Still, in response to journalists' questioning in that period, the government and politicians consistently had to defend their actions (publicly at least) on the basis of a strong desire to end the lockdown and get the country back up and running.

In July 2021 an early heralding of 'freedom day', in which the UK government would 'remove all legal limits' on numbers congregating and 'end the one-metre-plus rule on social distancing', was very quickly toned down to an 'urging' of nightclubs to impose restrictions and an 'expectation' of continued mask wearing on public transport, as public support for this vision of 'freedom' was shown to be limited (Stephens, 2021). In a final damning testament to what was described in a House of Commons select committee report in 2021 as 'one of UK's worst ever public health failures', ministers offered as a defence of the government's slowness to act its underestimation of the public's willingness to accept the lockdown (Sample and Walker, 2021) – an admission that the government was totally ignorant of the opinions and priorities of the people it was governing (quite bizarrely offered as a defence).

As I have noted, the period of the pandemic was unique in many ways, and, in this case, in spite of the early effort to construct a narrative around negative 'public opinion' towards the lockdown, the evidence in the opposite direction was just too robust to allow it to hold. The level of trust in scientists, given a prominent communications role, is likely to have been a key factor. Both the media and politicians conceded some ground (arguably it was too late). But in spite of the mismatch, a construction of 'public opinion' is regularly drawn upon to justify action. This can take the form of references to free-floating signifiers such as 'nanny state', a vague and broad-reaching term with no particular foundation in survey work, which couldn't effectively capture the range of complex views people have on state intervention anyway, or other forms of research. But this term is regularly drawn upon by journalists and political commentators to resist policy action which is seen to be restrictive of freedoms. We see this, for example, in relation to resistance to taxes on alcohol and food products, which mainly restrict the freedom of corporations but protect public health (my own research with Chatham House on a proposed meat tax indicated exactly the opposite attitude and that there was a lot of public support for such policy action: Wellesley et al., 2015). Here political action is simply undemocratic, especially when the power of corporate lobby groups, existing in a circuit of interest with the media in a structural sense, is factored in.

At other times, the discourse of 'public opinion' can be itself a factor in actually shifting what the public think or care about. In the context of more traditional media, there is a range of ways in which 'public opinion' is inferred to audiences, for instance through 'vox pops', a series of random short interviews usually recorded in places very accessible to journalists (e.g. in the street), and the category of the now clichéd 'Public outrage over [insert moral panic]'. Journalistic questioning of political figures routinely draws on a more subtle version of the latter, as we have seen, and is important in creating an expectation that politicians will respond. Across a range of rhetorical tools, 'public opinion' is loosely constructed, and is used as a vehicle for influence in different ways.

But when we turn our attention to social media, now the dominant mechanism for delivery of media messaging, the question of 'public opinion' – here understood as the impression gained of 'what other people think' – takes on a much more significant role and can be seen as a uniquely powerful tool of media persuasion. In many ways this is in essence what user-generated content on social media is – millions of utterances and demonstrations of 'what other people think'. These utterances construct perceptions of consensus on some issues, extreme and vitriolic division on others (perceptions which might differ from one user to the other, depending on the networks they are immersed in). They may not be authentic, but these perceptions ground us in relation to others around us. The way in which posts, comments, threads, likes and emojis on social media may influence users is exceptionally complex. But one thing that emerges from all of the work covered in this book is the importance of volume, consistency and reinforcement of messages or ideas. Immersion in this new digital opinion environment, combined with the tendency to invest trust in known quantities – people who are followed or friended because they can be trusted to act with good motives – can make the influence of these processes of immersion and trust extremely powerful (Bak-Coleman et al., 2021).

I would argue further that, while trust in mainstream journalism has been eroding and will probably never regain the levels of the previous era, social media as part of a system of power is less understood, less transparent and less scrutinised at the current time. There may be disquiet about their influence, but people continue to increase their reliance upon social media platforms, with young people in particular preferring to access information through 'side-door routes' rather than from news outlets' own websites (Newman et al., 2023). Here the agenda setters (or managers) may appear to be a democratic collective of users, and the practice of media distortion isn't so easy to see. But the social media information landscape is every bit as structured, by the design and ownership of platforms, moderation, algorithmic amplification, journalistic manipulation and foreign and domestic state bots and trolls. The distortions of 'public opinion' to manipulate social change continue, but the lack of clarity in who is controlling whom, and the groups battling for power, allows for a whole new set of possible outcomes to emerge.

Themes and approach

The fact that 'public opinion' is often distorted, weaponised and difficult to capture is for sociologists the strongest argument for undertaking the work of public understanding, belief and opinion. The more it is publicised, the harder it is to ignore. And social scientists have unique tools and methods to move beyond superficial understandings and illuminate the processes by which opinions are formed, and how they might shift as the conditions of their production change. The focus group method from which the data in this book derives examines the reception of new events and information to identify the way in which people organise their thinking around existing frames of knowledge and understanding so as to select and either endorse or reject the range of 'positions' offered to them by the media they have access to. Strauss (2014), an anthropologist who studies public opinion, describes the range of discourses circulating in public and private contexts as the 'building blocks' of opinion formation. People select particular discourses because they resonate in ways which move beyond prior exposure to ideas to the consideration of strategic goals – what we might call personal interests – and individual life experiences which 'endow some discourses with particular motivational and emotional relevance' (Strauss, 2014: 117).

Similarly in my own work, I have found focus groups a highly effective method for triggering disparate thoughts which can be traced back to language, imagery and framing from media, but which are also subject to other influences, motivations and resonances, which can be unpicked. Following the methods of the Glasgow University Media Group (Happer and Philo, 2013), I find that this process flows best when words and phrases are offered for consideration, rather than direct questions which tend to embed an existing position. These stimuli trigger group discussions aimed at integrating responses to form a relatively coherent if complex set of opinions. Here the role of 'opinion leaders', those who have the tools of articulation to shape some sort of coherence, is important, but for any position to be found acceptable to the group, it has to be close enough to the shared perceptions and beliefs which rooted the thoughts in the first place, and this can take some time to achieve. These kinds of exchanges provide researchers like myself with data which gets as close as possible to *thinking in action* – and take us far beyond the snapshots of formed and recognisable positions offered in opinion polls, of which Bourdieu was so critical.

Across all methodological approaches, the way in which social media engagement shapes belief and opinion is less well understood than the influence of professional media reporting. It is certainly less apparent to users who are emerged in these platform cultures – and even where cynicism of social media and personal data collection is growing, most people believe that there is 'no alternative' to having a platform presence. This makes developing an understanding of these processes ever more significant.

However, it is important to raise here a note about this empirical work: as my approach rests on the assumption that any media system is embedded in and reflects particular political and socio-economic contexts, the processes identified should be seen as similarly located. The critique here is one of Westernised norms and practices of journalism, and the book charts a particular historical phase in which the project of neoliberalism was in the ascendancy to later produce periods of crisis (Davidson, 2016). Even within liberal democracies with broadly similar political trajectories, such as the US and UK, global crises can be communicated and responded to in ways which produce very different outcomes (a topic which I examine in Chapter 5). I would make the argument that the processes by which opinion is managed more generally, particularly in the context of an increasingly globalised platform infrastructure, may have applicability beyond the contexts discussed in this book, and that control of information remains a key tool of power whether it is wielded through democratic means or in other political regimes. But only empirical research can answer these questions, and I welcome any dialogue with global scholars as to the applicability, or deficiency, of the model presented.

Accordingly, this book is not intended to be exhaustive but to add to ongoing discussions by presenting a model for the relationship between the structure of media, now largely digital but with information flows shaped by different agents, and what the public comes to believe. It is intended as much to raise questions as to offer answers. It emphasises the contexts, ideology and belief systems, priorities and objectives which draw people to positions and which are then taken up across a range of issues. It does not present a model of media accounts 'setting' public opinion. It argues that people come to hold opinions not just, or even primarily, because they perceive them to be 'true' but because they want to connect with others, because they want to be seen to be knowledgeable, because trust in authority has evaporated and they are looking for alternatives, because they want to conform and, in many cases, simply because it benefits them to do so. It shows evidence of a complete reworking of how people come to know about things, with the elevation of individualised research and expertise as a distinctive shift, and perceptions of trust and authenticity often prioritised over evidence and even judgements about 'truth' (or, in the absence of confidence, over claims of 'truth'). But always the argument is that media and information play a key role in shaping opinion, and in often unpredictable ways in driving social change.

Overview of chapters

In Chapter 1, I map out the socio-historical context of the period studied, and show the way in which the societal changes delivered by neoliberalism have been paralleled by a transformed communications infrastructure; these are mutually reinforcing to produce a disconnect between members of the public and those in power, with journalists impacted directly. In this, I set out the empirical and conceptual foundations of 'the disconnect' which underpins the thesis of the book in respect of how social change occurs or how it might be inhibited by the processes of opinion formation and management. I explore the important role of trust in shaping public sentiment and present evidence of a fairly widespread erosion of trust in the public sphere due to the gap between the rhetoric of the neoliberal media and people's real-world experiences. That absence of trust in the system, I argue, played a role in steering recent political shifts as the populist rhetoric of Trump and the Brexiteers mirrored and appropriated that sense of dissatisfaction – an example of the mis-management of opinion – though over time it discursively responded to public sentiment in ways which allowed demands for change to be accommodated into systems of power. Finally I look at how communities organised around questions of trust emerge in response to different circumstances, which can at certain times reconnect with a centred (or official) media culture and at other times draw in significant numbers of people far removed from it.

In Chapter 2, I develop a more granular model of how public opinion forms and shifts in the context of a digital media culture which operates across six filters, with different opinion outcomes for different groups. This underpins the analysis in Chapter 1 that assesses the societal outcomes of collective opinion formation, and the success or failure of political actors in managing these processes. I identify the filters which underpin or shape these processes: ideology, priorities and established value systems, interpersonal communities, identity and alignment, modes of media engagement and lived experience. The model offers insight into how patterns of opinion may be mapped across a range of factors including demographics, social contexts, identity and patterns in media consumption. I argue that, while people engage in often highly sophisticated and far-reaching modes of media engagement, interpretations free from the influence of representation and rooted in lived experience are less common than before – and opinion is more highly managed than ever.

In Chapter 3, I investigate in more depth two inter-related filters of opinion identified in the model outlined in Chapter 2: interpersonal communities and identity categories in respect of class, education and age. I examine the role of social class in shaping media engagement and the ways in which people interpret and respond to ideas and take up positions. I argue that perceptions of generational conflict obscure the role of formal education in constructing opinion communities and alignments which are cemented and sustained by media engagement in both historical forms of journalism (tabloid versus broadsheet) and newer platform cultures. An aspect of this is the way particular modes of social media usage, careful curation of profiles and entry into public discourse add value to those who have cultural capital gained in educational settings and can operate to marginalise those who do not possess these resources. However, these intensely reflective online performances must also be seen in the context of representations of class and increasing job precarity. Further, expanding the understanding of how opinion formation and management are implicated in social change, I make the case that the construction of this conflict as between generations sets those with shared economic interests in struggles against one another, and is a significant barrier to building collective demands for change.

In Chapter 4, I investigate in further depth the digital infrastructure providing the context for the processes which operate to manage opinion across social media platforms, connecting with the key themes of public trust, a disconnect from the centre and the ways in which users themselves promote existing forms of power and limit the potential for change through their own modes of engagement. To do this, I engage with the changing agents of power and influence within the digital media environment, presenting an overview of an expanded circuit of media and communications, including new players such as Big Tech, platform owners, AI and human moderators, and new forms of propaganda and content management. Drawing on my

Introduction

research with social media moderators and users, I examine the processes by which particular opinions and ideas and the groups of users expressing them can be promoted and amplified or marginalised and silenced. I argue that while the management of digital opinion through these processes is different in nature from that through control of information and thought – more rooted in the mirroring of acceptable forms of expression and avoidance of transgression – the groups which benefit and power represented are fairly similar to those that went before.

In Chapter 5, I bring these questions to bear on more recent developments with an examination of the narration of three inter-related global crises – climate change, Covid and the cost-of-living crisis – across different media cultures. Here we see the overall arguments of the book demonstrated in a more empirical way. First, I examine the way in which the ideological practices underpinning mainstream media reporting produce expectations about the nature and urgency of action to be taken in response to these issues (as well as closing down alternative solutions). This allows me to explore in more depth the final filter of the model presented in Chapter 2 – lived experience – and I examine how media can construct a sense of proximity and relevance which often overrides individuals' own experiences and observations. I further discuss the way in which the cost-of-living crisis has come into public discourse at a pivotal moment in which the need for real systemic change is being reinforced across public life; where moments of decisive change such as this are missed, I argue, the disconnect grows and resistance is likely to emerge. Finally, I explore the very different ways in which crisis and ideas of proximity are constructed in decentred cultures on social media platforms, with attention to the activities of young climate activists – whose disconnect and alternative visions of social change remove them from the conventional politics of policy and collective action.

Terminology

A final word on terminology. Talking about media is now immensely complicated. At the most basic level, it is no longer appropriate to make a distinction between digital media and traditional media (newspapers, television, radio), as everything is digitally produced, and everything from the BBC to the *New York Times* to Fox News and most newspapers works across a whole range of digital media. In some cases, I use the term 'professional journalism' when referring to the media produced by people who are paid for this and work broadly within the conventions and norms of journalistic practice. Importantly, it implies some form of access to politicians and other elite speakers and the kinds of relationships, formal and otherwise, that this might involve. There remains a limited group of people who get to speak and whose ideas circulate at the heart of our public culture and carry influence. 'Professional journalism' as a term includes television, radio and national press. Independent or local media outlets are named where they are relevant and may be seen as distinct.

At other times, I use the phrase 'mainstream media' or 'mainstream culture'. This includes all of the above as well as other professionally produced media (such as documentaries and entertainment shows). However, it is also to some extent a rhetorical device referring to the kinds of events, issues and understandings that circulate in our culture, which may or may not originate in the mainstream media – although they often do – and have a direct relationship to those who get to speak and their priorities. This is much more nuanced. An example in recent years would be reporting on the cost-of-living crisis, which circulated right across the culture, with the majority accepting that some response was necessary. Belief in climate change would be considered a mainstream belief as it is evidenced and accepted by most governments in the world. That is not to say that it's not countered in the mainstream media, or that there is a consensus around the form and urgency of action to be taken, and the mainstream does not represent a homogeneity of views.

'Mainstream' does imply, though, a wide reach in terms of how discussions circulate, and sometimes a mainstream culture can be clearly seen on social media platforms that are public-facing. We might also refer to 'mainstream knowledge', an example being the accusations of rape and abuse aimed at the comedian Russell Brand, which most people in the UK in the week of 18 September 2023, when the Channel 4 *Dispatches* programme investigating this was aired, would have known something about. This is true even though they won't necessarily hear the news from the same form of media or source (or agree on the accuracy of it).

This leads me to another term which is used throughout, and central to, this book: 'social media'. Here I begin with the most basic definition of the digital infrastructure, which enables individuals and collectives to come together to communicate, share and collaborate across a range of media forms and which can transfer previously private exchanges onto public platforms and transform their nature, legitimacy and reach in doing so (though sometimes they simply amplify what is already public). Like the widely used term 'media' this includes a whole range of platforms which embed distinct affordances and produce very different cultures and norms.

A key axis of distinction is the degree to which platforms are public- or private-facing: so Twitter (X) is largely public; Facebook, Instagram and

TikTok may be either public or private depending on the account settings; and WhatsApp is largely private, while platforms such as Discord and Telegram are invitation-only (though access to personal data may well not be). The voices that dominate in the platforms which are more public-facing tend to be more conventional elites (journalists, politicians, celebrities), and platforms such as Instagram and TikTok elevate 'influencers', figures who are less known outside platform cultures. In very private platforms influence might be exerted by those we know directly. I note where the private/public axis, although a crude distinction, is important, and I discuss these issues in more depth in Chapters 2 and 4. In places I refer to 'social media alternatives' in those circumstances where social media engagement has pushed people away from the narratives of mainstream news, or where they are more broadly representative of a 'decentred' culture (as opposed to a 'centred culture', a term which I also use in places).

To return to Russell Brand, here we had a YouTuber with many millions of followers. Before his channel was suspended in 2023, he undoubtedly had larger audiences than many mainstream news programmes. But the key point is that his ideas are not considered mainstream by those at the centre of the culture. It's also notable that he built his profile on Channel 4 and the BBC, and, while it is increasingly common to build this kind of profile without some mainstream foundation, it is currently relatively difficult to do so beyond youth audiences who ground their media consumption on platforms like YouTube. Is he influential? On the basis of my research, yes, he's likely to be very influential with his followers, and this could potentially impact on political outcomes. He also operates in a culture with other speakers who have influence and share the same views. They may be part of a decentred culture, but it's not an insignificant one. At the other end of the spectrum, we could consider a figure such as Greta Thunberg, who emerged more organically in the social media ecosystem. Mainstream politicians might regard her arguments as extreme, but among a growing number of young people, these ideas are accepted. Again it may be a decentred culture, but it is sizable and influential, and she is known very widely.

Things can move in the centre, however, and ideas that have historically been marginalised in professional media can become mainstream. What tends to happen, as with Trump, is that professional journalists aim to shoot down these ideas, concessions are then made by those at the centre of the culture, and what it is acceptable to say can change. In this respect the term 'mainstream' has clear links with the concept of hegemony, though I've chosen not to use the term 'hegemonic media' because this would imply that power lies only with those who are involved in the production of those ideas. In fact, the decentred cultures which people like Brand lie at the heart of have clear and direct links with capital. Those who control our digital infrastructure – the 'new frontiers of power' discussed in Chapter 4 – operate and benefit across all dimensions of content production. So the use of these terms is not accidental, and directly relates to the arguments being made in the book. They are not perfect, but the media world is now immensely complex.

1

The disconnect: mis-managing public trust

In this chapter I map out the socio-historical context of the period studied, and show the way in which the societal changes delivered by neoliberalism have been paralleled by a transformed communications infrastructure, which are mutually reinforcing to produce a 'disconnect' between members of the public and those in power, with journalists impacted directly. In this, I set out the empirical and conceptual foundations of the disconnect which underpin the thesis of the book in respect of how social change occurs, or might be inhibited. I examine the inter-relations between media and political rhetoric, public opinion and societal outcomes through a closer look at the campaigns of Trump and Brexit, both of which occurred within the period of research. For what we might describe as examples of the *mis-management* of public opinion – in that most mainstream journalists tried to steer their audiences away from these outcomes through their reporting – I then look at how the media discursively responded in ways which accommodated these demands for change into systems of power (though did not include a reckoning with their own culpability).

An argument made throughout is that the trust which traditionally lay at the heart of the social contact between the media and members of the public – crucially based on perception of intent rather than judgements of absolute 'truth' – collapsed in this period. The collapse in trust, and the turn to social media alternatives, produced an atomisation of thought and opinion and an environment in which questions of 'trust' and 'truth' were reworked. In times of crisis, such as during the pandemic where trust in science (and scientists) was prioritised, we saw a brief reconnection with a centred media culture (Newman et al., 2021). At other times, though – organised around isolated issues and/or in relation to questions of trust – opinion communities can draw in significant numbers of people who are positioned at quite a distance from the centre, and whose demands for change become much more difficult to respond to.

Conceptualising trust in media

Georg Simmel, one of the key sociological thinkers on trust, argued that:

> Without the general trust that people have in each other, society itself would disintegrate, for very few relationships are based entirely upon what is known with certainty about another person, and very few relationships would endure if trust were not as strong as or stronger than rational proof or personal observation. (Simmel, 1978: 179)

Trust not only is necessary *for* society but it is produced *through* it. 'Social norms', which emerge through social interaction as standards for behaviour, play an important role as a guide to how agents can be expected to act in any context (Bachmann, 1998). People become trusting as they observe and learn to expect consistency in the way in which institutions and agents act. As Luhmann (2000) notes, familiarity is a necessary precondition of trust, to which Giddens (1991) adds the aspect of technical expertise, or the know-how to produce consistent results. But crucially for Simmel this consistency in action must be perceived to be for the common good (Möllering, 2001). Trust has at its heart an expectation of *positive* intent. If social institutions are understood to be historically reliable in this way, less direct knowledge and observation become necessary. Here trust relies upon Simmel's notion of 'suspension': what we might call a leap of faith (Möllering, 2001).

Media and journalism are among the most important social institutions, and play a key role in representative democracies, which rely upon an informed electorate. In conceptualisations of media as 'the fourth estate', trust is founded on journalists' adherence to a professional ideology or to a set of norms which have historically placed a sense of 'objectivity' and 'truth-seeking' at the centre (Schudson, 1978; Deuze, 2005). Also importantly, a key element is that the version of empirical reality offered comes from a place of good intent (Kreiss, 2017) (though I would argue that this necessarily complicates questions of 'truth'; I will come back to this).

The twentieth century saw the development of mass media, and, across broadcasting in particular, a fairly homogeneous lens on the world emerged thanks to the standardised training, mode of recruitment and ownership models which underpin professional journalism. Trust was to a large degree rooted in familiarity in respect of how broadcast reports looked and sounded as evidence of adherence to a particular professionalism or expertise. As Stuart Hall noted, because of the visual nature of the medium, television news could convince audiences 'as if the referent of a televisional discourse were an objective fact' (Hall, 1973: 58). Here trust was founded on a leap of faith, in that most people relied on mainstream media accounts to inform them about events in the world that they would not directly experience.

Media scholarship, which emerged in parallel with mass media expansion in the twentieth century, started to unpick the constructed nature of news. Through conceptualisations such as gatekeeping, which addresses the range of influences which shape journalistic decision-making, and agenda setting, focused on the selection of and salience given to stories, this work began to challenge the 'objectivity' and 'truth' value of what was on offer (Shoemaker, 1991; Deuze, 2005; Shoemaker and Vos, 2009). Bourdieu (1998) argued that because they are immersed in the 'journalistic field' – a 'microcosm' in which its own rules and forms of capital circulate – journalists draw on a set of professional norms to assert their status and authority in delivering trusted news. Here journalists' assertion of their role as 'guardians of collective values' masks the influence of external forces and the locatedness of their own community to power (Bourdieu, 1998). In other words, trust is a strategic tool with which to manage manipulation and consent to domination.

Similarly in their work, Herman and Chomsky (1988) conceived of public trust (or the 'manufacture of consent') as based on ignorance and a lack of transparency in the actual processes which shape media content. A key factor for them was the absence (or suppression) of trusted dissenting voices in the mainstream environment. As noted in the Introduction, it was on this basis – that people form their ideas in part on imperfect accounts of the world – that Walter Lippman cautioned against the democratic reliance on public opinion. In these and other critical accounts, the interests lying behind news and the role of trust in promoting hegemony were emphasised. But while some of these critics gained attention in mainstream culture, for most of the twentieth century, the media which people had access to remained much the same.

Just after the turn of the millennium, Tim O'Reilly coined the term 'Web 2.0' to refer to the evolution of the digital infrastructure which allows for peer-to-peer engagement and the collective production of user-generated content. Users became plugged simultaneously into globalised and individualised news media ecologies, which in theory offered access to every single perspective possible on events in the world. Mobile technologies democratised access to the means of production previously reserved for professionals (which brought into question their unique expertise). I will talk more in Chapter 2 about how users confronted with such an overwhelming amount of available information develop strategies to make sense of what is going on. But the one belief this access inevitably reworked was the idea that there was one privileged lens on the world. If the demystification of journalistic 'objectivity' was once the preserve of a select band of media academics, in the digital age the constructed nature of news was made publicly visible.

I am, however, presenting this as contextual rather than causal and would approach with caution the argument that the advent of digital is directly implicated in any wider collapse in mainstream media trust, the complex reasons for which I document across this chapter. Even if bias in news is seen as inevitable, it does not necessarily preclude people trusting media accounts if they feel their interests are being represented. Media production involves making selections and editorial judgements, and these are inevitably bound up with the narratives and viewpoints which are on offer in the political landscape. But it is the distance from or closeness to them, and the degree to which they are operating in the interests of those who experience them, that will dictate perceptions of good intent and investments of trust.

Neoliberalism: ideology and practice

The most significant of these changes in recent decades is the socio-economic and cultural transformation of neoliberalism in the West. This represented a rupture from the post-war consensus of government intervention in employment and welfare systems and progressive spending and taxation policies. Well documented is the way neoliberalism emerged as a product of concerted effort by funded think tanks such as the Manhattan Institute to produce a counter-narrative, though the processes by which it spread and in particular was embraced by the very people it actively disempowered are less well articulated (Harvey, 2018). A current discussion point is the degree to which we've seen or are seeing the breakdown of the neoliberal era (Gerbaudo, 2021). The answer to that depends on what we understand it to be. Neoliberalism is a much-discussed concept without a consensual core (Mudge, 2008; Fine, 2010; Vanugopal, 2015). It's not possible to be exhaustive, so here I will consider divergence along two inter-related axes: the relationship between neoliberalism as ideology and a system or set of policies, and the relation between the economic and the cultural aspects of change.

Ideology here is conceived of as the lens through which the organisation of society is understood, perceived and rationalised. Ideology is therefore adaptable to different social and historical contexts, and different ideologies can co-exist, either in harmony or in competition: Fukuyama, for example, argued that for most of the twentieth century, liberalism was in competition with communism for global dominance. But within most nationalised or localised contexts, the ideas which exist to articulate the relationship between those in power and everybody else tend to cohere enough to appear as 'inevitable' or 'common sense'. In this, I draw on Gramsci's (1971) concept of hegemony in its reference to the process by which power is exercised through domination of the cultural sphere. Here ideology becomes hegemonic when it largely goes unquestioned. But it is also understood to be constantly vulnerable because of changes in social experience which might, if let loose, demand revisions to 'common sense'. Hegemony is constantly reworked and is never absolute; as Hall noted, it is 'the tendential balance in the relations of force which matters' (Hall, 2019b: 34).

The degree to which a dominant ideology actually reflects how things are underneath can therefore vary a great deal. If we look at the core signifiers of neoliberalism – 'free markets' and 'individual freedoms' – the evidence suggests that neoliberalism has been more established as an ideological force than as a system in practice (Philo et al., 2015). In fact, increased 'freedom' of markets was the product of a series of state interventions to redirect power to large global corporations. Governments in the UK and many other European countries first sold off and privatised key public assets, and then introduced market-based mechanisms into what remained of the public sector, for example in areas of health and education, in which patients and students were reconstructed as 'customers' (Happer, 2017b). The rise of private–public partnerships, such as PFI (Private Finance Initiative) schemes in the UK, to deliver public projects like new schools and hospitals, brought corporations into decision-making in public life in unprecedented and highly undemocratic ways. Corporate power and wealth grew exponentially with the support of the state. In practice, less state intervention meant leaving the market to its excesses through deregulation (and subsidising growth) while providing a security blanket if things went wrong. The 2008 financial crash, when governments intervened to save the banks (and the incoming government imposed austerity on the public as a solution), offers an illustration (Berry, 2012).

The neoliberal ideology of 'individual freedom' did have some structural foundation – in the broader move towards individualisation, by which is meant an institutionalisation of the individualism already inherent to liberalism in which social forms are increasingly organised around the individual (Fine, 2010; Dawson, 2012). This told people they could work where they wanted and when. A number of mechanisms designed to increase 'flexibility' in the workplace, enabled by technological change, culminated in the 'gig economy' in which work can be undertaken anywhere and anytime through digital platforms (Muntaner, 2018).

In actuality, such 'flexibility' represents freedom only when people can choose *not* to work in any post which is available, but because of low wages, and poor (or no) sick pay and security, for most it means being available 'any time', which reduces freedom and choice. This was compounded by reductions in welfare spending (as part of the neoliberal rollback of the state) which were rhetorically founded on the sense that people who took the freedoms offered were 'strivers' and those who didn't were 'shirkers' (Jowit, 2013). Here 'individual freedom' really meant individual responsibility (in contrast to the lack of corporate responsibility) (Bauman, 2001). These kinds of working conditions also led to an atomisation of the workforce, already set in motion by the neoliberal state's attack on the unions who aimed to bring workers together and fight for their collective rights.

And this is possibly where the neoliberal ideology has been most effective: in the cultural sphere. This is because whereas identity for much of the twentieth century was largely rooted in people's role in the workplace, as David Harvey noted in 2016, they now understand their identity through a series of individualised opportunities and conflicts which they choose to take part in. If 'individual freedom' in the workplace is largely illusory, people are more invested in the belief that 'freedom' lies in the identity groups which they align with culturally and which allow for the expression of their individualism.

As Nancy Fraser (2000) argued as early as 1995, demands for the 'recognition of difference' and the battle for cultural domination had supplanted class as the site of struggle. In this context a lot of attention has been paid to the new social movements which focus on single political issues, such as environmentalism, sexuality, gender and so on (Larana, 1994). Explaining in an interview how these have emerged, Harvey offers a proposition:

> What if every dominant mode of production, with its particular political configuration, creates a mode of opposition as a mirror image to itself? During the era of Fordist organization of the production process, the mirror image was a large centralized trade union movement and democratically centralist political parties. The reorganization of the production process and turn to flexible accumulation during neoliberal times has produced a Left that is also, in many ways, its mirror: networking, decentralized, non-hierarchical. I think this is very interesting. And to some degree the mirror image confirms that which it's trying to destroy. (Harvey, 2016: unpaginated)

This may be the real sophistication of neoliberalism as an ideological system, and it goes some way to explaining its sustainability in the context of consistent failures to meet the material demands of the widest sections of the population. As Fraser (2000) notes, however, it's not possible or even desirable to reject as unhelpful struggles for cultural recognition, not least because these are authentic responses to the circumstances people find themselves in. As I will argue in Chapter 3, these are the new fault lines along which people are filtering information and positioning themselves politically and so must be accommodated into any hegemonic project to rework power from left or right. But the conundrum remains that while the economic programme of neoliberalism is increasingly found wanting, as new concerns emerge, they often take shape as the mirror image of the neoliberal society.

The neoliberal media

As part of the circuit of power, media simultaneously shape and are shaped by these changes. There are two important dimensions to this in the neoliberal age. The first is the increasing consolidation of power at the top of society, which sees the flow of communications through corporations, political and social institutions and mainstream media narrow in respect of the range of perspectives. The 'short circuit' of communication channels enabled by private–public partnerships allows companies to lobby governments directly in their interests, and here the public and media are cut out of the conversation completely (Philo et al., 2015). These communications tend to surface in the media only when elite groups disagree – Brexit being a good example; another was the opposition to the Iraq war from sections of the military and intelligence agencies (Dinan and Miller, 2012).

Neoliberal policies on media ownership and (de)regulation also contributed to an increasingly corporate media, particularly in the US, which had already been governed by market mechanisms (Phelan, 2018). A key driver of a more ideological news product, however, has been the massive growth in public relations and communications agencies, particularly in the corporate sector, which operate to inform and direct news reporting. Not all public relations agencies represent vested interests – NGOs and charities of course do a lot of public relations – but they are not designed to be neutral and are in many ways in conflict with a traditional model of journalism.

A further aspect in the UK context has been the cultural shift in BBC journalism from presenting news from the perspective of people as part of a workforce to a reflection of the 'naturalising' role of the market in the political system. This played out through an increasing reliance in reports on expertise from the city of London or 'journalists' who previously worked there (Berry, 2012; Mills, 2016). Across media, politics and expertise there was a re-orientating of discursive mechanisms around the ultimate logic of finance and the free market, and the metaphorical construction of the public as financial subjects, as a 'nation of shareholders' with 'personal responsibility' for public debt (Clark et al., 2004). Even if the voices heard in public were different – across politics, journalism, business – they seemed to be saying the same things, not to mention attending the same schools, weddings and universities.

The range of influences intensely shaping media content (public relations, media ownership, politics, corporate expertise), and the integration of these interest groups into decision-making in public life, cut ordinary people and their perspectives out of the discussion. Media and political priorities were increasingly removed from the experiences of actual audiences for news and other forms of media content. The mainstream media functioned less and less as the vehicle for the expression of public feeling on the material realities of the neoliberal economic project.

Over the last two decades, however, the cultural expression of identity and individualism has found a very welcoming home in the digital landscape, which allows for new forms of knowledge production and peer-to-peer dialogue. Social media in many ways embody the ideology of individualism in their promotion of 'self-branding', where people are asked to post and upload content which presents them as professional, knowledgeable, attractive, funny, confessional and so on, depending on what works for the particular platform. On the basis of these 'brands', individuals select and are selected for inclusion in particular media ecologies in which forms of trust, information, ideas, evidence (or lack of it) and opinion circulate. The degree to which these ecologies are the product of individual choice, as opposed to being steered by a range of influences, is a theme I will return to in Chapter 4. But what is true is that social media users may invest a great deal in what is essentially the 'management' of public opinion about themselves, while engaging directly with others doing the same.

Constant brand management (of the self) and brand assessment (of others) are the essence of engagement (Khamis et al., 2017). The individual self is elevated to the highest level of importance, the core around which everything else orbits. Social media, while not necessarily inhibiting political activism, very much encourage a form of resistance which is characterised in Harvey's neoliberal mirror image as 'networking, decentralized, non-hierarchical'. In this, as Merrin (2021) notes, left and right share the same logic. Because of the design and affordances of social media in general – though of course 'social media' is a broad category and I'm generalising somewhat – there is also the tendency to simplify and flatten complex social phenomena. Taking a position on political issues is largely aligning with 'sides', the good guys and the bad guys, which are rooted in simple messages. That is not to argue that they are necessarily inauthentic, or that they can't be influential, just that they don't have much space to breathe.

The disconnect

The complex interactions of the distance between the promise of ideology and practice, along with the very real consequences of economic and political change for people's experiences, as well as the individualisation and fragmentation of digital media and their coincidence and mutual reinforcement, produced what I define as a growing *disconnect* between public institutions and media from the people they are supposed to serve. It is experienced to different degrees by different groups in society, but can be seen to play a role in facilitating a series of outcomes in distinct ways. These depend on the extent to which people will seek out and invest in alternative sources of information and the degree of distance from a centred media culture, but also on the way in which collective and individual opinions and beliefs will form and develop, which then has very real societal impacts.

This conceptualisation emerges from my empirical evidence in a holistic way and shows the value of research which is exploratory and longitudinal in nature. Across a series of studies, even when they are organised around different themes, narratives can emerge and identify themselves as salient. This was the case in this research, from 2011 to 2015 in particular, and even across geographical locations and socio-economic groups (Philo and Happer, 2013; Happer and Philo, 2016; Happer and Wellesley, 2019). The narrative was one of widespread distrust in institutions and public discourse: perceptions of a system which was dysfunctional at best, and corrupt at worst. Participants referred to public issues such as the banking crash, the UK MPs' expenses scandal, the Iraq war, the Leveson inquiry into media ethics in the UK, exposés of corrupt scientists and industrial lobbying. Repeated evidence that public figures could not be trusted to act for the public good – and that they aimed 'to line their pockets and better their selves', as one participant said – left people feeling they had little or no faith in the decisions that would be made.

While the broad narrative was widespread, levels of trust and the language and frames used to express these feelings and the impacts of them varied a great deal, reflecting the social, political and media environments in which people were immersed. A key area of divergence was the degree of social power that people perceived themselves, or the groups to which they belonged, to have; so, for example, wealthier university students had higher levels of trust and felt that outcomes would broadly reflect their interests, and urban groups who were active in the community felt they could shape outcomes in their favour. However, in the lower-income groups in the UK and US, perceptions that outcomes were always disappointing translated into feelings of powerlessness, a sense of a lack of control, and were expressed in ways which showed genuine anger. As one said, 'They'll promise you the world', but promises were always broken.

Feelings of frustration and indignation were palpable in the groups from more conservative areas in the US. A common reference point was of the 'agenda' underlying public life which the media covered up. Those most disillusioned described the media as being 'in cahoots with the military, the government' while others regarded the whole system as corrupt:

> You have to play by other people's rules ... it's just a big system of politics and funding and fundraisers. (Male, low income, US, 2015)

In-depth conversations showed the complex ways in which people negotiated information from different sources in accordance with their everyday experiences and observations to produce sophisticated and diverse opinions (which will be addressed further in Chapter 2). But these were often underpinned by this broader perception of the logic of the system in which *they* can do as they like while *we* have to stick to the rules. To put it succinctly: 'I couldn't trust them as far as I could throw them' summed up the views of many. Because people did not perceive good intent, the leap of faith which trust requires could not be made.

There was at this point no coherent political discourse on what the real issues were. This may reflect to some degree the illusory nature of neoliberalism, which was designed to be structurally opaque, with a lack of transparency built in. However, what was identifiable was a growing discontent with the system – but, importantly, accompanied by and entangled with a strong sense that media and political accounts did not reflect people's own experiences of it. There was also a discernible lack of mechanisms available to factor in the views of the wider public and importantly to contain resistance, which is a necessary part of any hegemonic political programme understood in the sense of an ongoing struggle. When Gramscian 'flashes' emerge from the contradictions of particular socio-economic systems, there opens up a space for alternative voices to be heard (Ives, 2018). For a period, different perspectives exist in a state of conflict, and there is a struggle over which assumptions will dominate and which interests will be served. The old beliefs may be reworked, with critiques of the system absorbed into a new set of hegemonic assumptions, or a whole new set may emerge; at these points, the possibility of radical ideas and outcomes emerges.

In the struggle over hegemonic ideas, Gramsci saw journalists playing a key role in attributing meaning and importance to the words and phrases that the public use to make sense of things. However, as I have noted, the neoliberalisation of journalism restricted the ability of certain sectors of the media to speak to the 'flashes' of discontent which appeared in this period, and in particular to those groups among whom they were most keenly felt. In this an opening was created for alternative forms of information, social media, and new political actors to articulate public sentiment. Political outcomes must be seen as the complex interplay of a range of factors, and it is not useful to make an argument for simple cause and effect. I also don't want to minimise the very significant differences between the US and UK political and social systems, and the outcomes they produce. Instead, I want to focus specifically on the disconnect in relation to media, information and beliefs around trust and perceptions of the system as one factor which may have played a role in the trajectory of social change from 2015–16 onwards.

Trump, Farage and the elites

Trump emerged as a potential Republican nominee for the US presidency in 2015, just after I conducted qualitative research in three cities across the country (Wellesley et al. 2015; Happer and Wellesley, 2019). His name did not come up in focus groups, which indicates just how quickly things happened. Watching from the other side of the Atlantic, I was immediately struck by the tone of his rhetoric. America, he stated in his speech to the GOP Convention in 2016, was:

> being led by a group of censors, critics, and cynics. Remember: all of the people telling you that you can't have the country you want, are the same people telling you that I wouldn't be standing here tonight. No longer can we rely on those elites in media, and politics, who will say anything to keep a rigged system in place. (Plumer, 2016)

And the media, he ranted in October 2016 at the third presidential debate between himself and Hillary Clinton:

> is so dishonest and so corrupt and the pile on is so amazing. […] It is so dishonest, and they have poisoned the minds of the voters. But unfortunately for them, I think the voters are seeing through it. (NPR Staff, 2016)

And on his campaign tour, he told his audience he was representing the 'people who work hard but no longer have a voice' because of the 'the special interests, the arrogant media, and the political insiders', echoing my focus groups (Trump quoted in Weigel, 2016). I used to do an exercise with my Media Sociology students in which I mixed up a number of quotes from the 2015 focus groups and from Trump's campaign speeches; the students almost never identified them correctly. In his construction of a system of elite power as corrupt, contemptuous, detached and untrustworthy, Trump effectively mirrored and amplified people's growing frustration and disconnect with the system, and for some he did so almost exactly in their words and in their framings.

An important point in this context is that, in spite of the broad narrative around trust which emerged through research, Trump did not of course appeal to all groups who were exposed to his rhetoric. This emphasises that communications are received within the context of existing value and belief systems, which allow for openness to particular ideas and closure to others. In this case, there are clear parallels between areas of support for white supremacist groups and patterns of voting in the 2016 US election, and scholars have produced a body of work highlighting the role of racist ideologies in the appeal of Trump (Tilley, 2020; Schertzer and Woods, 2021).

Commentators also saw Barack Obama's presidency as unleashing the country's (often not so) latent racism. But, as William Merrin (2021) notes, since the Clinton presidency, the tendency to promote conspiracy theories has also shifted right, often circulating in alt-right spaces online and later moving into mainstream media primarily on Fox News – which in 2017 dropped its original slogan of 'fair and balanced' (Grynbaum, 2017). Many of these theories in the period involved convoluted ideas about the 'hidden' aims of the elites' promotion of multi-culturalism and/or immigration. One of the most significant circulating during Obama's first term was the 'birther' conspiracy, rooted in the claim that because of his birthplace he didn't qualify to be president, though with clear implications about race. This too was echoed time and time again on Fox News, as well as the infamous 'Infowars' website. Often it was Trump himself re-stating the claims, bolstered with accusations of lies from the Governor of Hawaii among others, before he entered politics officially (Merrin, 2021). The underpinning assumption was: these people (the Democrats) are not to be trusted and the establishment is covering for them.

In the UK, there had also been a similar convergence of media, politics and factions of public opinion. From as early as 2013, the United Kingdom Independence Party (UKIP) leader and later campaigner to leave the European Union (EU), Nigel Farage, had been railing against 'metropolitan liberal elites', which he defined in a vague and broad-reaching sense bound up with conceptions of contemptuous politicians, detached expertise, corruption and crucially the liberal media. In parallel to Trump's rhetoric of giving 'voice' to ordinary people, Farage raged against the regulation of information and speech – the curse of 'political correctness' – which functioned to silence people's genuine feelings and concerns.

Here 'elite' groups were imagined to shape mainstream culture to dismiss problems that their privileged lifestyles protected them from. This integrated effectively with other rhetorical processes, including the 'othering' of immigrants, integral to which was the construction of a 'white working-class identity' under attack, with immigrants scapegoated for all society's problems (Philo et al., 2013; Virdee and McGeever, 2018). Elite groups, again with the media at the centre, were seen to have imposed uncontrolled immigration on the public and failed to recognise – or more conspiratorially deliberately stifled – the problems it caused. As Nigel Farage noted in a piece on the BBC for the *Telegraph*:

> When it comes to Immigration the bias is even clearer. They cover themselves with this idea that they are nice, and other people who differ, who believe that migration has gone too far, are in some way nasty. Is it nasty to think that the sheer volume of people arriving on our shores and impacting upon

our services, jobs and wages is wrong? [...] Maybe so if, like the average BBC executive, your experience of migration is a cheap au pair, cleaner, and a fascinating little restaurant down the road, but that is not the experience of this country's majority. (Farage, 2013)

In my own research, I found competing views on immigration in this period even within similarly positioned groups. Immigration was seen to be variously positive and negative in relation to different aspects of society and culture. In the UK groups, Britain was seen by many as 'soft touch' on immigration, but others could see the inequity in the challenges faced by people from other places which might bring them to the country. As in the work of Claudia Strauss on public opinion in the US, what emerged was a sense of the 'ways in which varying discourses could each capture part of a complex reality that cannot be reduced to a simple pro or con position' (Strauss, 2014: 5). Research shows that an anti-immigration discourse already present in UK mainstream media accounts gathered pace in the years leading up to the Brexit referendum: here public opinion became more consolidated around that emerging narrative and the proposed solutions (Philo et al., 2013). I discuss how this might be differentiated across geographical, ideological and social spaces in the next chapter.

Anti-immigrant sentiment was also central to Trump's platform, and the years before his campaign saw this issue become much more partisan, with Republicans much more supportive of stronger controls than Democrats (Gimpel, 2017). Again, Trump's rhetoric was underpinned by a perception of the interests served by immigration (Montanaro et al., 2016). A related theme was the prioritisation of free trade and globalisation over national interests and the global elite who benefited. In Trump's campaign, this was embodied in the nationalistic slogan 'America First'. In the EU referendum campaign, the slogan 'take back control' was similarly underpinned by a sense of the conflicted priorities inherent to the EU project, and a perception of global, metropolitan elites detached from the people they were supposed to serve.

An illustration of the way in which media, public opinion and politics can come full circle lies in the different roles and rhetoric of one man: Boris Johnson, anti-EU journalist, Brexit campaigner and finally triumphant in the public vote in 2019 as UK Prime Minister to implement the Brexit deal. As a *Daily Telegraph* columnist, for many years Boris Johnson fed the public a stream of hostile, usually completely unsubstantiated reports about the EU. Perhaps the most notable was the now infamous 'bendy bananas' story – about the supposedly absurd trading rules imposed by the EU – which symbolised power running riot (in contrast to ridiculous news reports and #bendybanana memes running riot in people's imaginations). In his first speech as Prime Minister, he promised to deliver Brexit as 'answering at last the plea of the forgotten people', leaving unacknowledged his own journalistic role in shaping this particular public 'plea' (BBC News Online, 2019a).

'The people' atomised

Scholars have drawn on conceptualisations of 'populism' to analyse the political rhetoric of Trump and Johnson, and as a way of making parallels with global trends as represented by political leaders such as Bolsonaro in Brazil and Modi in India (de Vreese et al., 2018). Even though their politics and contexts look very different, there is some merit in this analysis of the basic definition of populism as a belief system which 'juxtaposes a virtuous populace with a corrupt elite and views the former as the sole legitimate source of political power' (Bonikowski and Gidron, 2016: 1593). In different ways, these forms of rhetoric centre 'the people' as an ideological construction, to which a range of meanings are attached. Further, 'the people' is an exclusive category defined in opposition to what it is not, here in respect of 'the elite' who currently hold power and stand in the way of a representative system (Mudde and Kaltwasser, 2017). In this appeal to identity categories of belonging, we again see Harvey's neoliberal formations of political organising at play (Harvey, 2016).

But perhaps the most significant aspect of populism in respect of these movements is the degree to which, as Gerbaudo (2021) notes, they are ideologically very free-floating. This relates not only to the way populism can attach itself to different policy programmes (most often extremely right-wing and increasingly racist in recent times), but also to how the reality of 'the people' versus 'the elite' (or other adversary) is made sense of. In Johnson's rhetoric 'the people' is constructed as the ordinary people who wanted Brexit, which of course includes a massively diverse group with often very different motivations for voting for it (though he never quite went so far as to say that 48 per cent of the population make up the elite).

Trump's rhetorical constructions were nurtured by the affordances of social media. His use of Twitter (X) allowed him a direct call-out to those who might imagine themselves in this category of 'the people' and to manage public opinion around a sense of belonging to it (de Vreese et al., 2018). In this context, emotive, though often vague and unsubstantiated, accusations of corruption and wrongdoing flourish, and trust is built not on the production of 'facts', alternative or otherwise, but on uniting against a common enemy who is not to be trusted. Fragmented promises and slogans, appealing to different groups with different trigger points, can connect to people in ways which bypass the kind of scrutiny that comes from more traditional forms of political media coverage.

Polarisation has its uses as a way of understanding the cleavages which emerge in relation to these debates. However, this is a term which can lack nuance, neglecting the different ways in which this might occur beyond political partisanship, such as ideological and affective polarisation around key issues, and how particular groups might be drawn in to opinion communities which cross the fault lines of ideology and politics (van der Veen, 2023). As Rory McVeigh et al. (2014) note, at times, other identity categories can be evoked which produce party realignment, and some of this was happening in the period of research.

For my purposes here, 'atomisation' as a term is more helpful than 'polarisation', albeit used in a very specific way. I already talked about the processes of individualisation in the neoliberal era, which fragmented people in the workplace as well as in the digital arena. Hannah Arendt (1976), for example, talked about atomisation as a de-humanising process which leaves people without a connection to those around them, while Zygmunt Bauman (2001) noted that individualisation reduces the traditional markers of difference such as class, religion, history and so on and encourages us to join temporal (or 'coatpeg') communities of difference that actually leave us fairly rootless as we flit about.

My research indicates that the range of alternatives to mainstream culture circulating in the digital sphere, largely via social media, then exacerbated the disconnect between people's concerns and realities and the concerns and realities around which mainstream media discourse orbits, pushing people further into decentred opinion communities. Often these decentred communities are imagined to offer correctives to the inaccuracies and distortions of the mainstream. Sometimes they are quite divorced from conventional evidence, but in other cases, such as in the communities assembled around concern for the climate, they can be more evidence-based than the mainstream media (which I will chart in Chapter 5). Here different voices are trusted, though an important principle for some groups is that those in the centre aren't trusted at all.

As a body of literature in political science has charted, there is now a growing trend of news avoidance (Edgerly, 2022). As is always the case, a wide range of factors are implicated in this – such as information overload, for example, which I examine in the next chapter. Not knowing who to trust and how to identify what is credible has also been identified as potentially significant here (Benton, 2019). My empirical evidence indicates that even those who are highly political and well informed may fall into this category. Research shows that young people, who also must be seen in the context of an overwhelming choice of content, often just home in on their favourite topics (Edgerly, 2017). While the disconnect may be most obviously mapped to the support of Trump in this period, it has other outcomes too. People move fast in this space, often between different communities organised around changing concerns and interests, and how such communities are composed and what the relations between those within them are not always clearly understood. What I would argue, however, is that these processes of atomisation have enabled new, less directly visible agents of power to control thought in new ways (which I will discuss in Chapter 4).

Mis-managing public opinion

A key feature of the disconnect therefore is the direct implication of the mainstream media. Here Trump and Farage – as well as their left-wing counterparts Corbyn in the UK and Sanders in the US, who I will discuss later – again tapped into ideas already circulating across media, politics and publics in different forms. Trump's rhetoric of media as the 'enemy of the people' may have been hyperbolic but the sentiment was not new. In both the UK and the US, right-wing media historically positioned themselves aggressively against their liberal counterparts, which were also their rivals in the marketplace (though attacks should not be seen as simply one-way). In the US, it has been argued that Fox News was set up to counter the historical liberal bias in the media landscape, and commentators attacking titles such as the *New York Times* are a regular feature (Bartlett, 2015; Cameron, 2018).

The stable of newspaper titles owned by Rupert Murdoch in the UK consistently attack the BBC on everything from 'dumbing down' to staff pay scales, as well as the funding model (Petley, 2015). In 2011 the Leveson inquiry, which was set up to investigate media conduct in the wake of a scandal in which a major tabloid newspaper hacked the phone of a murdered girl, charted routinised unethical practices in news-gathering as well as a web of corrupt relations and information sharing between politicians, the police and the media (Department for Digital, Culture, Media and Sport, 2012). It was perhaps the most significant reputational crisis in British journalism in recent history. In parallel on social media and the blogosphere, often intensifying around key political events including the independence referendum in Scotland in 2014, there developed almost an industry in monitoring the distortions of mainstream media, as well as the space for legitimate and not so legitimate criticisms to spiral. Here we see a complex interplay of media narratives, people's own disaffection with media reporting and the very real and evidenced failures of the industry. As already discussed, in my own research, when people referred to a lack of trust in the system, they saw the media to be right at the heart of it, not outside looking in.

It was within this context that mainstream media began their soul-searching following Trump's election win in 2016, and to some extent in the UK following the Brexit vote. It is important to note the clear differences between the context and nature of the Brexit vote on the one hand and Johnson's and Trump's leaderships on the other. A key one is the degree to which in the media landscape in the US, the players identified as liberal largely map onto the Democrats, and right-wing outlets such as Fox align with Republicans, whereas in the UK, at the heart of the media landscape is the BBC – of which there is no US equivalent, as it is public service media at scale. The BBC is broadly liberal on social issues but leans right on economics and policy, and particularly so when a Conservative government is in power (Wahl-Jorgensen et al., 2017). Johnson, for example, received largely positive coverage from the BBC (and most of the press), and this may be one reason why his rhetoric did not much echo Farage's in respect of attacks on elites (Oborne, 2021). But, in spite of these differences, there were parallels in the way in which these 'liberal' or otherwise outlets responded to these unpredicted outcomes, and a perception that, as the Bureau of Investigative Journalism noted: 'journalism, just like the pollsters, failed' (Oldroyd, 2016).

In this, the mainstream media's defining of its own election reporting as a 'failure' exposed much about what they understood journalism's role to be. In an unprecedented open letter to its readers after the shock election, the *New York Times* stated its 'aim to rededicate ourselves to the fundamental mission of *Times* journalism' (Sulzberger and Baquet, 2016). For outlets such as the *New York Times*, CNN and the BBC, the 'fundamental mission' is based on a broad understanding of the liberal model of 'the fourth estate', which brings us back to the earlier discussion of the expected practices and norms of journalism in producing 'objectivity'. In relation to this, there was some acknowledgement of the simplistic personality-led coverage of the election obsessed with a candidate 'so crude, spiteful and intemperate [that he] could never be elected' and their own 'naivety' when that translated into votes (Sullivan, 2016).

The CEO of CBS, however, offered a simpler explanation: 'it may not be good for America, but it's damn good for CBS' (Bond, 2016: unpaginated). Simply put, Trump received more coverage because he is a product that sells. A similar argument could be made about Farage's disproportionate prominence on the BBC, with over thirty appearances on the BBC flagship politics show *Question Time* since 2000 (The Jouker, 2019). He didn't win a seat in the House of Commons until 2024 but he had a huge Twitter (X) following and sold newspapers.

That media, public service media aside, operate to generate profit is undisputed – but, as noted in the Introduction, they are also agents of influence, and these two forces can pull in different ways. The comment from the Bureau of Investigative Journalism is telling in that it parallels journalism with pollsters, who are uniquely focused on predicting who will win elections. The comment indicates a shared interest in outcomes. Journalists are not concerned solely with faithfully covering an election campaign and informing the public in an impartial way: they are concerned with influencing the outcome of it. Here they failed both to predict and to *persuade*. This was a *mis-management* of public opinion.

Some journalists did acknowledge that their complete lack of understanding of why such a candidate could ever triumph over their anointed candidate, Hillary Clinton, emphasised a disconnect with audiences (Oldroyd, 2016). But discussions of the 'failure' did not directly refer to influence, as this would necessarily preclude some reckoning with the way in which the media operate in normal times to manage public opinion: that is, in the closing down of options and perspectives which might speak to people and reflect their interests. To return to a previous point, the kind of rhetoric which was promoted by Trump and to some degree by the Brexiteers was relatively apolitical in many ways. The appeal to the crisis in trust, calling for a fairer system to represent 'the people', could have manifested itself in different leaders and different policy programmes, and at the time, alternatives were offered.

In the US, Bernie Sanders ran to become the Democrat nominee twice, to run first in 2016 and then in 2020. It is very feasible to see how the following form of rhetoric might have been very appealing among the disaffected groups:

> [C]orporate and billionaire-owned media often tilts coverage against candidates [...] who push a working-class agenda – an agenda that threatens the political power of corporations and billionaires. (Greve, 2019)

In his emphasis on the corporate '1 per cent' and corruption of the system, Sanders also mirrored the concerns of some sections of the public. In 2016, as noted, the low level of mainstream coverage of Sanders's campaign was completely out of step with polling and the large crowds he was attracting (Byers, 2016; Chang, 2019). In 2020 the coverage was fairly negative, and particularly so in comparison with that of his rival for the nomination, Joe Biden (Johnson, 2019). One difference between Sanders and Trump was that Sanders moved on from simply attacking the liberal media to exposing their links to big business – Amazon and others – and offering policy solutions in the form of higher taxation.

In the UK, in 2015, Jeremy Corbyn was voted Labour leader on the promise of a radical change in direction. In response to the question of the groups in society going unheard, Corbyn proposed solutions such as open and participatory conventions on key issues from the environment and the economy to social policy and a move away from top-down leadership. On delivery of his manifesto prior to the 2019 election he said:

> the most powerful people in Britain and their supporters are going to tell you that everything in this manifesto is impossible. That it's too much for you. Because they don't want real change. Why would they? The system is working just fine for them. It's rigged in their favour. (Rodgers, 2019)

His position on the gap between the elite and public opinion on the economy was a key aspect of his popularity among Labour supporters. In response to this, he received coverage with echoes of Trump's in respect of demonisation and attacks on his character where the press moved from 'watchdog to attackdog' (Cammaerts et al., 2016: 2). Again, coverage was light on policy analysis and, when it was there, it was decontextualised and distorted. But oddly, after the 2019 UK election, the media spent less time lamenting their own 'failure' and questioning what they should do next than they did following the outcomes of Trump's campaign and the Brexit referendum. In these cases they saw a successful *management* of public opinion. In their eyes, the coverage had worked.

These outcomes were of course the product of a range of factors. And in Trump's case, the reliance on social media, often bypassing professional media, and a completely new form of political campaigning within the context of broader discussions about 'post truth' became the primary focus of the liberal media in this period. There were some initial interesting discussions about the way in which coverage of Trump's campaign had called into conflict two norms of journalism – that of reporting truth and remaining impartial – and these had echoes of the scholarly critique of balance as bias and the dangers of giving serious attention to unevidenced and unrepresentative views. But over time, these moments of reflection gave way to a discursive shift to the more defensive focus on the external threat of 'fake news' in a 'post truth' world.

Fake news, 'truth' and media trust

The term 'fake news' is conceptually fuzzy: it can refer to one of or a combination of disinformation, misinformation, and state and market propaganda, and for some people is simply conflated with media bias. When 'fake news' emerged as a central concern around the time of the 2016 presidential campaign, the focus was the circulation of stories with no evidence base, which was seen to play a role in influencing political outcomes. For example, the story that the Clinton supporter George Soros was paying

Trump protestors was believed by over a third of Trump supporters (Public Policy Polling, 2017). But as the discussion progressed news agencies such as the BBC and *New York Times* waged war on 'fake news', which played out largely in endless 'fact-checking' of news and opinion, underpinning which was the foundation of mainstream journalism and the norm of 'objectivity'. This was a discourse which was all about the management of public opinion – with the aim of reconstituting liberal journalism as the anchor of the public conversation on any issue.

In retaliation, 'fake news' was co-opted as a weapon by Trump and his team to discredit the legitimacy of the mainstream media and their version of 'truth'. As my co-authors and I argued in our book *Trump's Media War* (Happer, Hoskins and Merrin, 2018), Trump, for a time at least, was more effective in his approach here, as he understood that the battle going on was not for claims to be guardians of 'truth'. The use of the term 'alternative facts' by a member of the Trump team in relation to their own information supply was much mocked across social and mainstream media (Swaine, 2017). The comment by Michael Gove during the Brexit campaign that 'the people of this country have had enough of experts' (Jackson and Ormerod, 2017) was condemned, but in office Johnson governed with a similarly low level of respect for evidence and with consistently high approval levels, at least before Covid (Oborne, 2021). Both men demonstrated a finer understanding of the 'post-truth' environment and what was at stake than did most liberal journalists: that the issue was one of trust as much as one of 'objective' truth or checking 'facts'.

If this sounds like a radical shift, I would argue that it is and it isn't. As I noted earlier, trust has always been at the core of audiences' investment in media accounts. In the twentieth century trust was organised around conceptualisations of a singular 'truth' – rooted in familiarity and a belief in its unique form of expertise, but the context was one of few alternatives. In response to the recent body of scholarship (Kahan, 2015; Kreiss, 2015) arguing that the erosion of journalism as the centred orientation of democracy is founded on the mistaken notion that there could ever be such a centre because other factors such as identity or partisanship become the lens through which we decide what is true and not true – that it is an *epistemological* difference – I would counter that how people process and judge the facts they are offered was never the most important thing. Only a minority of people (and we might squabble over the size of it) pore over facts and evidence. Trust as involving a leap of faith is first and foremost dependent upon the perception that people are acting with good (or ill) intentions.

This is not an argument about whether or not we can verify that real things happen; that is 'truth' by the most basic shared social definition, and most people still feel cheated when they see evidence of distortion about actual events (whether they ever see or listen to it of course cannot be assumed). But where journalists' claims to 'truth' are now questioned is in how they make meaning of those events, and whether and how much attention they give to them. These can't be separated, as journalists must make meaning through their selections and the context and explanations offered.

These questions of truth played out in interesting ways in focus groups in this period (and beyond). While some participants distrusted media and politics on the basis that they didn't tell the truth, just as many engaged with the question of what truth is and how to recognise it. Participants drew on a negotiated concept of truth – what one described as 'partial truth' – and another noted that he always looked to see 'if there is a slightly different version of the truth'. This comment sums up how some people saw it:

> I have to say no one is really wrong and no one is one hundred per cent right, there's a little bit of truth in everybody's argument. (Male, low income, UK, 2015)

If 'truth' is not seen to be absolute, trust requires an even bigger leap of faith. It is conferred when people become convinced that whoever is speaking can be relied upon to be consistently fair and acting in the best interests of their audience. Especially where bias is widely perceived, trust dictates who is listened to.

And people continue to care deeply about trust. They often go to considerable lengths to source trusted information, as I will document in Chapter 2. As I stated at the start of the chapter, trust is at the heart of any social contract. But more than that, people feel anchorless without a sense of trust in place. For some this can lead to disengagement – at the extreme end, some participants in focus groups said they just no longer cared about anything in public life – and for others it leads to a deep concern about what might happen when systems and agents can't be trusted. To the difficult question of whether liberal democracies should even aim to produce some form of recognisable and shared vision of reality, when it will necessarily be selective and over-representative of powerful voices, this provides the answer. It must be yes, because we are social beings, and society can't exist without a common orientation point. There can be no identifiable public consciousness and consensual prospectus for change without it.

But that doesn't mean that it will necessarily always look the same or represent the same power bloc. It doesn't inevitably lead to the same forms of legitimacy and knowledge production. I return to my earlier point about the importance of making the distinction between the construction of public opinion and its management. Even 'public opinion' must have some foundation in what people experience, perceive and believe. To reinstate the hegemony of liberal media and politics in a public that journalists had lost in the US at least required a clearer reckoning with what was going on in people's lives, with what they felt and thought. In this journalists had to contend with the widely felt dissatisfaction with systems in which media were seen as complicit. They also had to compete with actors who built their whole ideology on the media's historical complicity. Without addressing the root causes of the absence of trust, the obsessive drive to 'fact-check' in this period was always unlikely to win the consensus.

The pandemic response: trust on trial

However, people's perceptions and priorities change. In early 2020 the collective and individual experience changed, and perceptions and priorities changed very quickly in parallel. The advent of the global pandemic, registering on the public consciousness in different contexts at different times in early 2020, put trust to the ultimate test. Collective investment in the system and trust in decision-makers to act in the public interest were at the heart of any mitigation and response efforts throughout the countries of the world. Across the pandemic, public acceptance of measures such as varying degrees of lockdown, mask-wearing, social distancing and latterly vaccination uptake was vital. It was, in many ways, the very worst time to have an ongoing crisis in public trust, but the context also produced outcomes in not always predictable ways. Here I would reiterate the key arguments about trust:

- first, that people lose faith in systems to act for the public good when there is a collective sense that media and political rhetoric do not match their real-world experiences;
- second, that people do not want to abandon trust and care deeply about it, as without trust they feel anxious about what might happen in society; and
- third, as a result, people must find ways to attribute trust, and usually this will be invested in those who can be relied upon to be consistent and relatively predictable in their interpretations of what is right and fair.

Trust in governments and media in the West remained low at the time when the pandemic hit (Edelman, 2020). Both Trump and Johnson were however polling relatively well, and with Trump's approval rating at 49 per cent in March 2020, claims that he might have been on course to win his second election were not completely unfounded (Borenstein and Fingerhut, 2020; Dzhanera, 2020; YouGov, 2022b). The primary importance of economy, jobs and opportunity to the electorate may be summarised in the oft-repeated phrase 'it's the economy, stupid'. But in times when public health is under threat at the collective and particularly at the individual level – as almost everyone will tell you when asked directly – that is the top priority. Of course, that is not to say that health is prioritised at the expense of the economy, and people will disagree on where the balance should lie, but the aim of saving lives is broadly accepted as something those in power should put first.

It's important here also to re-state the context in the US, which was one of fragmented and partisan information sources and, in a very large country, very different value systems. Also, there was an election in the midst of the pandemic, the result of which was very close and doesn't allow for strong claims to be made about majority sentiment or simple causation. There is a rich and expansive literature documenting why the president may have lost, but here we are interested specifically in trust – and what polls showed is that Trump suffered from a significant lack of trust in his handling of the pandemic (Langer, 2020; Strandberg, 2020). As noted above, Trump's rhetoric had, as a central element, the promotion of distrust in elites and even liberalism as a system. During the pandemic, where anxiety about what might happen was at its highest, one group were trusted by a majority. These were the scientists, a group that Trump had continually tried to silence and delegitimise in his time in office, particularly those who spoke out on climate change (Barrie et al., 2020; Johnston, 2017).

Again, it's important to stress that scientists are not trusted absolutely, or equally by all groups in society. This was very apparent from the body of data I draw on here. Scientists were the most trusted of all sources referred to in discussions (a finding which is also replicated by the Edelman Trust (Edelman, 2020)). However, in the lower-income groups and in the Republican-leaning parts of the country in particular, there were disputes over the integrity and trustworthiness of scientists, and in the 'agenda' rooted in vested interests. This discussion in a Dallas focus group about climate scientists illustrates the point:

> Female speaker: I don't see the money or the political gain that [...] if we're talking about a huge number of scientists, we're not talking about one or two or three, we're talking about 80 per cent of scientists think this. What would they gain from that? I just don't see – I don't see the money.
> ...
> Male speaker: I know, but ... but you've got an agenda out there that's willing to spend money on it, right, so, you know, they're going-I can get these guys approved as I can start this and get all this money so the scientists ... the scientists are always looking to get a grant. (Middle income, US, 2015)

But while some felt that 'scientists, they can lie just as easily as anybody else', most gave them the benefit of the doubt, as this participant said:

> Like, if they gave us facts like so and so, it's been researched, scientists so and so, like I'd want to believe it. (Male, low income, UK, 2015)

At this stage, before the pandemic, politicians 'listening to the science' were broadly believed to bring better public outcomes.

Johnson in the UK similarly saw levels of trust fall in relation to his handling of the pandemic, though less significantly than Trump (Woodcock, 2021) (at least prior to 'Partygate', which exposed the way in which members of the government had simply ignored all the restrictions imposed on the public). While a looming election can consolidate public sentiment in distinct ways, Johnson at least rhetorically emphasised the importance of 'listening to the science'. In fact, the October 2021 House of Commons report into the failings of the UK's Covid response showed a fairly dysfunctional relationship between scientists and government, which was a factor in the resulting excess of deaths. As noted in the Introduction, an important factor was the tendency to overestimate resistance to measures such as the lockdown and the vaccination programme (Sample and Walker, 2021). However, Johnson did not openly delegitimise scientific advisors as Trump did, for example, in the case of the leading infectious disease expert Anthony Fauci (BBC News Online, 2020a). Johnson also had not significantly parted ways with liberal media which put scientists at the heart of their reporting. A key factor in outcomes is always the presence (or absence) of legitimate alternatives. In this too Johnson did not face a media which enthusiastically supported an alternative candidate, as was the case in the US with Biden.

But while Trump may have lost the election, the US media that he described as 'enemies of the people' have not necessarily undergone the kind of restoration of trust they may have hoped for – and that indeed the media received in some other countries, where trust and desire for accurate information went up in this period (Newman et al., 2021). According to the Reuters Institute Digital News Report of 2021, after the pandemic, the US had the greatest distrust in news in the world, and this sentiment was felt particularly among those who were right-leaning and the young. Despite the study finding broad support for the 'ideals of impartial and objective news', many news consumers conceded that they were drawn to more partisan content (Newman et al., 2021). In other words, they believed news in theory but not in practice.

Again in 2021, where the news media were broadly supportive of audiences' own preferred speakers or political parties, they were more likely to listen and pay attention to them. When they didn't, as before, they were put off by perceptions of bias (Ralph and Relman, 2018). In the UK, the BBC's centring of scientists bolstered its legitimacy. The corporation largely followed the government in this, indeed in a very real sense, as the main channel broadcast its briefings with scientists daily. The BBC, which scored very highly on trust in the Reuters study, is unique in many ways. First, it has a global reputation built up over a century for trusted news and expertise which carries great weight, and second, as a public service broadcaster it would have the dissemination of public guidance about Covid as part of its remit.

The media, as I noted in the Introduction, do not hold power independently, nor can they construct public feeling from nothing (though they can manipulate and shape understandings of what it is). In this, the media exist in a circuitry relationship with politics, political speakers and public response, depending on the range of factors I will document in the next chapter. Media outlets can selectively promote and marginalise ideas, they can critique the leaders, or they can support their agendas to differing degrees, but they are bound into the political ideology and culture as it exists. Levels of trust can be restored only when the disconnect between the story of neoliberal politics they are selling and the public's experiences are addressed and new possibilities offered. If this idea of a unifying core now seems impossible to imagine, the early period of Covid demonstrates how close we might get: where trust is the unifier, and not that the nature of information, channels of access to it and interpretations of 'truth' will all look the same.

Conclusion

Here, finally, we return to an earlier question: are we seeing the end of the neoliberal era? We also ask: what did the responses to the disconnect and desire for change actually mean for systems of politics and power? Paolo Gerbaudo in *The Great Recoil* (2021) tackles this question and argues that Covid illuminated some of the vulnerabilities of the populist right. This would include the demeaning of science and expertise but also the prioritisation of profit over people's lives and welfare. He argues that we have moved into a new era in which:

> from the collision between neoliberal thesis and populist antithesis a novel synthesis is now emerging in the form of a protective neo-statism that aspires to displace neoliberalism in its role of defining our shared ideological horizon. (Gerbaudo, 2021: 36)

It's important to note that neoliberalism is, after all, just the latest stage in capitalism, and so this is not to suggest a radical overhaul to the current system, but more an allowance for shifts in emphasis. For all the rhetorical antagonism between the right and liberal left in both politics and media, neither poses any challenge to capitalist hegemony. In both the US and the UK, concessions in respect of social investment and a more protectionist approach to production and trade have been built into political programmes to some degree, as reflected in the shared slogan of 'build back better' for example. In 2021 even the *Wall Street Journal* and the *Financial Times* intimated that the neoliberal consensus was ending or at least needed modifying.

However, as Ajama Baraka, the candidate for US vice president on the Green Party ticket in 2016, noted in 2021:

> not because capitalists have suddenly experienced a scrooge-like transformation but because they are recognizing that even the absence of a militant movement putting pressure on them, they have to have stop-gap measures to address the now glaring contradiction of neoliberal capitalism. (Baraka, 2021)

The situation is changing even as I write, but one thing that persists for now is the neoliberal form of fragmented resistance and demands for change in respect of questions of identity, nationalism and so on. In most cases, these are absorbed into systems of power, and the mis-management of opinion is addressed with concessions as necessary (or other events simply changing the course of events).

I have argued that a disconnect, affecting different groups to different degrees, has pushed people to invest in alternative sources of information outside the mainstream, often via social media and atomised public thought and opinion, which can produce fragmented communities organised around particular issues of concern and less conventional assessments of trust. If this makes it more difficult for professional journalism to manage public opinion, as I argue in Chapter 4, power operating in a less visible way continues to manage opinion and thought in the digital environment and exerts influence with a remarkable lack of transparency or accountability. In the next chapter, I'll look more closely at the processes by which opinions are produced in the intersection of trust, ideology, context, values and modes of negotiating information which position people either further away from or closer to the centre.

2

Filtering for opinion: a new conceptual model

In the previous chapter, I made the case for trust or lack of trust as an important factor in shaping responses to media accounts and argued that a disconnect which positions people at a distance from the mainstream, affecting different groups to different degrees, can play a role in facilitating societal outcomes. In this chapter, I develop a more granular model for understanding the way in which media and information are sought out negotiated and (dis)connect, and the conditions under which opinions may form or change. In doing so, I return to a central question that I set out in the Introduction – and that is largely addressed as a conceptual concern in the literature cited – the degree to which opinion is manipulated by media and communications and the degree to which it may form independently of them. But I move beyond concerns with how mainstream media, still relatively consistent in the perspectives which tend to be elevated, manage public opinion to an understanding of the new mechanisms for constructing thought and opinion in social media environments.

This inductive model, informed by a significant body of empirical research, operates across six filters which locate these processes in socio-political systems as well as everyday interpersonal exchanges and experiences to produce different opinion outcomes for different groups. These filters work in different ways and, as I will demonstrate, come to the fore at different times. Ideology is the foundational set of societal understandings, and along with collectively produced priorities and value systems, underpins consideration of the positions that present themselves for people to take up. Interpersonal communities, and in particular those constructed around identity and alignments, negotiate and interpret the range of information circulating in the culture in an ongoing way. Modes of media engagement, understood here as strategies that people develop to access, manage and assess content, are particularly useful for understanding how media messages are confronted as they come in. Finally, lived experience can, when striking enough, lead to a distrust of the information and knowledge in current circulation and a re-arranging of established positions.

Ideology

The first filter I want to look at is ideology, with the media understood as a key mechanism for its transmission. I return to the earlier definition of ideology as a lens through which power relations in society are perceived and rationalised as common-sense or inevitable, or what Mark Fisher (2009) described as 'capitalist realism', the sense that there is no viable alternative to the system that we currently have. Here the focus is the role of ideology in shaping people's beliefs and understandings. In this respect it is useful to imagine a spectrum along which people might sit. At one end, in respect of Hannah Arendt's conception of ideology as 'literally the logic of an idea' (1976: 469), it provides an explanation for everything that happens, and experience can teach us nothing. For thinkers such as Gramsci and Hall, who sit closer to the other end, ideology is taken up by and invested in to different degrees according to where people are socially located. The key factors are the extent to which the dominant ideology in any social context is contested, and the level of its embeddedness into the structures within which we live.

At the most basic level, the degree to which the 'no alternative to capitalism' ideology works depends upon the stakes people have invested in the system and what they perceive they have to lose. This is about the kinds of things people want out of a society and how they believe their interests will be met. I discussed in the previous chapter how the dissatisfaction with the free market ideology of neoliberalism led to a disconnect because the political and media rhetoric did not match the reality on the ground. At the same time, evidence suggests that any alternative which didn't promise to protect the benefits of competitive employment and the housing and education markets – with rising house prices being a core benefit – would still largely be rejected by the majority. This was shown in in a circular way after the financial crash of 2008 in the UK, when initial media outrage over the greed of the bankers gave way to a discourse of necessary measures to get the economy back on track and protect markets (Happer, 2017b). Other positions were closed down in British media and politics, and the public delivered a new government led by the Conservatives on a promise of austerity to deliver on that agenda (Berry, 2012).

This point also came across in my own focus groups, particularly those with participants of working age, where taking measures to tackle climate or other political issues in the context of unresolved public debt was said to be a bit like 'fiddling while Rome burns'. In some groups, which took place well after the crash as priorities shifted, participants continued to caution that any measures should be 'realistic' or 'pragmatic'. Interestingly, conversations here often followed a familiar pattern: they began with some consensus that action should be taken and change was necessary, and after consideration of the implications, this final comment was typical: 'realistically it's not going to work'. There was a fear of losing freedoms and economic gains in a highly competitive environment. As one participant said:

> I mean, it's easy to sit and say that we should do x, y, and z but the reality is we all like our home comforts. (Male, middle income, UK, 2015)

In the younger groups, where there was a much wider consensus that measures to mitigate climate change should be taken, these attitudes were bound up with the perception that climate destruction is a threat to all future interests. The stakes are very high. Do young people still however aspire to the same things as older generations, such as home ownership? It's interesting that much of the research that is available on the latter – which suggests they do – seems to be commissioned by banks and building societies (see, for example, Brignall, 2019). Here Bourdieu's critique of polls representing the interests of those who commission them may be most keenly felt. But what has been apparent in my own research is a sense of frustration from some young people that they can't enjoy the economic gains their parents made. In this, the analysis of the problem is much the same:

> I think the problem is just the people [...] people are just lazy and they don't actually care that much about the future generations and what's going to happen, they care about the here and now. (Male, student, UK, 2015)

This perception runs in parallel to a widespread media discourse of a 'generational divide' portraying 'boomers' as selfishly hoarding all the benefits of the modern welfare state (Martin and Roberts, 2021). Again, the ideology that what other people will do, what they ultimately want and what they will be prepared to give up is a strong determinant of what is seen to be possible and what is realistic in terms of the wider system. It may be argued that this represents a complicity with the system, and certainly somewhere the collective deal was made that to protect individualism in liberal democracies means to give up actual liberty to markets (Deneen, 2018).

Most people have little direct knowledge of these questions, which are ultimately rooted in the economy and financial markets, and so they are particularly reliant on media narratives to guide their thinking. But I want to also to look at a relatively uncontested ideology which has become a form of 'realism' in recent years, and which everyone has direct experience of. This is the ideology that having a digital presence is essential or at least inevitable. Again, there is growing evidence of public opinion that social media and a wider digital society have brought many negatives such as fake news, increased anxiety and toxic online abuse (Brey et al., 2019; Donovan, 2020; Jayakumar et al., 2021).

In focus groups, people brought up these negatives, and young people in particular described very challenging and stressful online experiences. But when asked whether it was possible to have no social media presence, almost all said no. A pattern emerged in which a response began with 'I would really like to get rid of Facebook/Twitter/Instagram but I find it really useful for …' and then listed the reasons such as 'news', 'messenger' and 'friends' which made it 'impossible' for the participant to stay offline. This description by a young woman of how she managed her accounts was quite typical:

> I go through phases like sometimes I'll like use it a lot and other times I'll be like, right, I need to kind of purge myself and I'll delete the app and then I'll end up reinstalling it. (Female, student, UK, 2013)

These offline periods offered proof that in fact life continued to function without social media. Still, people returned. As conversations deepened, some participants struggled to articulate what social media gave them. But a word that came up quite frequently was 'validation'. As one young woman noted: 'you get that validation and you feel good about yourself'. For others, it was validation of opinions and ideas, and I will return to this later in this chapter.

More generally, there was a sense that staying offline meant missing out on something or an absence of something. Ultimately it was in people's interests to be present on at least some selected platforms – even where experiences were largely negative. Of course, we need to understand this in the context of the design and affordances of social media, which promote addictive behaviours (and the need to be online for access to basic services, though it is possible to argue that this is separate). But I would argue that the structural embedding of social media in the everyday is accompanied by an ideological set of assumptions about digital identities as essential for contemporary lives, and often it was this, rather than patterns and conveniences of usage, which drew people back. Cross-media discourses around social media largely parallel this contradictory position where, as Jorge notes, 'disconnecting is portrayed and even promoted as useful as a *temporary* experience' (2019). In this, they confirm that it is just not 'realistic' to lack a digital presence – an ideological position which serves new forms of power very well.

These ideologies of 'realism' about the workings of the system underpin the mainstream media messages circulating in the culture, connecting with the public thanks to their familiarity and taken-for-grantedness (Hall, 1973). They emerge in conversation in ways which help to position people around new ideas. However, these ideologies are contested to different degrees in public and in private, and are subject to a range of other filters which can either cement or overwhelm them in respect of interpretations and opinion forming in different contexts.

Priorities and established value systems

The second filter is value systems and related priorities. These are distinguished from ideology in their explicit nature – they are not unsaid and unquestioned – and in not necessarily being in service of power. Jaspers offers a useful definition: 'values give direction to the way that individuals, organizations, and societies act; what they strive for; and what they deem important' (Jaspers, 2018: unpaginated). Priorities involve some ordering of values, and are reactive to changes in environment. They are also rooted in cultural assumptions about how people do and should live, though they can also be very localised to families, workplaces, peer groups and so on.

One broadly shared value, and one which is particularly prioritised when it is seen to be under threat, is preserving good health, of individuals and of their families and loved ones. I referred in the Introduction to the mismatch between the journalists' prioritisation of getting the economy back on track and the widespread public prioritisation of saving people's lives. Early in the pandemic, at the daily briefings by the UK government broadcast on the BBC, the corporation's political editor, Laura Kuenssberg, echoed the wider media landscape in persistently pushing the government to manage the 'trade-off between protecting people's health and protecting people's jobs' (Happer, 2020: unpaginated). Meanwhile a YouGov poll in April 2020 found that the large majority of the UK public supported Covid measures even though they also believed that the economy would suffer as a result of them (Stone, 2020). Health – not allowing people to die needlessly – was a priority for most of the following year, though public concern about the economy started to grow to similar levels not long afterwards (Smith, 2020).

Similarly across focus groups prior to Covid, discussions about priorities for political action and motivations for behaviour often included some reference to health. In these, feeling healthy and maintaining health were key themes, and for many the sense of the immediacy and personal nature of health was a factor. As these participants noted:

> Like my view just usually isn't that big [in relation to 'bigger picture' concerns]. So the only thing that [...] affects me more is just like the idea of health. Like that's a personal, like okay, I'm gaining too much weight, I might not

be able to survive, or this is going to do this to certain organs. (Male, low income, US, 2015)

You know, health is first because it is what is happening to me right now. (Female, middle income, US, 2015)

This was sometimes countered with the claim that income always came first, and the conclusions varied between individuals and within groups. But to return to the previous discussion, for most people, in the moment of very real and serious threats to health, even arguments about the economy, jobs and income were secondary. The UK mainstream media discussions of Covid were also distinctive in their fairly widespread understanding of preserving health as primarily a collective responsibility. At other times, and again this is where the degree of ideological embeddedness is more significant, it is rooted in the sense of individuals acting in the interests of their own health, which can take on a moral character.

This element of moral considerations is again significant in respect of another value which emerged across different waves of research: the importance that was placed on people behaving honestly and decently. This value, as a standard for behaviour and one upon which societal outcomes should rest, was often vehemently expressed and could be influential on a range of other judgements. As emphasised in the previous chapter, the belief that people in power should behave well was a key factor in loss of trust in the system. Talking specifically about a range of issues including MPs' abuse of the expenses system in the UK, this participant summed up the way in which political messaging was received:

If you have not got moral probity in other things, then you have not got moral probity. (Male, middle income, UK, 2011–12)

As noted, there was a strong sense of injustice in respect of powerful groups operating with a different set of rules. Another example of this can be found in the fall in popularity of Rishi Sunak as a candidate for the Conservative party leadership: he was a front runner as potential leader at the start of 2022, but when news of his wife's non-domiciled status, which saved her paying millions in tax, was revealed, his popularity with so-called 'red wall' voters fell significantly (Kirk, 2022). This illustrates an important point about fairness. Across groups, behaving with decency was an explicitly stated value.

This also extended to judgements on how ordinary people should live and the consequences of not adhering to acceptable standards of behaviour. In a research study focused specifically on opinions about crime and punishment, across groups there was a degree of consensus in respect of those breaking the law which was rooted in a sense of fairness and individual responsibility (Happer et al., 2019). Views on the objectives and nature of punishment, as well as the sympathy given to those offending, however, were to some degree differentiated along the lines of income group and patterns in media consumption; for example, those people who read the tabloids tended to perceive prison as too easy and to support harsher sentences. But this also related to where people situated themselves in relation to those committing the crime, as this truncated exchange illustrates:

> First male speaker: From my point of view, as a normal human being trying to battle life, keeping house, keeping my family healthy and my wellbeing, there is no one actually saying 'oh come on let's do it, let me help you' and stuff like that. We have to battle for everything to be honest you know what I mean. Day to day, go out from my bed, whether you want it or not you're going to your job because you need to earn money [...]
> Second male speaker: Maybe you don't need the help, maybe he [the person committing the crime] does.
> First male speaker: Well, if I commit a crime no one's going to look on me like 'oh, he's been grow up in bad society'. How many people there are growing up in bad society and still make a living, and doesn't commit a crime? (Middle income, UK, 2014)

This discussion also shows the way in which moral values are bound up with responsibilities within the economic order – the responsibilities to play a role in a functioning society and/or family unit. But judgements about right and wrong can supersede these too. As the sociologist Andrew Sayer (2004) notes, to treat morality as simply a set of rules of ideas, backed by sanctions, is to ignore the way in which morality has its own internal force.

In other words, how people treat one another, what should be prioritised and why it matters to do the right and just thing cannot be dictated by media or ideology. Certainly values are influenced by societal belief systems including tradition, religion and gender roles, but within families and communities, expectations and judgements will vary. In one group made up of cleaners and janitors, for example, the degree to which a dirty home was connected with morality quite took me by surprise but perhaps shouldn't have done (one participant had such high standards that she refused to use a washing machine and cleaned all of her clothes by hand). An important thing about values is that they tend to be prioritised when they are seen to be under threat. But alignment with value systems is crucial for new ideas and perspectives to connect.

Interpersonal communities

The next filter is interpersonal communities. I refer here to those communities which are naturally occurring and largely originate in offline spaces. These include family networks, educational and workplace settings, and the social contexts where people meet. Taking into account all of the ways in which these communities might engage, this includes consideration of the communications that happen in social media cultures, where relationships may even come together and develop. Online and offline are of course intricately interconnected and difficult to separate. However, I approach them as at least conceptually distinct, with the focus here on those communities that would have some rooting in the way society is organised around physical settings (even more difficult when so many of us now work remotely). Here, though, I will start with the historical and ongoing importance of interpersonal communities in respect of interpretations of media messages.

The communications scholars Lazarsfeld and Merton (1971) identified the importance of interpersonal communication on media interpretations as early as the 1940s. The 'active audience' tradition which emerged in the 1980s represented a more widespread move towards a focus on how 'communities', organised around shared characteristics, experiences and interests, might generate alternative interpretations of mass media messages (Livingtsone, 2013). A body of empirical research showed the way in which social locatedness, and the 'active' everyday exchanges it produced, constructed a lens for processing media texts (Morley, 1980; Ang, 1985; 1991). A necessary corollary of this is the importance of language – the words and the phrases that people are familiar with and are comfortable using in their everyday lives. A major weakness of this work, particularly as it progressed, was its neglect of ideological issues in respect of interpretations – which led to an imbalance in respect of the power attributed to the public in its relationship with media. However, the essence of social locatedness, and the influence of everyday exchanges and the language used in shaping our perceptions and the positions people take up, remain a critical filter for understanding media power.

In the Introduction, I emphasised the role of 'opinion leaders' in influencing the ideas that collectives settle on. Lazarsfeld noted that this could involve offering information and authority on particular subjects (Lazarsfeld et al., 1968), which might shift the direction of a discussion or opinion (Zhang and Dong, 2009). In all of the focus group studies, there were examples of participants offering thoughts which were directly influenced by family members, friends, colleagues or teachers, who brought insights often derived from their proximity to the subject matter. Expertise and related experience close to home carry considerable weight. Similarly, when participants were asked about sources of information, 'conversations with other people' was a frequent response. The degree of immersion in any context of regular dialogue is a significant factor in shaping responses. Workplaces, school playgrounds and family homes nurture particular ways of seeing the world and negotiating new information.

Within my research settings, however, the situation in which a participant has shifted their opinion entirely through the influence of someone else in a group discussion has been relatively rare. The most significant role of any leader in the context of interpersonal communication, I would argue, is that of articulating a position which emerges through discussion and then persuading others that the position is an acceptable one. This requires a particular combination of confidence and communication skills. In these scenarios, once the balance of opinion is expressed, it is neatly summarised in a way that represents a compromise, though often one which is slightly tilted in the direction of the person articulating the position.

The degree to which the position is accepted relies upon its proximity to people's original thoughts – but also on how the position and those who hold it are located in the wider context of opinion. This process may involve a simple construction of participants as a collective through the use of 'we', as for example in 'I think we're saying …'. But the language used here, where one participant is summing up how the group responded to arguments about the impacts of meat consumption on climate change, for example, ascribes a kind of exclusive reasonableness to those within the discussion:

> Yeah, a lot of people just don't accept information anyway. I don't mean the people in this room [of focus group participants], I think we are all receptive to the information but there are some people like, not to be stereotypical, but there's a programme I was watching last night about [the] working class. (Male, low income, UK, 2015)

This comment also illustrates the way in which positions can be organised around perceptions of what other people think and do, even when they are not present. People care deeply about what others think, and this is not just about access to more compelling or new information; it's also about how individuals like to see themselves in relation to others.

This becomes ever more acute in the social media environment, immersion in which, my research would indicate, is increasingly transforming traditional interpersonal communication rooted in the societal organisation of work and leisure (which should be seen in the context of the reduced role of workplace communities and shared physical spaces in recent decades – reaching a pinnacle during Covid). Social media exchanges resemble offline conversations in some ways. The influence of family, friends and articulate others remains significant, and particularly so in those platforms and/or account settings that are relatively private (e.g. WhatsApp versus X, private Facebook accounts, etc.), and the investment of trust in their authenticity and recognition of their expertise or knowledge operate on a similar basis.

Research has shown that interpersonal communications online help people develop and reflect on their own views in respect of political information and may also boost their chances of getting actively involved (Vaccari and Valeriani, 2018). Social media also present positions as acceptable, though this can be less focused on dialogue, which leads to emerging compromise, and more on a constructed sense of consensus (or division). This impression of what other people think and believe creates a perception of what is a reasonable opinion. This relates back to the question of 'validation', as this exchange about Facebook shows:

> Facilitator: Do you feel it's a guide to what other people are doing?
> Participant: What they're thinking maybe. It's good to know what other people think of the same thing you've heard.
> Facilitator: Is that for validation?
> Participant: Yeh, it is validation. It's a personal thing. If you're thinking it's not accurate or whatever and then you compare your thoughts with somebody else it validates it. (Female, small business owner, UK, 2013)

The qualitative difference from offline conversations lies in the volume of comments and the extension of interpersonal networks. Survey research has shown that social media users perceive numeric aggregations as being representative of public opinion (Zerback et al., 2015). My own focus groups added some nuance, in that this broad perception of their representativeness was also accompanied by an awareness of the range of influences on social media discourse, to which members themselves were also subject (and which I'll discuss in more detail in Chapter 4). As one participant said, 'it sometimes feels that there's almost two completely dual cultures' in respect of the divergence between what people say and think online and what they say and think offline.

But in spite of that nuance, the key point was that the perception of representativeness was very influential. As I noted earlier, the degree of immersion in any context in which people's thoughts are aired shapes individual opinions, but this effect is significantly exaggerated as people access a large volume of comments and identify positions which are common, normal or acceptable – or which are uncommon, abnormal or unacceptable. Opinion leaders continue to play a role, but it is the impression of collective opinion which carries most weight, as ultimately people are social beings who adapt to their surroundings. This is not the same as assessments of trust, though of course the two are related. It should be understood more as a process of socialisation through which people absorb a sense of what is acceptable to think, express and believe as well as the words and phrases used to articulate this.

Identity and alignment

A further and directly related filter is that of identity and alignment. In respect of the previous filter of interpersonal communities, I have used the term 'naturally occurring'. In the original 'active audience' work of which Stuart Hall and then David Morley were originators, the emphasis was on class analysis. Class groupings are in many ways naturally occurring in their relation to people's position and organising in the workplace, but of course they are much broader and operate on the basis of self-identification too. Other identity positionings which the researchers in this tradition were interested in – and which empirically were shown to shape meaning-making – included gender, race and age (Ang, 1985; Bobo, 1995; Buckingham, 2000). More recently, work on intersectionality has highlighted the importance of considering the way in which these overlap and interact in respect of their influence on social experience and understanding. In the next chapter I will examine in depth the influence of these identity and other shared characteristics on negotiation of information, opinion formation and attitudinal patterns with an emphasis on shifting fault lines, in which arguably class has become a less predictable marker of social and political alignments. I will therefore keep this section relatively brief.

I want to highlight here communities which are more directly rooted in self-selection and identification and are more fluid in nature. These processes of selection and identification can be particularly significant in communities constructed through social media. Such communities are not exclusively distinct from those which are naturally occurring or demographically rooted, and often they represent an amplification of these divisions as well as sharing some characteristics such as the absorption of a familiar mode of language and expression. Indeed, boyd (2017) argues that people now self-segregate in new ways enabled by digital technology which allow them not only to continue to prioritise the cultures they already belong to, such as those rooted in existing friends and family, but also to actively exclude new people they might meet in changing physical environments. However, they can organise themselves around political beliefs, cultural practices, worldviews, and interests in ways which conflict with them too.

The degree to which social media users construct platform cultures in their own image and reinforce their own beliefs and opinions – so called 'echo chambers' – has been consistently addressed in academic literature (and mainstream media) (Bruns, 2019). While research indicates that the claim of lack of exposure to alternative ideas is largely unsubstantiated (Dubois and Blank, 2018), commonalities in respect of similar language, ideas and issues discussed are more apparent (Erickson et al., 2023). If there is some evidence for what we might describe as an active immersion in communities of 'friends' and 'followers' who think and see the world in similar ways to oneself, it affects people to very different degrees and even at different times (Flaxman et al., 2016). I will return to this in the next section. For my purposes here the important influences are the perception of social media discourse as 'representative' of what other people think and believe, and perceptions of socially acceptable opinions. So how does this relate to the communities people choose for themselves?

Most people, online or offline, know of course that their own selected groups are not representative of a wider population: they know *because* they have selected them. However, in many ways, the basis upon which these opinion communities are selected makes them even more powerful. They are founded on a perceived similarity – in politics, in worldview, in experience, in status, in self-expression – and this identification is founded, in part, on who people imagine themselves to be, and how they would like to be seen. So while these communities may not be seen as broadly representative, they are seen as representative of the people who are most likely to make the right decisions, and as a consequence, the views of other communities can be more easily dismissed where they are encountered. These are groups which are seen as desirable to be aligned with. A question that might be asked is: what might people think of me if I hold opposing views? How might I be seen?

The way in which this element of alignment and identity in the construction of communities adds desirability to volume of opinion is significant. But the importance of this contradictory consciousness – the 'two completely dual cultures' – should also be taken into account, as people do carry an awareness that can be seen to represent a form of resistance to the influence of social media consensus. Most people have a fairly sophisticated approach to making judgements about what information is to be trusted, what information is credible, which opinion communities to be aligned with and when to keep their distance, and they can move between these at speed. My research also shows media practices that aim to seek out ways of assessing the credibility of information, which indicate a continuing investment in mainstream culture as well as approaches to coping when the volume of information becomes overwhelming.

Modes of media engagement: holistic, centred and decentred

The next filter is modes of media engagement, and refers to the strategies people develop to access, manage and assess information. These relate primarily to assessments of trust and credibility, but also to how people manage being confronted with an overwhelming volume of content. Even with the range of processes operating to select, amplify and promote content built into the platforms, there is too much to engage with, much that is contradictory and much that is unverified. The filter of modes of media engagement is particularly useful for understanding how information may be assessed as it is confronted. However, before moving more directly to these modes of engagement, it is worth addressing the question of more general responses to this transformation in the access, volume and nature of content.

When asked directly in my research settings, most people welcomed access to a greater range of content, ideas and perspectives – and there was a sense from some that it was a freedom previously prohibited. This was, however, often accompanied by an acknowledgement that there is 'just too much information' and that navigation had become time-consuming and complex. A minority across the samples in which this was raised noted that they had found themselves responding with confusion and, in some cases, apathy:

> I think it's because we're exposed to so many opinions from people and, you know, a lot of the time it is conflicting opinions, you don't know who to believe, so it's a case of believing nothing instead of believing anything. (Male, office worker, UK, 2013)

In those groups it was broadly felt that this had contributed to the low level of trust in public life. This is supported by previous research suggesting that, across areas of mainstream media coverage, where the message is highly disputed it can lead to disengagement (Philo and Happer, 2013). But in some cases it was also related to a perception that the value of public information had been devalued more broadly and that access to an unfiltered range of content had clouded sensible judgement and understanding. As one participant put it:

> I think the internet [...] it encourages people to put them [opinions] forward as if anybody cares and you read them to pick up this ignorance, bias and they're there to get a reaction or to spout whatever nonsense they have in their head ... all it proves is that when people have an agenda, they can't think clearly. (Female, student, UK, 2014)

Certainly the argument that a less restricted public sphere leads to more informed decision-making is not one that the evidence here or elsewhere suggests. But that is not to say that some people don't *feel* more informed by their immersion in the digital media environment. Here I return to the argument in Chapter 1: that people care deeply about trust and will go to great lengths to source what they perceive to be trusted and credible information. The independent strategies they engage in can also produce a feeling of empowerment. My research would indicate that most people don't just give up and disengage, though I would still warn of it as a possible outcome of the current political and technological climate. To return to the discussion in Chapter 1, evidence would suggest that many are avoiding all news or at least all political reporting (Edgerly, 2022).

Of course, there are lots of reasons for engaging with media, but the focus here is primarily on assessments of trust and credibility of information, and I will document three broad categories in respect of engagement– which I will describe as holistic, decentred and centred – emerging from my qualitative research. The first two may seem opposing in some ways, but are both founded on the principles of self-directed (re)search. It is also worth noting that individuals should not be seen as firmly belonging in a single category.

Holistic

The first category is rooted in questions of consistency and involves a relatively holistic approach. For a growing number of people, the majority of news and other forms of content is delivered via a news aggregate such as Google news, a friend's post or a notification from a preferred platform, and evidence shows that people increasingly do not begin their news journey with news outlets' own websites (Newman et al., 2023). For some, these notifications can trigger a dynamic process of cross-platform and/or cross-media engagement, which is from that point onwards self-directed (though increasingly led by news aggregates). Here a participant describes how this might work for clarity around news stories:

> I don't know about anyone else, but I would go on to quite a few of them and try to build my own picture a little bit so I'd take pieces from … […] if there's a consistent message across four or five different news sites, then you've got to think it's probably pretty much that that is fact. (Male, office worker, UK, 2014)

In line with my previous argument that media bias is seen as largely inevitable, and that journalistic objectivity is increasingly questioned, one aim was to strip away the 'agendas' of the different news outlets in their reporting. In doing this, it's not unusual for people to look beyond their selected and trusted sources, and news aggregates encourage this further. Those more interested in less news conventional content, such as personalised videos or infographics, may access a range of platforms. But for those in this category too there is an emphasis on consistency. This is something the producers of propaganda understand all too well, with a common tactic in the digital world being to bombard users with messaging across outlets and platforms.

Decentred

The second category similarly involves self-directed (re)search and is engaged in by those most likely to align with decentred media cultures. This group, while embracing the world of information and content that digital environments have to offer, do not aim for consistency across sources. To describe the strategies they engage in, I draw on William Merrin's concept of 'me-dia' (Merrin, 2014), which refers to the way in which digital users immerse themselves in an individualised information environment orientated to their own interests, beliefs and desires and which allows them to take control over delivery of content and interactions. As Merrin notes, users tell themselves it's their role to assemble the truths, evidence, claims, ideas and arguments that explain the world to them (Merrin, 2014). To return to the question of news avoidance, of course, some don't aim to do that at all and instead watch cat videos on TikTok back to back, a mode of consumption made possible by the affordances of these kinds of platforms.

For Merrin, 'me-dia' is the dominant mode of digital engagement, and his argument is that people increasingly exist in their own constructed 'hyper-realities'. The empirical research which has investigated this, albeit from a range of competing conceptual positions, is inconclusive but suggests that the degree to which this actually happens can be exaggerated (Flaxman et al., 2016; Dubois and Blank, 2018). From my research, I recognise these strategies as being employed to different degrees at different times. I would also argue that there is still a stronger orientation to what we might call a mainstream or centred media culture, though it varies greatly by age (Newman et al., 2023). But the tendency to engage with content in ways which are led by beliefs rather than the other way around is something I have quite commonly observed in focus groups. For some people, such as those particularly interested in climate and environmental news or LGBTQ+ issues, this is simply a way of prioritising topics of interest. For others, it reflects a more participatory approach to political action which is coordinated online. But it does result in an intense and focused engagement, which can begin to close down alternative perspectives. This is exacerbated when people inhabit private or invitation-only communities, a feature which is built into platforms such as Discord and Telegram, but is increasingly common across the social media landscape, most recently being offered by the more established platforms (Wheelwright, 2023).

An interesting example from my own groups is those who self-identify as 'climate sceptics'. These are people who are highly engaged and motivated as well as often scientifically literate: in groups they were keen to talk extensively about the topic and had a tendency to consult many sources. But over time, they search for evidence which aligns with the position they have taken, and hold conflicting evidence to much stricter standards which make it easy to dismiss. As this position can be (though is not always) aligned with other forms of scepticism, it also makes more accessible the type of content which more generally casts doubt on the credibility of information from official sources – not just mainstream media but also all those groups producing evidence for consumption in the public sphere. It is not difficult to see how this kind of engagement can lead to an embrace of ideas and perspectives increasingly divorced from conventional forms of evidence, such as conspiracy theories. Taking these positions of course would involve some influence from the other filters in the model, with most likely an emphasis on a move towards online communities and away from friends, family and colleagues.

Centred

The final and third category involves perhaps the most traditional way of engaging with media and is employed by those most rooted in a mainstream or centred media culture. It involves a tendency to rely upon legacy news outlets (mostly now online), which are wedded to official sources of information and evidence, centring organisations and voices which are elevated as authoritative and credible. At the top of the hierarchy are government ministers and other politicians, and so their policy announcements and the actions they take have particular importance (though importantly they are not always agreed with!) – although it should also be noted that the category of 'experts' has been to some degree reworked in the neoliberal era. People in this category may or may not consume media widely, but they return to these mainstream sources for confirmation and clarity.

In the UK context, when it comes to news, the most commonly cited source across my studies was still the BBC. This was most pronounced in the older and professional groups, though education also appears to play a role (Newman et al., 2023). A lot of students were included in these studies, and the BBC seems to be a source of at least relative trust among them, as this student said: "cause obviously it [the BBC] does have bias like any other organisation but not quite in the same way as the newspapers do'. However, the audience data shows that younger people are less likely than others to use the social media platforms which bring attention to news from websites like BBC Online, such as Facebook and Twitter (X), and instead use platforms such as TikTok, Snapchat and Instagram, where other influencers and alternative voices tend to dominate (Newman et al., 2023).

Again, trust should not be taken for granted, but people do make decisions on the basis of information they receive.

These categories are not intended to be exhaustive: the role of imagery in assessments of credibility is important, for example, for all categories, and I discuss this in more detail in Chapter 5. Also, my research does not provide the kind of data that would allow for some assessment of the relative sizes of the groups falling into these categories, or the level of movement between them. The picture overall is one of a much more individualised, self-directed and highly active range of strategies for finding and assessing credible information than in the past – but one in which the prioritisation of issues within the media culture people are located in remains intensely significant. It is one in which people orientate themselves to a mainstream culture to different degrees at different times, and some, most of whom sit in the second category, may become very alienated from the centre. As I argued in the previous chapter, it is likely that people on the whole will become more wedded to a centred media culture in times of crisis.

Lived experience

The final filter is the presence or absence of lived experience. By this, I mean an understanding of the world gained through direct, personal involvement in or observation of events in day-to-day life. This relates directly to the theme of the first chapter but must be considered as a filter in its own right. A key argument there was that over time, when collective experience clashes with the public narrative, trust in the system is eroded and demands for change arise which may stand in opposition to the solutions offered by the mainstream. But we should also consider lived experience as a factor in influencing the knowledge and understanding of individuals, and how it interacts with media messaging to shape the positions they may take.

In Chapter 1, I talked about trust as developing in sources which could be relied upon to be consistent and relatively predictable in their behaviours and the related outcomes. Here lived experience should be seen as the ultimate in trusted sources. Of course, it should not be assumed that lived experience comes unfiltered and with its meaning always easily recognisable. As I will argue in Chapter 5, journalists orientate themselves to, but also elevate, issues and events in ways which make them seem as close to people's experiences as possible (this is what they call 'proximity').

The argument here, though, is that experience becomes most important when the other filters fail to provide an adequate explanation of what is going on. This brings us back to Lippmann (2010), who argued that where experience contradicts existing beliefs, one of two things happen: either people dismiss the contradiction, discredit the source and return to their pre-existing perceptions, or, where the evidence is 'striking', they begin to distrust the accepted way of looking at things, feel discomfort with the established beliefs and re-arrange their position accordingly.

So the question is what might count as 'striking evidence' and where the limits lie. To use an analogy, if we are confronted with a long, thin plank of wood, and a broad consensus of public, media, expert voices and collective and/or the relatable sources we rely upon for verification tells us it is a poker for the fire, we are likely to accept that. If we're told by those same sources that it's a table, then there is still a good possibility that we will accept that the legs are simply missing. But if we're told the plank of wood is a skipping rope, after we have made repeated attempts to skip over it, the evidence from our own experience may be said to be 'striking' and is likely to overwhelm all other sources. In this and other cases, repeated experience is particularly powerful and becomes the basis for logical assumptions which may carry over into other areas.

Across my research groups there are many examples of situations in which something which people had long been convinced of collapsed in the face of lived experience. A good illustration is the fairly well-established political argument that welfare benefits are generous, there is ease of access, and many recipients exploit them. For those who have not had reason to question this explanation, this can lead to shock and disbelief if they are ever forced to use the benefits system themselves: the gap between experience and rhetoric is comparable to that between a plank of wood and a skipping rope. Interestingly, the evidence suggests that direct and personal experience is very important here, as research has shown that even those who experience the benefits system through relative and friends still carry some of their original assumptions (Briant et al., 2013).

Another area in which people often had quite established beliefs challenged was in relation to the legal system and justice. Where people have the kind of background which does not force them to confront the police and/or legal system on a regular basis, they often assume that the system will be generally be fair and just. In other words, it will be on their side if they behave well. This tends to be the case even where they are immersed in a media context which emphasises the leniency of the system towards criminals, often framing this as a travesty of justice (Happer et al., 2019). When they directly experience the police and/or legal system, however, and the role of money in accessing justice comes to the fore, this again can lead to an indignant disbelief which radically re-orders preconceptions. Over time, where lived experience conflicts with media reporting on a more regular basis, levels of trust can dip significantly.

Conversely, it has historically been this absence of lived experience which has made it more difficult for climate scientists to persuade people in those contexts in which impacts of climate change are less tangible. Where people directly experience the impacts, and even when they are immersed in a political environment which tends to dismiss the science, the former can take precedence, as this comment shows:

> Let me tell you something, if there's anybody who's a real advocate about burning fossil fuels it's me. I have – I have ten cars and eleven motorcycles and I play with them all. [...] But the fact is, is that I lived in Alaska for five years before I moved down here thirty-eight years ago. I've been in Texas for almost thirty-eight years. And I have seen the glaciers recede from places that I used to stand on, who in the last thirty-five to forty years these same glaciers that I used to stand on and take pictures and have fun with are four or five miles – four and five miles, not feet or yards – have melted. (Male, professional, US, 2015)

In focus groups which aimed to communicate the impacts of livestock on carbon emissions (Wellesley et al., 2015), many people simply refused to accept that they could rival emissions from transport because they didn't experience them in that way. As one respondent from a Brazilian study noted, 'you can see the fumes coming out of cars but not animals'. Conversely, respondents felt that they directly experienced the climate impacts of transport. Similarly in questions of managing the economy, arguments can be made because most people don't have direct knowledge or experience of the intricacies of running one. The metaphor of the 'household purse' – which was used frequently in political justifications for austerity in the UK following the financial crash – is a very good example of persuasion based on a comparison which sounds feasible on the face of it (Happer, 2017b).

The key point here is that lived experience can and does play a role, and can be a central factor in changing opinions – but the fact that in many cases it is not the only or even the dominant influence does make a good argument for the power of the media. In a study of media representations of crime and non-custodial punishment (Happer et al., 2019), for example, one woman confessed that, even though her own son had successfully completed a period of community service and had since stayed out of trouble, she found repeated media reporting about its lack of efficacy more convincing. As one of two facilitators, I found this surprising and asked her the same question again. Her final conclusion was: 'It's only worked for Patrick [her son].' In taking her own lived experience out of the equation as credible evidence, however, she was not very unusual. As I noted previously, experience often becomes more important when other explanations become inadequate.

The corollary of this is that the more we are immersed in a media culture where ideas are verified in a range of different ways and evidence is produced for most arguments that exist, the more our own experience as a source has to battle powerful alternatives in order to get through. The more our lives are mediated, the more our understandings are mediated. Although we do have a number of terms in usage to distinguish 'real life' from online life – such as 'IRL' – many people now think that what they hear on social media is 'direct experience' because it comes from 'real people'. Most of the time they refer to things they've encountered on social media without distinguishing them from things they've encountered offline. This is particularly true in the more private platforms and account settings. In addition, even where people are convinced by lived experience, longitudinal research shows that its influence will wane as people return to a media culture in which the already established ideas are reinforced and consolidated (Happer and Philo, 2013).

Applying the model

Having set out the model of media and opinion formulation, I will finally offer two examples of how this may work in particular groups in a generalised way. Nothing, of course, is completely predictable, and these are fairly crude applications, as my key argument is that opinions and the positions we take are highly complex and often very individualised. But these examples may offer some insight into how patterns of opinion may emerge or be anticipated when the filters are known or can be known. They can also be applied to individuals. I will begin with opinions in relation to the highly contentious issue of immigration, and then I will look at Covid measures.

Example 1: immigration

Ideology: At least two dominant and competing ideologies which underpin positions on immigration are circulating in the media and broader culture: a liberal internationalism that welcomes diversity and open borders, which overlaps with a neoliberal promotion of open markets and opportunity; and a protectionist economic approach rooted in the nation state, which can overlap with a nationalistic attachment to tradition and a perceived threat to interests, often inter-related with racist ideologies.

Values and priorities: These may include openness, kindness and a belief that people should all be treated the same regardless of circumstances, and/or a sense that those closest should be prioritised, and/or an idea of fairness in which people should earn support and protection.

Interpersonal communities: Existing opinions about immigration have some relation to naturally occurring communities – for example, positive attitudes are more common in educational settings, and attitudes among older age groups tend to be more negative (Doherty et al., 2018; McLaren et al., 2020) – and allow for conversational exposure to and affirmation of particular positions in everyday contexts.

Identity and alignment: Key political debates such as those about Brexit in the UK and Trump's presidency in the US – as well as broader and more established political positioning around parties and left-wing/right-wing or liberal/conservative axes – polarise self-selected communities both offline and online. This can construct an impression of like-minded people thinking the same and produce linguistic mechanisms for promoting and reinforcing a sense of cohesion and belonging around shared beliefs (e.g. Brexiteers and Remainers).

Modes of engagement: A holistic approach in which information may be assessed in comparison to a broad range of sources reinforces the balance of positions across the media environment. These positions can vary, though in recent years in the UK and the US the media landscape has been broadly negative in respect of immigration as it mirrors the discourse of politicians as primary definers. But a further factor is the degree to which the landscape prioritises (or deprioritises) particular issues. In the UK context, for example, the intensity of broad feeling on immigration reduced after a peak in 2015–16 and the Brexit vote (Binder and Richards, 2020). Alternatively, some people are immersed in decentred media cultures with selective exposure to information which is rooted in existing beliefs and/or interests. This immersion can promote positive or negative views, simplistic or complex, but runs the risk of veering away from conventional forms of evidence. This lies in opposition to those who prefer more centred or official accounts and forms of expertise – which can contradict the media where reporting is not rooted in credible evidence, but can also reinforce narratives promoted by trusted media outlets such as the BBC.

Lived experience: The filters above can be a powerful collective force in respect of attitudes to and expectations of immigration; however, the experiences of those who live and work with migrants and refugees, particularly when they are direct and intensely felt, can contradict and challenge stereotypes and assumptions. Lack of lived experience can increase the media's influence: in the Brexit referendum, for example, Leave voters who had negative attitudes to immigration tended to live in areas with the lowest levels of it, which, it may be assumed, translated into relatively little experience (Lawton and Ackrill, 2016).

Example 2: Covid mitigation measures

Ideology: There is a significant ideological divide between libertarianism on the one hand, which relates to freedom of markets and limited powers of the state and also to individual freedoms and devolved power with a perceived threat of authoritarianism, and, on the other hand, forms of collectivism, which prioritise collectively acting for the public good and/or state welfare and security. However, these ideologies should not bseen as inherently distinct, and they can present contradictions in thought while also overlapping with other ideologies in circulation.

Values and priorities: In the face of threat, the prioritisation of individual and public health and well-being initially dominated for most people, but the competing priorities of generational fairness and protection of jobs and incomes led to shifts over the period of the pandemic and for different people at different times.

Interpersonal communities: Opinions about Covid restrictions also have some relation to naturally occurring communities: for example, evidence suggests that adherence to the guidelines was lower in younger age groups than in older ones because they perceived the threat to themselves as less serious (Mavron, 2021). However, in lockdowns and the ongoing periods of working from home, the influence of interaction in workplaces and educational establishments may have lessened for those less exposed to them.

Identification and alignment: The first year of the pandemic in the US saw differences in opinion towards restrictions between Republicans and Democrats; however, this alignment was perhaps less stark than might have been expected (Schaeffer, 2021). The need to protect public health was prioritised in as close to a consensus as is likely to be achieved, and this was also the case in the UK. As the pandemic progressed, these partisan divides became more pronounced (if still not dominant), and self-selecting identity-based communities around issues such as vaccination consolidated. For example, membership of the online community of 'anti-vaxxers' indicates alignment with a range of opinions and sources of knowledge and a relatively sceptical view of expert voices (Tyson et al., 2022), indeed more than it might indicate actual choices or behaviour, for which there is a range of reasons. Opinion leaders such as Joe Rogan saw a growth in influence and reach in this period, though in Rogan's case this was in part due to an exclusive Spotify contract.

Modes of engagement: Holistic assessments across a wide range of sources again reinforce the weight of evidence and public support for Covid measures in the UK at least, but less in the US, where the mainstream is more polarised. For those immersed in a decentred media culture, a whole range of evidence and theories are circulating which can intensify people's original positions and their resistance to what may be regarded as the official position, and these are readily accessible to those who are motivated to seek them out. On the other hand, those more rooted in a centred mainstream culture of media and politics may invest particular trust in scientists and a general belief that their recommendations are for the public good.

Lived experience: As already noted, many people re-orientated themselves to digital life in the early days of the pandemic because of remote working and socialising, with lived experience more limited than before. Media constructions of crisis are likely to impact directly on public fear and concern. However, fear of experiencing death and ill health from Covid directly, and indeed the sense of personal fear which may underpin this, is a likely key factor in influencing positions on the measures.

Conclusion

In this chapter, I have offered a model for how opinions may form in the context of a highly mediated environment. It offers some insight into how patterns of opinion may be mapped across a range of factors including demographics, social contexts, identity and modes of media engagement. It does not argue they can easily be predicted, but that analyses applying this model may be useful for anticipating these patterns.

To return to the main theme of the book, in many ways it is more challenging than before for powerful groups to manage public opinion in their interests, as the core of information, knowledge and opinion is increasingly fragmented. The mass media systematically edited and interpreted the vast range of information available, making some sense of the world for audiences and promoting certain truths over others – and digital media have shown that in fact there is an endless stream of circulating, disjointed and often contradictory information with no order or clear sense to it.

At the same time, whereas experience is more mediated than before, and understandings free from the influence of representation are less common, opinion is more highly managed than before. While the range of groups and spaces battling for legitimacy has increased, when powerful groups consolidate, their messaging can be all-pervasive, consuming people's attention and time intensely. The original claim of 'agenda-setting' theorists – that the media may not tell us what to think but they do tell us what to think about – continues to carry weight in the contemporary media environment.

People do however still have alternative resources to draw on. I return to a key point I made in the Introduction: public opinion is not wholly manufactured, in that it cannot be built on nothing. The filters which are less directly founded on media representations, such as knowledge or expertise gained from family, friends and colleagues and lived experience, are particularly important here, but historical and repeated access to different forms of credible information also plays a role. A totally baseless claim is still unlikely to be accepted. But in many cases, all that a claim needs is a kernel of 'truth', by which I mean something that connects on the basis of some relation to truth, to be accepted.

It is also the case that different people need different levels of evidence or credibility in order to be convinced, and here I refer back to the discussions on the complex relationship between truth and trust in the previous chapter. The filters outlined in this chapter also vary in significance in response to contextual influences and individual approaches. The latter is important because the degree to which people choose to be immersed in media – versus spending time talking to family and friends, being outdoors, reading books or even attending church – does vary a great deal. It is rare for people to be completely disengaged from digital media, but the extent to which they engage in self-directed strategies to source, assess and respond to information can be quite different.

To reiterate, though – and perhaps counter-intuitively – more self-directed engagement should not necessarily be seen as empowering. More significantly, it cannot be relied upon to produce good outcomes or clearer understanding. Often the opposite is the case, where people online become invested in distorted, prejudiced or inaccurate accounts. However, I would not want to offer the opposing argument – that thought independent of media is inevitably the fairest or the most accurate. People, unfortunately, are capable of finding prejudice all by themselves, and, as I continue to argue, credible information and some shared perception of what is going on are important for consolidating legitimate demands for change.

3

Class, education and media cultures: 'them' versus 'us'

In the previous chapter I offered a model for understanding how opinions may form in the context of a highly mediated environment, and I identified a series of different filters which may influence these processes. In this chapter, I investigate in more depth two inter-related filters: those of interpersonal communities and identity categories in respect of class, education and age (though these should never be seen in complete isolation from the other four filters). The term 'interpersonal communities' refers to those groups which we are organically located in (workplaces, schools, families) and which now extend into online spaces, and 'identity and alignment' refers to groupings around shared political beliefs, cultural practices, worldviews and interests, which may align with the former or conflict with them both online and offline. Both of these filters emphasise the way in which immersion in particular communities, organised around shared characteristics, might produce patterns of opinions, beliefs and responses to media and might represent identifiable 'cultures'. In Chapter 2 I emphasised the importance of perceptions of representativeness in respect of thought and opinion, and I made the argument that as our lives become more mediated, the communities we identify with become constructed more through media and communications, and less through the institutions and environments that shape our lived experience.

In this chapter, more specifically, I will examine the changing role of social class in shaping a sense of shared culture and political outlook, and then I will address other forms of identity and alignment, with a particular focus on the popular contemporary construction of a generational divide. A key question will be the degree to which these produce identifiable patterns in media engagement and the opinions and positions people then go on to form and orientate themselves around. I will also identify the processes which amplify and consolidate some categories of identification – 'boomer' versus 'millennial', for example – and those which minimise identifications, including forms of marginalisation and distancing. Through these mechanisms, we can see how social value is accorded to certain groups and how those without cultural resources are marginalised, while the essence of structural power goes unchallenged.

In the second half of the chapter I will steer the analysis towards the findings of my own empirical research in more depth, with a focus on the work on the UK, and explore how they might shed light on some of these questions. The way in which the groups were sampled and recruited is set out in the Appendix. As is shown there, the studies were not all approached in exactly the same way. Class is obviously an enormously complex thing to measure, and goes far beyond income and occupation to include qualifications, professional status, and related cultural and ethnic traditions. Questions of community and geography also directly and indirectly impact class alignments.

Across my empirical work, participants were recruited on the basis of income and occupation, though they were organised necessarily by geography because of the emphasis on 'naturally occurring' groups. In some studies there were lower-income and professional/middle-income groups, and in other studies there were groups of 'cleaners and janitors', 'call centre workers', 'IT industry' and so on. Students were usually taken as a separate category, however, and this included both groups of university students at prestigious universities and groups of students at further education colleges in inner-city areas. Some young people were included in the lower-income or occupational groups too if they were not in education. These modes of sampling and recruitment must be taken into account in the findings that are presented. For example, sampling by educational status may obviously be likely to produce insights into education and culture. Groups were not separated by gender or ethnicity, and hence I do not offer a coherent analysis by these factors.

Working-class culture

First, I want to return to a key tradition in media and cultural studies, which began with an emphasis on the importance of social class as an identity in influencing interpretations and attitudinal positions. The roots of this were a very public debate throughout the twentieth century about what a working-class culture looked like or even whether it could be said to exist. In 1957 Richard Hoggart published *The Uses of Literacy*, an ethnographic account of working-class life between the 1930s and 1950s in the north of England. He showed how at that point working-class cultures retained a certain authenticity through their emphasis on the internal logic of domestic life. However, written at a moment of rapid social change, his book was also a warning about the growth and influence of a more constructed mass culture. He was concerned that the working classes he documented might be predisposed to the 'invitations of a candy floss world' (Hoggart, 2009: xiii) – that is, to the promises of advertising and sensationalism – than other groups. In many ways, his account documented the coming of a post-industrial class structure founded on corporate capital and mass consumption (Hall, 2019a).

In sounding this warning, Hoggart was, in some ways, aligned with thinkers from the Frankfurt School, who saw mass culture as constructing 'needs' which are then sated through consumerism offering false freedom and choice, while simultaneously diminishing critical and independent thinking (Adorno, 1991; Marcuse, 2002). But a key argument of Hoggart's book was that, because the producers of mass culture would always come from a different background to those of the working classes (the 'Them' and 'Us'), there would always be some differentiation in the way media accounts were interpreted and used. In other words, the culture which was produced in the interplay between mass production and its negotiation by those who engaged with it must say something authentic about the attitudes, experiences and feelings that were already present in working-class lives. For Hoggart, politics was also an integral part of this culture and would be played out in the institutions which structured working-class lives such as trade unions, workers' social clubs and so on. These were the interpersonal communities of that era in respect of shared ideas, beliefs and knowledge. However, he was also one of the first to hint at a more 'classless' society, at least in respect of culture if not economics.

In 1963 E. P. Thompson's *The Making of the English Working Class* similarly argued that while class was determined by economic structure, class sentiment and identity played out in people's everyday lives and their social relationships. Class solidarity was a product of their shared experiences and common lens on the world. As Virdee has pointed out, this common lens was largely that of a white working class, and studies by Thompson and others examining class consciousness in this period neglected the role and experience of ethnic minorities and considerations of race (Virdee, 2014). This absence is replicated in much of media scholarship from the period that followed. However, as Stuart Hall (2019a) noted, these texts were crucial in laying the foundations for Cultural Studies as a field and the shift towards questions of culture and identity in understandings of class.

It was Hall himself who applied these understandings directly to the power of mass media, most significantly in the development of an analytical model which showed how class as a set of shared ideas and experiences might shape interpretations and responses. Hall's 'encoding and decoding' model, first published in 1973, was a pivotal point. It represented a paradigm shift in the way in which the influence of media and communications could be understood.

Media and the struggle for meaning

Like Hoggart before him, Hall (1973) was interested in the negotiation of meaning in the formation of organic cultures. In line with thinkers such as Gramsci, he understood these processes as representative of ideological struggle and was most concerned with the way in which consent for change is won by groups in power. His approach was structuralist in nature and foregrounded the role of language as the site through which these battles primarily take place. In his 'encoding and decoding' model, Hall rooted media ideology in the language and imagery encoded in media texts. However, ideology is understood to be powerful only when it is made meaningful by audiences in the moment of reception. That is, a successful decoding has taken place when the message connects with the experiences, ideas and values – what Hall called 'the map of meaning' – that are already present in people's heads. For example, the word 'democracy' used on the BBC conjures up very different associations – fairness, representativeness and so on – from those it evokes when used on Chinese state television, where it might simply mean Western states or even dysfunction.

There are two important points here. The first is that interpretations can vary and will reflect people's different positioning within social contexts, producing the 'map of meaning' already present, and so what Hall called 'clusterings' around socio-economic, ethnic, geographic and cultural groups are likely to form. The second point is that texts are still 'structured in dominance' (Hall, 1973), and so ideological messaging which connects with the ideas and beliefs which are already in circulation in the culture will connect successfully in the majority of cases. This is a nuanced argument – that media carry great influence, but through contextualised forms of reception subordinate groups also have the capacity to resist social power. My own model, as presented in Chapter 2, broadly inherits these two basic principles. I also follow Hall in the claim that the situation where an entirely new interpretation and/or way of thinking is produced – what he called an 'oppositional reading' – is relatively rare. I am of course working in a qualitatively different technological and political landscape from Hall's.

An early text which applied this model, David Morley's *Nationwide Audience* (1980), emphasised the role of class positioning in shaping the interpretations of television programmes. In this study, trade union membership, naturally occurring in respect of physical environments but also in respect of shared ways of seeing, was a key factor in shaping interpretations. These oppositional readings were seen as the product of a resistant working-class culture and the basis for political action. This body of work, however, which came to be known as the 'active audience' research, gave more emphasis to other identity positionings including gender, ethnicity and race as central to meaning-making (Ang, 1985). This work was important in highlighting that audiences are not wholly predictable, and in its empirical demonstration of Hall's key point about the need for media texts to speak to audiences, to talk their language and connect with their experiences. This allows us, for example, to move beyond crude analyses of the Brexit outcome, which characterise those who voted for Leave as idiots duped by the false arguments of the tabloids. This knowledge forces us to confront often difficult questions of why these narratives connect with people's experiences, values and beliefs.

This work has fallen out of favour, however: in part because these studies were primarily products of the broadcast era, and in part because in spite of some breakthroughs in respect of gendered media and the organisation of women's leisure time around domestic work, they focused on increasingly niche audience groups and failed to speak to wider patterns of experience. This became particularly problematic in an era in which in the social science questions of intersectionality, and the complex interactions between categories of identification and forms of oppression, moved increasingly to the centre. Ethnographic studies of distinct audience groups – that is, those organised around particular texts – often limited the ability to address these relations, and a more flexible, adaptable and critical research strategy for moving beyond single categories of analysis was needed.

But perhaps even more crucially for critical media researchers, the field began to seriously neglect questions of power and ideology, and the kinds of patterns in interpretation, response and opinion formation which allow us to analyse processes of social change. In that respect it does not help with the fundamental questions of this chapter: to what degree is class a continuing factor in shaping a culture and/or set of communities which produce positions for people to take up, and conversely, to what extent have other forms of identity and culture defined as shared experience and ways of seeing become more significant factors? And what is the role of political views and organisation in these processes?

Politics and the generational divide

A useful place to start is with an exploration of one of the most commonly articulated positions on these questions right now – that divisions of age and generation, between so-called 'boomers' and 'millennials', have replaced class as the most significant cleavage in opinion, belief and demand for change. We must always be wary when examining voting patterns and class. The charting of a progressive dealignment between the two in the second half of the twentieth century is often countered with the claim that the predictability of voting along traditional class lines was always based on an imagined past (Heath et al., 1988). But recent trends certainly indicate that there appear to be changing fault lines in respect of voting patterns.

After the 2017 election in the UK, just one year after the Brexit vote, YouGov stated that 'class is no longer a very good indicator of voting intention' (Curtis, 2017), while Ipsos MORI charted the middle-class swing to Corbyn's Labour (Skinner and Mortimore, 2017). But underpinning both analyses was an emphasis on age as the new dividing line in electoral politics in the UK. There is no question that divisions by age were stark – with 66 per cent of people aged eighteen to nineteen voting Labour versus 19 per cent opting for the Tories in 2017, and 67 per cent of the over-seventies opting for the Tories in 2019 (Curtis, 2017; McDonnell and Curtis, 2019). While it is difficult to get away from the dominant influencing factor in respect of Trump's support, which was its overwhelming whiteness (Cineas and North, 2020), a range of studies of the demographics of his vote in 2016 showed that his supporters were also discernably older than Clinton voters (Gould and Harrington, 2016; Tyson and Manium, 2016). Similarly Biden in 2020 appealed much more to younger voters, while Trump lost support in those groups (Bryant, 2020). But prior to his nomination, Biden was also losing the support of young people in the primary race to Bernie Sanders, who was much further to the left (Levitz, 2020).

These patterns in voting are underpinned by structural changes which have been instigated by neoliberal politics across the West, and which, as discussed in Chapter 1, constructed a highly financialised and individualised culture in which those without capital increasingly struggle to compete for resources. This certainly does not only or even disproportionately affect the young; however, it does have particular impacts on the experience of education and the workplace for young people. Access to discernible rewards for effort and work has been significantly reduced in recent decades. People work harder for less and will work for longer.

According to my own research, a key aspect for young people is their orientation to the future, and crucially their expectations and investment in that future. I talked in the previous chapter about young people's sense of frustration that the economic gains of their parents are no longer available to them, with home ownership and job security particularly emphasised in student focus groups. Concern about the future, in a world which in recent years has been so full of disorder and uncertainty with political upheaval, war and conflict, the pandemic and climate change, seems to have particular resonance for young people who have more years in front of them and perhaps feel they can still do something about it.

To return to questions of class identity and shared interests, what can be said about age as a determinant of a shared culture, viewpoint and most crucially solidarity? In this, of course, we have a very rich tradition of sociological works on young people and politics, with *Resistance through Rituals: Youth Subcultures in Post-War Britain* edited by Hall and Jefferson, first published in 1975, a key text. In this collection the authors explored the cultural practices of youth movements such as punk to assess 'in what sense was the generational disaffiliation a sign of broader social contradictions?' (Hall and Jefferson, 2006: xi). Class resistance was one aspect of the movements examined, though it was stressed that no simple articulation of class in respect of economics underpinned the analysis. Through these very rich and varied studies, what in fact emerged were expressions of individual autonomy and cultural diversity which mostly had no clear class-aligned roots. In a later edition published in 2006, the authors were clearer still that the movements were much more fragmented than they had imagined in respect of class (or anything else) and, further, that as societies became more individualistic and pluralistic from the 1970s onwards, class and culture became more disarticulated than they had been. Muggleton, who offered an important critique of the original study and was cited in the later edition, noted that an emerging phenomenon had in fact been the convergence of a working-class subculture rooted in increasingly middle-class or 'bohemian' values (Hall and Jefferson, 2006: xiv).

Much has changed of course even since 2006: the change in voting patterns previously referred to is one example, and the nature of communications is even more significant. If perhaps the most visible shift has been the politicisation of young people around climate change, the degree to which there is a generational divide in respect of levels of action and concern is disputed: in fact a 2021 study from the Policy Institute at King's College London published in *New Scientist* magazine claimed that such a divide on climate change was a 'myth' (Duffy, 2021). But what that study and others, including my own, do show is a real difference in the ways in which the issue is expressed and responded to, and in the channels of communication engaged with – the social media platform Tiktok, for example, having recently been a major vehicle for expressing views on climate change (I look at the way in which this operates as a decentred culture in Chapter 5). These modes of articulation and contexts of negotiation are exceptionally important and, I believe, provide some insight into other factors which might position people politically and culturally (and the connections they may have). Here Muggleton may have been on to something.

Cultures of education

To return to voting patterns, the traditional markers of class, such as income and employment status, indicated that Trump supporters were among the most affluent US voters in 2016 and 2020, while both Clinton and Biden attracted those in the lowest-income groups (Zhang and Burn-Murdoch, 2020). But analyses of Trump's electoral win in 2016 on various measures of health, longevity, and intergenerational mobility and in respect of the community context showed that they were not necessarily the most prosperous (Misra, 2016; Rothwell and Diego-Rosell, 2016). Looked at overall, however, the analyses show a potentially significant axis around which the other factors can be mapped, and that is access to education. Exit polls dating back to 1980 showed the widest gap recorded in support for the two candidates between college graduates and non-college graduates (with race again overwhelming all other factors). It was particularly marked in respect of postgraduate study (Tyson and Manium, 2016). Trump's supporters were empirically less educated.

An analysis by Rothwell and Diego-Rosell (2016) argued that not only were Trump's supporters less educated themselves, but they lived in communities where they engaged less with those who were educated. The authors noted that Trump's supporters tended to live in culturally isolated communities and in commuting zones with limited access to a diversity of racial and ethnic groups, migrants and college graduates. Students returning from college with opinions, experiential knowledge and friends from the more diverse and liberal environments they have inhabited, which may potentially forge attitudinal change, exist in relatively small numbers. Previous studies have shown that increased contact with diverse groups limits the development of prejudicial stereotypes of the kind Trump espoused (McVeigh and Estep, 2019). While the geographical and cultural divisions characteristic of the US are not paralleled in the UK, Brexit voters were similar to Trump supporters in some respects, one of which was their educational levels and those of the areas in which they lived (Statista, 2016; Rosenbaum, 2017).

In voting trends, therefore, age emerges as a key factor, but to some degree this focus can operate to obscure the potential role of education, as younger generations are, because of the increased numbers going into further and higher education in recent decades, by definition more formally educated than their older counterparts (Pew Research Center, 2019; Clark, 2023). Education does not map clearly onto social class, or even onto outcomes in life, in ways in which it perhaps used to, though it may construct expectations of outcomes and may, similar to age, conceal the importance of social class in the translation of educational success into economic benefits (Crawford et al., 2016). This is especially true in the context of a significantly expanded higher education sector in the UK, where there is an unspoken hierarchy of institutions which employers recognise (Blackmore, 2016).

At this point I want to return to the importance of the interpersonal communities within which people are immersed. In this, education extends far beyond what goes on in the classroom, to the cultures, ideas, dialogue and people that individuals and families are exposed to through it. If class solidarity was once developed around the physical forms of organising which took place through unions located in the workplace, an increasingly fragmented workforce has made this more challenging. This can only be exacerbated by the drift to remote working fast-tracked by the pandemic, in which jobs are now sometimes advertised as remote, with the prospect for new recruits of *never* meeting other employees when they start work. Education currently offers both physical and online contexts for people to come together in dialogue and develop shared sensibilities and political objectives, if not necessarily a clear sense of a collective group. In contrast to the previous more transient engagement with 'student politics', digital technologies allow such alignments to extend far beyond people's time in education and into more established and expansive cultural formations.

The social media theorist danah boyd (boyd, 2017) has developed a theory of digital self-segregation which offers some insight into how this might work in a more sustained way. She looked at the US college housing system, which had historically operated as a diversification project with allocations designed to bring students from different backgrounds together. Students were thus thrust into the same new world in ways which united them, and this represented a break from the culture of the home. From her fieldwork on teenagers and young people going into formal education once Facebook arrived, however, boyd noted:

> What I wasn't prepared for was how quickly they would all get on Facebook, map the incoming freshman class, and use this information to ask for a roommate switch. Before they even arrived on campus in August/September of 2006, they had self-segregated as much as possible. (boyd, 2017: unpaginated)

She also found that, with constant access to mobile technology, they continued to prioritise the cultures of connectivity they already belonged to, keeping in contact with friends and family sharing similar values rather than connecting with the new and often very different people in their new physical environment. This has two potential implications for the questions addressed in this chapter: first, that the contexts in which people are brought up continue to shape their connections and alignments, suggesting a cementing of social class and race; and second, that the extension of cultures of education which may overlap with the former are likely to extend much further through life than in the past. As a period of study at university can often be one in which discussions of values, politics and new ideas are particularly intense, it may be a time when young people's perspectives become consolidated and tend to stick.

These changes coincide with arguments that in place of a focus on the traditional left–right politics rooted in economics, social movements built around gender, race, sexuality, environment and so on have begun to dominate as forms of resistance and alignment (Harvey, 2016). Certainly since the Occupy movement of 2011–12, which emphasised social and economic inequality and the injustices of the neoliberal system as evidenced by the global financial crash in 2008, young people have not been orientated so visibly around failings of the economic system. I use the word 'visibly' because there's no question that arms of the youth climate movement are anti-capitalist in nature, and I have already mentioned the considerable youth support for political candidates such as Jeremy Corbyn and Bernie Sanders, both of whose rhetoric and policy programmes are rooted in wealth redistribution. It is clear from my own work that young people care about these injustices, many of which they are experiencing through precarious working and poor life outcomes. But the media play a key role in constructing alignments which minimise the connections between those who share those experiences, and amplify those which cut across them. I'd argue that in this professional media and social media construct and cement these alignments in a circular way.

Differentiated media cultures: continuity and change

In this section I will consider my own empirical work in more depth. I want to first address the importance of increasingly differentiated media environments. In the previous chapter I talked about divides in respect of how far people were rooted in a mainstream culture, introducing the categories of holistic, decentred and centred modes of engagement. The latter category includes those who might be thought of as traditionalists, and, within that group, as one might expect in view of the name, there are historical divisions which continue to have relevance (Happer et al., 2019).

Tabloids, which were once read by the majority, have suffered falling readership with the move to digital media. For the most part, they came up as reference points only in the lower socio-economic groups, and largely in older groups (I should clarify that this is not a claim that only these groups read tabloids or see their content, but just that they were referred to and discussed in these groups). Often the tabloids were dismissed as nonsense, and not sources of credibility and trust, as this janitor noted:

> I think sometimes when you read media stories, you don't believe a thing they say anyway, so you read them like you would read a piece of fiction. (Male, low income, UK, 2015)

But on the other hand, tabloids were read because, even if they were not seen to be telling the truth, at least they were speaking the same language as those groups and did not feel alienating, as this cleaner described the broadsheets:

> A lot of these papers they're all financial things, about the financial world and money stuff, I'm not really used to it, [more used to] reading murders and stuff, kind of thing. (Female, low income, UK, 2015)

Similarly, a student noted that 'I read *The Guardian* [...] I trust it to pander to my predisposition', something which further discussion clarified referred to what and how things were presented rather than a particular political position. As noted in the previous chapter, those in the lower socio-economic groups also shared with the tabloids a relatively stable sense of morality, which underpinned their interpretation of many issues and could be almost instinctive – for example, with Brexit, a sense that it 'just feels wrong' that important aspects of people's lives in Britain should be decided by people in Europe. This is an important point: language, approach to story, value systems and key reference points are as important as political alignments in determining where people will go to for information. An important factor is what the other people you associate with read and what you might know and talk about, even if you disagree.

As noted, this orientation to tabloid or broadsheet consumption and class (at least in aspiration if not actual status) is long-standing and self-perpetuating. As someone who grew up on a council housing estate, and whose father had *The Guardian* delivered to the house, I was constantly asked: *who does he think he is?* Clearly in some communities this attitude continues in a fairly recognisable form. In other places social media, which the majority of all groups consume, seem to have disrupted these formations significantly. However, I would argue it's not that divisions around language, story, values and reference points are no longer important; it's more that the axes around which they are organised have shifted and diversified.

For example, owing to the emphasis on 'naturally occurring' groups, I had a number of lower-income groups from inner-city areas which were made up of largely Muslim participants, mainly small business owners. My research does not extend to a fully formed analysis of ethnicity, but I was struck by how distinct the media culture was as regards language, sources, values and reference points. These groups were orientated to Al Jazeera and a number of independent online media sources and had very different perspectives on political events from other groups. The lack of trust invested in the mainstream culture was very stark and was rooted in direct experience of authorities, as this quote shows:

> I think newspapers, TV, news channels I think they all have their own political agendas nowadays, and it's up to you to work out which one is telling the truth, hence we have four or five different choices of TV channels and BBC. I couldn't trust them as far as I could throw them. They're in cahoots with the military, the government, they toe the line and they don't tell you the truth. I couldn't trust them as far as I could throw them. (Male, small business owner, UK, 2013)

In this case the participant was from Govanhill in Glasgow, an area with a historical migrant identity, and it is possible to relate these findings to evidence from migration and media studies on the under-representation and misrepresentation of migrants in mainstream news media. as well as the importance of digital alternatives as a 'connective presence' and source of information (Riegel, 2019).

These kinds of differentiated media cultures also emerged in very significant ways during the pandemic, when it was found that black and ethnic-minority groups which were particularly affected in respect of employment, discrimination and so on were a very difficult cohort to reach with official guidance. Public Health England's (2021) appendix to its report 'Beyond the data' noted that participants in its study:

> made continual assessments of the accuracy and credibility of the guidelines based on their levels of trust. These levels of trust varied on a range of factors that included familiarity with the source and when information was corroborated through trusted relationships. (Public Health England, 2021)

Some reported getting information from WhatsApp groups with friends and relatives because of their low levels of trust in official health guidance, though they also realised that they were subject to a great deal of misinformation, which worried them too.

Again, these divides are not new: in some ways, they can be seen as an extension of loyal consumption of local newspapers. The *Digger* magazine was talked about in groups in Glasgow, for example. But they are amplified by the move away from a mainstream culture that is imposed to some degree by lack of choice. This also indicates the degree to which the mainstream isn't inclusive of the diversity of voices across the country, in direct relation to the loss of trust, something which my work would suggest most affects lower-income groups, who feel the impacts of intersectionality keenly.

Perhaps in direct relation to this, research produced by Yates and Lockley (2018) has shown that lower-income groups tend to use social media more than they engage in internet use overall. They also use it differently from other groups, engaging across a more limited range of platforms, and are less likely to use the public-facing ones and those most associated with professional contexts, such as Twitter (X), which is the key platform for academic use. Again this came through in my research: for those in the lower-income groups, social media cultures were more an extension of oral cultures, stories, experiences and pictures of the self and family, rather than an extension of the professional media discourse. WhatsApp is a preferred app among these groups. The social circles and references points engaged with are often close to home rather than outward-looking, as this exchange between two female cleaners shows:

> You'd get a wee bit of something but my man is well into world news and radio's never off world news, can tell everything that's happening in Pakistan or Japan or whatever, doesnae interest me in the least.
> Naw, you just want to know what's going on round about you. (Manual workers, UK, 2014)

Skeggs and Yuill (2019) have charted the way in which these differentiated social media practices amplify socio-economic status. Users who are more inward-looking are seen as lacking cultural capital, and this reinforces their status as people without value or unworthy of attention, while those with a formal education often use the highest-profile platforms in ways which signal them as people of worth who are part of a more public conversation.

While in my findings the use of social media as brand management was evident in all groups to some degree, the more careful and reflective curation of profiles (treated as entering a space in public discourse) was more pronounced among the student and middle-income groups, albeit in different ways, with the latter notably having a greater tendency to protect and limit what was published about themselves. It was explicitly stated in more than one group that social media use 'varies quite widely within our demographic of age group and social class or whatever'. Both Facebook and WhatsApp were described as 'boomer places', obviously indicating the importance of age. However, in patterns in platform usage more generally, including key talking points, education was again a significant factor.

The battle for scarce resources

Here I am going to suggest a hypothesis which I believe is of value, if not a fully adequate explanation of what is going on. This is the thesis of 'Professional-Managerial Class' originally conceptualised by Barbara and John Ehrenreich in the US in the 1970s to chart the expansion of a workforce who use their intellect to gain better-paid salaried jobs, including roles as media producers, academics, doctors, lawyers and managers (Ehrenreich and Ehrenreich, 1979). This group have similarities with – as well as important differences from – the knowledge specialists identified by thinkers such as

Reich and Castells, who are essential to the project of globalisation (Webster and Robins, 1998). As this group do not own the means of production, they are therefore working class in the Marxist sense, but they do not have an antagonistic relation to capital and so are not really a class, and they can take either side in a class struggle (Hochuli et al., 2021). With the growth of the service sector and the structural expansion of higher education in the UK and the US in the last thirty years, these jobs expanded and, the authors argued, this 'class' grew very powerful (Ehrenreich and Ehrenreich, 2013). However, the financial crash of 2008 saw a contraction in respect of the opportunities for this group, and in particular for the younger generations who might aspire to gain access to it via education.

The members of this disenfranchised group are distinctive in that their material circumstances – rising rents, precarity, low pay – look like very traditional working-class conditions, but they themselves sound – in language, culture and values – middle class. In what is perhaps a fairly ungenerous account, Catherine Liu (2021) has argued that in order to protect the social hierarchy and any opportunities that may present, this group police the boundaries of language and culture – what she calls 'virtue hoarding'. In other words, they engage in practices of exclusion towards those who do not possess the cultural capital that they have – which as an argument brings us back to the role of social media practice and the differentiated modes of engagement previously discussed. I describe this as an ungenerous account because, according to my experience of working in a university, the culture of young people is one of hard work, and this group collectively express regret for missing out on much of what the previous generation of students expected and enjoyed, rather than exhibiting a sense of entitlement. Also, importantly, young educated people are not a monolith and they are certainly not all leftist purists, an idea which owes a lot to the right-wing tabloid construction of 'snowflakes'.

Social media as cultural capital

But there is something more structural in relation to changing forms of media which gives weight to elements of this thesis. One aspect of this is the affordances of digital technologies, and social media platforms in particular, which lend themselves very well to the public monitoring and control of language use and views, and which seem to offer power to those who have the most capital in respect of social media expression. In the next chapter, I will talk more about who really holds power in this landscape, and the ways in which this is obscured by the design and management of the platforms. But when educated and professional groups use social media as an extension of public discourse, they can amplify this form of power in ways which promote their own social value and diminish the value of others – knowingly or otherwise.

In some ways, this can be seen as extension of the way in which the media industry has, particularly in the neoliberal era, represented the working class so as to promote exclusion and distancing. For example, a lot of work in British sociology in recent years has looked at the phenomenon of 'poverty porn', television programmes which focus on those living in poverty, with a particular emphasis on the lifestyles of those who do not work and are claiming benefits (Skeggs, 2009; Jensen and Tyler, 2015; Tyler, 2020).

A key aspect of the critique is that these are shows about working-class people made by middle-class people, whose gaze is presented as 'normal' while those being looked at are 'abnormal'. The latter are specimens for the rest of us to judge, and as seen through the lens of neoliberal ideology, they have failed to have 'normal' lives because they haven't worked hard and garnered achievements like the rest of us. Here their ways of expressing themselves, of dressing, of living, are seen as having contributed to this failure. Beyond the extremes of 'poverty porn', everyday representations casually refer to the moral and individual failures of the working class. Labour's Angela Rayner, for example, is described by the *Daily Mail* as 'a socialist grandmother who left school at 16 while pregnant', with her 'comprehensive school' education rarely left out of the story (Owen, 2022).

If a now common phrase is 'you need to see it to be it', there are limited positive representations of the working class with which people can identify. The class scholar Mike Savage (Savage, 2015), who investigated the question of class consciousness in the twenty-first century, found that, rather than there being a consolidation of class solidarity in the neoliberal era, fewer than a third of people actually see themselves as belonging to any class. This quote from one of the participants in Savage's study illustrates the active distancing from working-class alignment:

> If I put myself as working class I don't think I would want to be in the same class as somebody who takes what they can and takes the attitude of 'Well, I'm better off not working' … 'cause, you know, I take a pride in what I do, and … I can't think of anything worse than being home all day doing nothing. (Savage, 2015: 384)

In my studies, I also found that people didn't refer to their own or others' class status very much (though that must be seen in light of that fact I didn't ask specifically about class even if groups were organised according to income, which is one measure of it). When 'class' was referred to, it was applied in different ways. At times it was used to evoked sympathy as a shorthand for those in need or having a very tough time. In the previous chapter, I also discussed how focus group participants used the term 'working class' in a way which distanced themselves from those who might be seen to occupy this category. This quote also shows this to some degree:

> So one of the guys on our subReddits, he is very much against immigration, and he blames the immigrants instead of ... so he's like, he sees himself as like part of the working class and things like this, without realising that a lot of the immigrants that come in are also working class. He blames it on race and his circumstances on that, rather than the other things that cause what circumstances he has. (Male, social media moderator and user, UK, 2019–20)

This is quite representative of discussions among student groups – though usually the reference is not to class but to age – where these young educated people perceive those in older age groups as culturally distinct from themselves. By 'culturally distinct', I broadly mean lacking in understanding or vulgar in expression. In the context of this discussion, without falling into the unhelpful dichotomy that presumes either that all Brexit voters are racist idiots or that Remainers refuse to listen when the working class speaks authentically, there are different ways to analyse what is going on here with media as the focus. Those groups who are more exposed to the tabloid press and associated media cultures will tend to understand immigration through the lens repeatedly offered to them. *Bad News for Refugees* (Philo et al., 2013) charts the significant influence of repeated media coverage that stigmatises and blames refugees and migrants for a range of societal ills including unemployment and low wages.

To return to my point in earlier chapters, however, public opinion should be seen as managed rather than constructed from nothing, and such coverage also taps into direct experience of scarce resources and competition, which is felt most keenly by lower-income groups. Again, the ways in which this shaped responses in my research varied: in one focus group from 2012, when a group of cleaners was presented with media materials showing the plight of people in Bangladesh losing their homes because of climate change, there was a real willingness to offer donations on the basis that 'people who don't have much should stick together' (in higher income-groups in that particular study, the emphasis was on what the Bangladeshi state government should do).

The middle-class professional habitus is one of cultural pluralism and the opportunity it presents, and a media culture which promotes this discourse too. However, if racism is a structural presence, it is inevitable that it goes beyond expressions of prejudicial attitudes (Bonilla-Silva, 1997; 2012). It is very difficult here to ignore evidence from my own institution. In a Glasgow University report of 2019, it was found that half of all minority-ethnic students had received racist abuse on the university campus, and its

Class, education and media cultures 89

publication led to much reflection and commitment to reform (University of Glasgow, 2021). There is also a quite shocking lack of non-whites in elite roles at UK universities as a whole (Adams, 2017), though this still cannot rival the lack of diversity in the film and television industry (Friedman, 2020). These are distinct elements of the professional sector, of course, but the evidence does not suggest that racism is purely a problem of those without education (or indeed of any particular age group).

And yet, in the culture of social media, the discourse around 'social justice issues', of which race is one, was repeatedly cited as a cleavage around which groups could be clearly situated. The quote below indicates where those cleavages are seen to be:

> Yeah, I mean definitely lines get crossed, but then the majority of the time, at least for me, they're from an older generation that's ... which, I kind of like, you can't change people when they're almost dead so ... (Female, young social media user, UK, 2019–20)

In one study I conducted with computer science colleagues from 2019–20 with young and intense social media users (Happer et al., 2021; see Appendix), a central theme was the way in which the older generations needed to be 'educated' out of their views by younger generations:

> But educate and if ... I think the problem is that a lot of the time, if it's a younger person trying to explain a situation to an older person, there's an idea of like, that's just being too PC or that's going too far, and we can make jokes or we can talk about this. And maybe they're right because they have the benefit of years of experience but they don't seem to have a lot of sensitivity a lot of the time, and openness to accept people for whoever they say they are. (Male, young social media user, UK, 2019–20)

This quote shows an unusual level of reflection on the way in which these groups may interact on social media platforms. Again, it's not helpful to make simplistic interpretations. Young educated people, who are more likely than others to be immersed in public discourse, are more aware of social injustice and progressive values: they are not just observing positive change: in many ways they are driving it, often in confrontation with elite speakers. The current 'culture wars' represent a continuation of historical battles over the ways in which, and speed at which, we should manage social change.

This is not an argument that bigoted views, racist or otherwise, are no longer heard: as noted, the mainstream media platforms these views repeatedly, and it's easy to think of a range of high-profile individuals who have built their followings on that very basis (Philo et al., 2013). The latter include members of the Conservative government, with Boris Johnson before and after he was elected Prime Minister saying the kind of things that would get him rightly sacked from many other jobs. This is the mainstream culture that many young people rail against and despair of, resistance to which fuels their move to decentred cultures. But there is a difference between the protections received by those with cultural resources and those who have none, and these processes have a tendency to push to the margins the voices of the less formally educated people, who often reside in the lowest-income groups.

The key argument here is that people are socialised into ways of thinking and talking which are shaped by the online and offline cultures they are immersed in, and these also reflect how they want to be seen. If part of that consists of learning not to align yourself with the groups who are seen to possess little value or worth on social media (and do not engage in that careful curation), then that is in part self-preservation, even if it is not fully conscious. The distancing in this case is by younger people from those in the older age groups, but as I have argued, the latter can to some degree be seen as a proxy for a particular segment of the working class. The point does not extend to all older groups.

In some cases, this may be seen to have exacerbated the moves of some people in those groups who lack this kind of capital towards political leaders who are not working in their interests. To return to the question of the de-alignment of Labour from the traditional working class, culture as a way of talking, seeing and thinking remains important, though this is a complex question. Very few Labour leaders historically have been drawn from the working class, and working-class people have still voted for them. In my lower-income groups, however, a feeling of being distanced from all political discourse – and an expectation of not being listened to – was a common theme. It is important to note that any blame and anger I identified was directed at those in power – not at groups of people marked by youth or educational status (beyond young people being seen as 'naïve' or university professors as 'fat cats'). But some in these groups are increasingly distanced from the tone and nature of public discourse as a whole. In reflection of the fragmented and multi-faceted nature of the current media environment, of course, young people feel similarly removed from the mainstream culture and established power. The problem lies in perceiving of where the conflict lies.

Constructions of conflict and solidarity

My data suggests that groups organised around age and education inhabit very different media cultures, and perceive themselves as not only distinct but also in conflict. I further want to argue that these processes exacerbate the atomisation of thought and opinion and produce a distancing between groups who may share experiences of economic injustice, which limits solidarity. Again, this has also been promoted by a mainstream media narrative (and amplified by a series of memes such as 'ok boomer') which sets 'boomers', those born in the post-war period, against 'millennials', who orientate themselves around economic and climate inequality (Elliott, 2021). Here 'boomers' are characterised as selfish and individualistic and as having benefited from a generous welfare state, affordable housing and relative prosperity, but as then voting to prevent the following generations benefiting from them too (Airey et al., 2021). While the circumstances of this period are unique, what Bourdieu describes as the 'clashes between systems of aspirations formed in different periods' (Bourdieu, 1993b: 99) are historically typical, as cultural change often reflects an intensity in the battle for scarce resources across generations (Turner and Edmunds, 2002).

But the key factor is scarce resources, and what is at stake. In order for there to be genuine conflict, in the Marxist sense, one group will be structurally exploited by the other. This is not the case here. As Rebecca Elliott (2021) notes, the construction of generational conflict:

> elides important intersectional inequalities that shape the conditions people face, even people who were born in the same year or cohort. While it is broadly true that today's young adults and children will face much more dire planetary conditions than their elder relations, intragenerational differences of class, race, gender, nation and region profoundly shape who will face the most significant forms of loss as the climate changes. The impacts of COVID-19 – and the economic recession in its wake – have also shown considerable socioeconomic and racial disparity. (Elliott, 2021)

In my own groups, I observed overall a fear of the future and a sense of things getting worse, though the focus and explanations offered could be very different. In some groups of older people (especially the higher-income groups), there was a fear of losing what they had gained in respect of what form climate action and other economic policies might take. There was less emphasis on what would work best for the majority than on the problems of different groups, and this may have been because workplaces, opportunity and the political and media culture are so fragmented and stratified, as much as because of fear of loss.

If this can be seen to represent a particular combination of the first five filters addressed in Chapter 2 (ideology as stakes in the system, priorities, shifts in interpersonal communication, the rise of identity-based communities and decentred media cultures), moments can emerge when collective experience clashes with the public narrative to form new and resistant positions. If the global crash failed to produce such a moment (Berry, 2012; Davidson, 2016), it will be interesting to see what will emerge as the after-effects of the pandemic, the war in Ukraine, climate change and the worst ever cost-of-living crisis in recent history all bed in across the globe. In the UK, the solutions offered by a stale Conservative party in power for over a decade are not in any way adequate, and the story of neoliberalism, already disrupted, is crumbling further. At these points new ideas and new speakers begin to be heard, and are not easy to silence.

Work conducted by the Glasgow University Media Group in the 1970s and 1980s showed the way in which media reporting was consistently hostile to representatives from trade unions, referring to them as 'militant' and 'dispute' organisations and emphasising the 'disruption' caused by strikes rather than their intended outcomes (Philo and Hewitt, 1976; Glasgow University Media Group, 1985). Unions are far less powerful in Britain now as a result of a series of policies designed to restrict their activities from the Thatcher government onwards. There are now only just over 6 million people in trade unions, compared with over 13 million in the 1980s (Statista, 2023). The work of Tom Mills (2016) showed the way in which the BBC, as it shifted to the neoliberal agenda in both form and tone, marginalised the voices of trade union leaders as it amplified the voices of business.

However, in April 2022 a new voice – new to a mainstream audience at least – entered the public discussion in the context of the growing discontent about the cost-of-living crisis, and of a distinct growth in industrial action (albeit still low in historical terms: Wall, 2022). Mick Lynch, General Secretary of the National Union of Rail, Maritime and Transport Workers (RMT), began to appear on a range of media, including BBC, ITV and Sky, in connection with the RMT's series of strikes. His interviews were widely circulated on social media as notable for his 'owning' of journalists asking questions which produced the kind of biased coverage that the Glasgow University Media Group and Mills had rigorously exposed.

The *Sun*, in what looked like a photocopy from the 1970s, talked of 'militant unions' 'causing chaos' (Ferguson, 2022). On a fairly representative item on ITV's *Good Morning Britain* entitled 'Are the unions wrong to strike?' the presenters consistently referred to the 'misery' caused by striking and 'holding the public hostage'. In a later interview for GMB, Richard Madeley asked Lynch if he was a Marxist. The Sky reporter Kay Burley pushed a line of questioning which implied that striking workers would move beyond reasonable persuasion in an explicit reference to the miners' strike (and claimed to be asking 'on behalf of the British people'). On *Question Time* in June 2022, Lynch faced a hostile audience comment about 'dinosaurs'. Each time, he briskly explained the causes of inflation, the role of taxation and the nature of employment law and industrial relations while exposing the bias of the questions and openly using the terms 'working class' and 'pro-boss line'. The ideological construction of strikers in conflict

Class, education and media cultures 93

with working people, as opposed to strikers *being* working people, was starkly exposed across the coverage.

The empirical research to assess how Mick Lynch was received across different audience groups – such as age, education, class and the foci of this chapter – is not in place. However, a poll by GMB at the end of June 2022, when many of these interviews took place, revealed that support for the RMT strike had increased (Tingle, 2022). Similarly support for striking teachers and doctors, in recognition of how difficult their working conditions had become, was in the period fairly high, though it was not consistently high for those in all professions (Ibbotsen, 2022). In what is likely to be indicative of a recognition of Lynch's success in steering public opinion – or a *mis-management* on the part of the mainstream media – the latter took a more personalised approach with a focus on his relatively high earnings, the living arrangements of his deputy and his 'pro-Putin' leanings. But these attacks broadly failed to connect with a wider audience. Again there was a mismatch in respect of what journalists assumed public opinion to be.

Of particular interest, with respect to this chapter, is Lynch's position on the EU. He is an open supporter of Brexit, and the views he has expressed on this are still a fairly certain way of losing the support of educated, liberal groups. This comment from a listener to James O'Brien's LBC show may offer insight:

> Fully agree with him on his views on the strike and workforce protection. And I don't mind his views that are against mine, e.g. on Brexit, as they're obviously honestly held. (Hickey, 2022)

It's not often now that we hear statements such as these:

> The working class is back. We're not just back as an idea, we're back as a movement. They act in their class interests, it's time we acted in ours. (Mick Lynch at the #EnoughIsEnough launch rally, August 2022; Wilson, 2022)

For some reason, Lynch is allowed to express these views where many others sharing his broad outlook, background and culture usually aren't. Whether he is correct remains to be seen.

In the Introduction I referred to the mismatch in respect of 'public opinion' as presented by journalists (to politicians and their audiences) and what the public thinks. At some points empirical evidence is just too robust in the opposite direction for people to be swayed by media accounts. In August 2022, before the dramatic rise in charges later in the year, already one third of people in the UK were struggling to pay their energy bills (Borrett, 2022), while in Scotland 90 per cent were very concerned about the cost-of-living crisis (Gray et al., 2022). The example of Mick Lynch illustrates the recognition given to the reasons as to why people might strike and how difficult the current conditions are for everyone. In these circumstances – with inflation riding so much higher than wages – the media narrative of 'greedy' workers can't be sustained. Consistent attempts to defend journalistic questions framed in this way as representative of public opinion were exposed by Lynch's exasperated response but also clashed with the 'map of meaning' already present in people's heads (Hall, 1973). This represents a failure to manage opinion. It is at these moments that disparate groups come together in recognition of shared interests and shared struggle, though of course one voice is not enough.

Conclusion

In this chapter, I have examined the role of social class in shaping media engagement and the ways in which people begin to think about and respond to political ideas and positions. I have argued that divisions by age obscure the role of formal education in constructing opinion communities and alignments which are cemented and sustained by social media engagement. An aspect of this is the way particular modes of social media usage, careful curation and entrance into public discourse add value to members of these communities. Identity as communicated through this intensely reflective online performance must also be seen in the context of shifting mainstream representations of class and increasing job precarity. Unquestionably, one outcome is that those without cultural resources – still mostly from lower-income groups – often have their stories, culture and experience silenced. However, these processes are often understood as a conflict between generations, where the discourse of ignorant 'boomers' is seen as in need of disciplining (as simultaneously it is amplified in the wider culture). Power is relatively untouched, although individuals may benefit in different ways. I will talk about the way in which social media platforms discipline public discourse more generally in the next chapter.

The key point is that the more public discourse is facilitated through a fragmented digital media, the more atomised the positions that people will take up. If the mass media have been traditionally understood as a mode of social control through mechanisms such as folk devils, moral panics and stigma, social media operate on the basis of constructed conflict and division. In the context of diminished workplace cultures, the building of solidarity on the basis of shared interests and opinion communities becomes much more challenging. In some cases, disaffected groups move to a decentred culture and are lost from the mainstream altogether, and as Covid has shown this can have exceptionally damaging impacts. Finding a widely shared cultural space is much more difficult than in the past, with big spectacles such as football tournaments representing some of the rare opportunities.

Is there still a discernible working-class culture? To offer an apparent contradiction, what seems to exist is a mass global individualised culture: we all plug into the same narrow range of platforms, but find our own little corners within it. Consequently there will be cultures of working-class segments sharing language, reference points and outlooks – and even when these cultures are intensely managed by social media platforms, they cannot be fully imposed by them. As Hoggart noted, because the producers of culture will always come from a different place from the working classes ('them' and 'us'), they will always reflect something of their origins.

4

The new gatekeepers of digital content and opinion

This chapter will focus on the changing agents of power and influence within the digital media infrastructure, offering an understanding of the new circuit of media and communications and the key elements and processes which are implicated in decision-making and societal outcomes. Here I will build on the understanding of new forms of media influence operating through perceptions of representativeness and acceptability of opinion and thought. As noted in the Introduction, the circuit previously involved the flow of information from, between and through social and political institutions, media organisations, the public and decision-makers at all levels and was primarily organised around the production work of media professionals (Philo et al., 2015).

First, I will map out a new set of elements, including tech companies, platform owners, AI and human moderation, and new forms of propaganda and content management which expand the circuit. It is not possible to be exhaustive but, as always, a central question is the way in which such processes are underpinned by state power and/or market power. Drawing on my own empirical work, I will pay particular attention to an important cog in the wheel of these new systems of power who in some ways share characteristics with journalists and media workers (though with important distinctions): social media content moderators. Social media content moderation is a relatively new role which is important to an understanding of the complex dynamics in respect of how power circulates and is maintained through the construction of platform cultures.

I will then relate these processes more directly to my central question of opinion management (in respect of both thought and expression) in this expanded circuit, where we can see more direct connections with the positions laid down in the previous chapters. Again on the basis of my own research, I will focus specifically on the processes by which particular opinions and ideas and the groups of users expressing them can be promoted and amplified or marginalised and silenced. This relates to the affordances and design of platforms as well as the power relations underpinning platform policy and the implementation of forms of moderation (deleting, hiding, intervening in threads). But crucially they are also founded on the way in which people internalise and respond to the discussions they see and the treatment they are subject to and perceive others to be subject to (withdrawing, self-censorship, conformity). I will explore trust and understanding of moderation and its relation to the authenticity of platform cultures, perceptions of cancel culture, and the silencing of women and marginalised groups in interpersonal and public cultures as illustrations of how this works. Ultimately I will argue that while management of digital opinion through these processes is different in nature, the groups which benefit and power represented don't vary too much.

The circuit of communication

The foundation of this conceptualisation of an expanded circuit of media and communications is the model set out by the Glasgow University Media Group in 2015 (Philo et al., 2015). Here media and communications are understood to sit within a system of capitalist power in the West, and while they do not simply represent power, their role and function is underpinned by it. So the media landscape is always a contested space, and often a site of conflict, but resources and visibility are weighted towards those in power. In the neoliberal era, which I discussed in depth in Chapter 1, media have got closer to power and further away from the public they nominally represent.

On this basis, the model identifies four key elements of the communication process: (1) the social and political institutions and the elite speakers who influence the supply of information, which include government, business, lobby groups and think tanks, trade unions, universities and so on; (2) the media and their content, which refers to the key agents such as media owners, editors, journalists and the work they do to produce content for newspapers, radio, television and so on; (3) the public, which is organised around key demographic and identification categories such as class, gender and ethnicity as well as professional and political alignments; and (4) decision-makers, with consideration of the people who are positioned to decide and the nature of decisions they make; this element includes local, national and international governing bodies (city councils, state governments and organisations such as the UN), but also community groups and the voting public. Decision-makers are therefore similar to those who feature in (1), though not exactly the same, and decision-making is controlled by a range of structural factors and is to varying degrees accountable to all of the other elements.

These elements constitute a circuit in that they connect with, lead into and are determinant upon each other. However, the circuit operates in sometimes complex ways, so for example the way in which journalists construct a sense of 'public opinion' may be based on the information that is available on what members of the public think and believe (surveys and polling, for example), but it is also shaped by the interests of those who control the information supply (and what they want 'public opinion' to look like). But all of this feeds into decision-making. The interactions which shape societal outcomes vary, and sometimes groups can influence decision-making quickly and directly. During Covid, support for lockdowns was built by a concerted effort of media and government almost overnight. In other cases, outcomes and social change involve years of research and information-gathering, often battling with a range of influencing agents, a significant volume of communications aimed at the winning of public opinion, and a number of decisions involving policy and individual behaviour change. The shift in attitudes, behaviours and restrictions in relation to smoking is a good example of this.

An important point in relation to this original formulation is that the elements can interact in a non-linear way, and the model was to some extent developed as a counter to linear models of communication and power such as neo-Marxist approaches, which imagine a fairly one-way process by which ruling ideas reproduce capitalism. But ultimately the model was constructed with the flow of information and other forms of content produced by journalists and media professionals at the centre and as the organising principle. In this it was aligned with traditional 'gatekeeping' theory, which examines the complex range of factors which shape decision-making at the institutional, organisational and routine levels of media to select and filter the information that reaches the public (Shoemaker and Vos, 2009). There was a concession to the transformed role of the public (or audiences), now positioned simultaneously as both consumers and producers of content; however, this was not extended to a significant rethinking of how power is exercised through media and communications to produce a range of (sometimes competing) political, social, commercial and other outcomes.

'New frontier(s) of power'

Thinking has evolved quickly, and we now have a range of conceptualisations which imagine new forms of power and control. A key writer in this respect is Shoshana Zuboff (2019), whose model of 'surveillance capitalism' reworks the logic of power in which the aim is control of user behaviours by automating the range of choices we routinely make. Control is organised around the collection of user data, which is used to predict future behaviours and then to influence and steer them towards commercial ends. In this mutant version of capitalism, we are herded towards doing things which are separate from our thinking, and which are unquestioned because they are rooted in the things we (and others like us) already do and the data they produce; for instance (to give a very simple example), when we type a search term into Google, Google doesn't wait for us to finish our thinking, instead offering a range of options based on searches done previously. In many cases, we simply go with the thinking offered to us.

This expands to the kinds of books, clothes and food we order, and then what our bedtime routines look like. As discussed in Chapter 2, many people may object to the intrusion of data collection into everyday lives and are aware of the controlling power of it – I will come back to this point – but are so embedded in online systems ideologically and structurally that opting out does not seem to be an option. Zuboff calls this new form of power 'instrumentarianism', and it looks quite different from the power which aims to manage public opinion and win consent for outcomes. In liberal democracies, Zuboff argues, this market-based form of power is one on which conventional politics impacts very little (though in countries like China these mechanisms are utilised to extend state power as a mode of surveillance).

Zuboff's identification of predictive algorithms as the organising logic of the economy on the internet which produces a new form of capitalism is convincingly articulated. But her argument that these global corporations operate 'free of democratic obligations, legal constraints, moral calculations and social considerations' (Zuboff, 2019: 327) implies a degree of separation from the business of the companies of Silicon Valley and the state, which is at best contestable. Certainly, there may have been a naivety, as Zuboff suggests, when, as the US constitutional debate around the role of behavioural modification began, its focus was limited to questions of state power. As a result, politicians did not see its embrace by corporations, and their business in this area was largely left to grow untouched.

Questions of data privacy, legality, morality and social impacts in relation to platforms and their corporate owners are, however, increasingly the subject of political debate and policy formation as well as media coverage. Facebook in particular has been under endless regulatory scrutiny since 2017, with significant intensification in relation to the livestreaming of the New Zealand massacre in 2019 (Guo, 2020). In fact, in this period, digital media have been subject to what is sometimes called the 'regulatory turn' – a reference to a raft of policies at the national and the supranational level, including the ongoing development of the UK's Online Safety Bill (Happer et al., 2022). In the EU, a body of regulatory mechanisms known as the

General Data Protection Regulation (GDPR), introduced in 2018, puts limits on how personal data can be used, with a particular emphasis on transparency of use.

So, while these companies have largely proved too big and too complex to properly regulate – and have often been successful in their resistance to it – they are not simply left alone. It is, however, true to say that the main objectives of regulation – striking the balance between freedom of expression and online safety, and the market dominance of companies such as Google – have led to a neglect of' limits on data-driven behaviour modification. Even GDPR, which does have intent in this respect, does look, as Zuboff notes, a little like David versus Goliath in the face of surveillance capitalism's 'unprecedented asymmetries' of knowledge and power (Zuboff, 2019: 11). This is not to mention the fact that there is currently no direct equivalent in other major economies, including the US.

However, in respect of what might look like a lapse in state oversight, there is one exception, and that is when these mechanisms of control move into the political sphere. This happened most notably in the runups to the Brexit vote and the election of Trump, when whistle-blowers exposed the way in which the data-mining company Cambridge Analytica had been using algorithms to predict and influence voting preferences via Facebook (Cadwalladr and Graham-Harrison, 2018). Here data analytics moved back into the more traditional and recognisable form of power in liberal democracies: controlling the information environment in order to manage opinion. This, more than any other incident, brought surveillance capitalism out into the open, and forced state actors to respond – with the US consumer regulator, the Federal Trade Commission (FTC), imposing a significant fine and the Facebook founder Mark Zuckerberg, in a show of unity, committing himself to structural changes in how the company handled personal data (Davies and Rushe, 2019). Similarly, as I will discuss below, state forces regularly intervene directly in the business of these corporations when it comes to the promotion of information or ideas that might compromise their interests (York, 2021).

One factor in the lack of priority given to data capture for commercial imperatives is likely to be that from day to day it doesn't challenge state power, or that state and market interests might align in these activities. But I'd argue that what it shows more directly is that there is no one overriding explanation of how power works in a global, digital age, and while Zuboff's work represents a significant 'new frontier of power' it does to some degree deprioritise a range of others. For example, production is fairly marginal in this analysis, though the production of goods and services, including content for circulation on platforms, remains a significant sphere of power (Morozov, 2019). It's not the intention here to present a new thesis of capitalism or to be exhaustive in respect of the processes and groups who continue to reproduce it. My focus in this book is on how opinion is managed to win consent for social and political outcomes and thereby serve power. Accordingly, I want to make the argument that, even though algorithmic mechanisms for control of publics as consumers are in the ascendant, and indeed are increasingly important for the delivery of content, we need to cast our gaze in other areas too.

But these discussions have other implications for the original circuit in that, in spite of its non-linearity, it featured a centralisation of information production, with a nod to the production of content by users themselves as supplementary or marginal. This implies some singular coherence or core to the flow of information which simply no longer exists. In other co-authored work, I have charted the fall of a mainstream media culture and the evacuation of its centre ground (Happer et al., 2018). This relates to the erosion of trust in the mainstream politics and culture and the disconnect which I documented in Chapter 1, but also to the affordances of digital technologies which allow for the construction of a series of decentred cultures of opinion organised around new forms of legitimacy, trust and consensus.

As I argued in Chapter 2, there is still an identifiable mainstream culture, but it is one which some groups almost never engage with in normal times, and for many people the core of their media engagement is the content produced collectively by those in their own chosen community (what Merrin, 2014, calls 'me-dia'). As Ford and Hoskins (2022) note in their book *Radical War*, thanks to smartphones everyone has their own 'war' built on their pre-existing perceptions, knowledge and alignments, with what is going on in the ground almost incidental to their digitised experience of it. But if professional media production is no longer the organising principle of the circuit, and people sit at varying distances from the centre, it is still possible to talk about the infrastructure that facilitates everything else. In the next section I will chart some of the key elements involved in the production of content and opinion management, with particular focus on a group – the content moderators – who operate as an increasingly important cog in the wheel of this infrastructure.

The circuit of communication expanded: the new gatekeepers

To reiterate in presenting this indicative map of the expanded circuit of media and communications, I am looking specifically at one dimension of power which engages with opinion management and the persuasive power of different forms of content to produce political and social outcomes. Here we have a quite different starting point from the suppliers of information who are set out in the original circuit. Instead we begin with Big Tech, the five dominant global companies which largely construct the infrastructure through which we access the internet. In 2020, during the pandemic, these five companies made up 20 per cent of the stock market's total worth, a level not seen for a single industry in seventy years (Eavis and Lohr, 2020). The companies are Google (the embodiment of Big Tech for Zuboff), Meta (which owns Facebook and Instagram), Amazon (the marketplace for everything), Apple and Microsoft. These companies each oversee a range of apps and platforms which compose an ecosystem that facilitates what people can do and see, and the parameters within which they operate online. Though users move between different platforms, they are often 'locked in' to Apple or Google ecosystems, and this situation also relates to brand choices (whereas Amazon has a wider reach) (Merrin, 2014).

Most people in the world – as well as most organisations – would be cut out of parts of the internet if these companies chose to implement restrictions on access. This increasingly includes companies which dominated in the broadcast era. The BBC has its own streaming service in the form of iPlayer, and much of its content is already accessed through platforms. But with the corporation announcing in late 2022 a strategic move away from its broadcasting arm, combined with the acknowledgement that it does not have the funds to compete with Big Tech, it will become more and more reliant on their ecosystems to distribute its content (Waterson, 2022). Though it may be well hidden from users, this distribution of content comes with its own conditions. In *Silicon Values*, Jillian York (2021) documents how these conditions are rooted in the values and interests of the range of actors that hold influence in the corporate platform landscape dominated by Big Tech.

In her book, York, similarly to Zuboff, notes that in spite of Big Tech being subject to an evolving suite of regulatory mechanisms at the national and supranational level, the speed with which platform cultures have grown and the extent of their truly global operations and reach have made them difficult to contain. As early as 1995, the US introduced legislation to protect the right of platforms to moderate, which Reynolds described as 'an obscure law that created our flawed, broken internet' (Reynolds, 2019: unpaginated). At the heart of this legislation was that platforms were understood as distributors and not publishers of information. As York notes, it gave platforms the 'right' but not the 'responsibility' to remove or not to remove content as they chose. At this point, long before the advent of Web 2.0, the internet was still fairly niche, so this level of control was not flagged as being of social concern. However, as the internet, and social media platforms in particular, came to operate as a global public sphere, facilitating all of life's conversations, this lack of accountability began to look highly unusual.

In fact, what York calls these new gatekeepers constitute an unrivalled power base in respect of contemporary controls on the range of information and content ordinary people can access (York, 2021). If Facebook – which developed community standards only in 2011 – used to rely on users of the platform to moderate the site via a culture of 'snitching' on perceived violations, policy which dictates moderation decisions is now much more centralised and top-down:

> the rules are ultimately decided by actors close to the very top of the hierarchy. And these are actors who, as many have observed, come from relatively homogenous backgrounds, are not chosen by the people they serve, and are accountable to almost no one. (York, 2021: 21)

However, as with the old gatekeepers, standards and policy are shaped by a range of factors and influence agents – from both above and below as I shall discuss – even where they might look autonomous (Shoemaker and Vos, 2009). In this, again, the decoupling of state and corporate interest is in some ways very real, and in other important ways simply removed from view. One aspect of this is mentioned in the York quote above: the 'relatively homogenous backgrounds'. These young, largely white men are broadly liberal, pro-business and crucially pro-West. In their decision-making, like those who go on to be successful in journalism, they instinctively reproduce these values in their work and head off any real challenges to them in a dynamic way. York notes how quickly the Facebook team responds to situations in which white people from the Global North are seen to be at risk in comparison with events on the opposite side of the world.

Unlike in China, where state censorship of social media – and indeed the use of platforms as tools of surveillance – is widely recognised, in liberal democracies the degree to which states directly interfere in social media is relatively unknown. However, in her book York also charts how state governments often lobby social media companies such as Facebook to intervene in problems in their own territories, and how the 'policy team' at Facebook is often too busy engaging with the loudest states such as Germany, and of course the US, to give due attention and time to states that are less well resourced. York notes also how quickly those at the top of platforms can change direction in policy in response to these interventions.

Again, these negotiations (and we of course don't know much about their nature) are not only predicated upon a shared set of assumptions and values, but also taking place in a shared legal, moral and political location. York (2021) offers an interesting example of how this works in practice through moderation policy as set by platform executives. She notes that the definitions of 'terrorism' and related ideas of 'violent content' are in direct alignment with those of the US and/or broader Western understandings.

This has led to the de-platforming of groups such as Hezbollah, which has an immensely complex history with both a militant and a political arm and which continues to play a key role in contemporary Lebanese politics. A strictly imposed moderation policy extends not only to censoring the group itself, but anyone who mentions it to praise or condemn. This operates not only to shut down discussion of local politics, potentially impacting electoral outcomes, but also to silence dissent on the US's political interests and activities in the Middle East, and in particular in relation to the state of Israel.

The relationship between corporate aims and state interests was shown in a very public way during the latest phase in the Israel–Palestine conflict triggered by the Hamas attack on southern Israel on 7 October 2023. Again indicating that political bodies may become particularly interested in the harms of social media when their interests may be in question, on 10 October the EU issued a public warning to Elon Musk, owner of Twitter (X), of consequences including a significant fine and/or EU blackout of the platform if disinformation, repurposed imagery and illegal content on the Hamas attack were not removed (O'Carroll, 2023). Musk had taken over on a platform of free speech, and one of his first acts was to reinstate Trump, who had been banned from Twitter (X) in 2021 following the January riots in which his supporters stormed the US Capitol.

Initially Musk was resistant to political pressure, but as it mounted and advertisers became involved because of posts of his own which were deemed anti-Semitic, Twitter (X) banned Hamas-affiliated and Hezbollah-affiliated accounts, citing UN rules and definitions concerning permitted political groups and terrorism (Scott, 2023; Kwan Wei, 2024) – in a move which perhaps did hint at what governing bodies were really getting at when they railed at fake news and disinformation. In recognition of the complex clash between personal, corporate and political aims, Musk conceded that it was a 'tough call' (Kwan Wei, 2024).

I will move more directly to the work of content moderators in the next section, but it is worth noting at this point that there was also evidence in my own empirical work with moderators themselves of how this more direct top-down censorship was supported by moderation carried out by ordinary users – who are also immersed in largely Western political, media and cultural environments, in this case, sitting in the UK and moderating content on Reddit. As one participant in this moderator study noted, moderation aiming to stifle anti-Semitic content could translate into hiding or deleting any discussion of the Israel–Palestine question – and again by extension any detailed critique of Israel as an occupying state.

In this concerted way, policy works with moderation (in interaction with users and other influence agents in complex ways, as I will show) to produce a fairly conventional form of 'agenda setting', understood as the capacity to focus or inhibit attention to topics which might shape people's preferences and opinions (Lukes, 2005). Of course, there are significant differences between journalists who produce content themselves and the outcomes of policy, algorithms, moderation and self-censoring or promotion. But, as with traditional media, omissions, content which is *not* included, are every bit as important as what *is* included in respect of constructing ideas of which perspectives are important and worthy of attention. It is, then, those perspectives deemed important and worthy of attention that stay in people's minds and direct their thoughts and opinions.

On matters of politics, the bottom line is that Facebook is as interested in disrupting US state power as it is in developing a moderation and information control system led by the values of fair and free expression. If it does either, it is accidental in the case of the first (what we might call a mismanagement) and convenient in the case of the second. It's not simply that, as Zuckerberg says, Facebook is merely a 'conduit' for information, though if it is this, it is one that has become increasingly censorious and political (York, 2021). Facebook has also seen a major shift in recent years towards the active promotion of professionally produced content over that generated by users. This culminated in 2021 with Facebook signing a deal with Rupert Murdoch's News Corporation to pay for journalism (Meade, 2021), somewhat debunking the idea of it playing fair in a level playing field of the marketplace of ideas. What is true is that all of this is secondary to its overall aims. While the design of algorithms which arrange, (de)prioritise and deliver content based on relevancy and interest is famously kept secret, it's reasonable to assume that these are broadly similar in principle to the data-driven mechanisms described in Zuboff's book. The ultimate objective is maintaining visibility and generating engagement.

Communities of moderation and influence

This new element of Big Tech within the expanded circuit also leads into, interacts with and determines the processes and agents involved in moderation. Algorithms also play an increasing role in moderation, which is in theory concerned with the opposite of Big Tech's ultimate objective – reducing visibility or removing things completely – though usually in combination with other forms of community and human moderation (Caplan, 2018; Gillespie, 2020). Human moderation takes many forms. It can include a number of activities which are more or less intrusive, depending upon the design and oversight of platforms, and range from hiding or deleting comments and banning users to actually altering or contributing content.

In her important study, Roberts (2019) documents the low-paid and low-status army of commercial content moderators employed by global corporations such as Facebook, many of which are outsourced in countries such as India. This is a truly exploited workforce with very little autonomy and very real emotional costs. As Roberts notes, the role does, however, also come with significant responsibilities and expectations. Workers must have knowledge of particular subject areas, localised cultures and languages, relevant local or national legal and policy parameters and user guidelines, and are required to make value calls on political commentary, inflammatory speech and so on. They do all this of course under the overarching principle of growing and maintaining revenue.

At the other end of the moderation spectrum, there is a growing body of literature which highlights the way in which the volunteer moderators relied on by platforms such as Reddit perceive and inhabit their role on social media platforms as possessing forms of cultural agency (Matias, 2019; Seering et al., 2019; Squirrell, 2019). These groups of moderators conduct similar tasks to Roberts's exploited workers, but their perception of their role and responsibility is very different.

In 2019, along with colleagues in sociology and computing science, I conducted a study involving a survey and follow-up focus group work investigating content moderation which included both moderators and users of social media. We were interested both in the factors shaping moderator practice and user behaviour and in users' perceptions in their interactions with it. This study focused on Reddit, which of course is a distinct if significant part of the wider social media environment, but we did also include some qualitative work with paid moderators from a reputable media company. We found a number of similarities between these moderators and the Reddit moderators, particularly in respect of their decision-making and role perception – though of course there were also significant differences, most of which related to the paid moderators' overall objectives in representing their employer. This work illustrates more than anything the diverse range of activities, understandings and experiences of those in this now huge contingent of content moderators. However, it perhaps also indicates that there are insights that can be drawn in respect of the broad structural role played by these moderators in shaping our new media landscape.

A good starting point is to set out a profile of the moderators in our sample. Only Reddit moderators were surveyed (more details are given in the Appendix), but the key empirical point is that these volunteers were overwhelmingly young men based in North America. In this, their demographics were broadly comparable to that of Reddit users (Barthel et al., 2016) and of the tech industry as a whole, including platform executives (Stempeck, 2019; York, 2021). This relates to another notable feature of Reddit moderators (more likely to be replicated in those platforms that rely on volunteers, rather than platforms like Facebook which don't):that they are invited to their role by the moderator community and/or they set up their own topic-specific subreddits, and so are of necessity active and experienced users of the platform already. They not only are the type of people who are initially drawn to Reddit and find it a 'fit', but they have, through their engagement, absorbed the culture and expectations of the platform in a fairly organic way before beginning their moderating role.

This has important implications for the practice of these moderators. In our study, we found that, while this group tend to use language and framings to construct moderation as a collective endeavour (and in particular we noted the repeated use of 'we' rather than 'I' in discussions), as individuals they were very confident in making decisions independently. They rarely escalated cases for review or consulted with other moderators. As one said, it was not their role to 'sheepishly defer to a higher authority in every case' (male, moderator survey, 2019, USA).

Some of this relates to the mode of recruitment, in that the moderators were selected on the basis of shared understandings and adherence to the platform 'norms' which embed them (Lee and Hyunjoo, 2010), and the expectation that this would play out in their practice too. The following comment emphasises this sense of autonomous decision-making rooted in the shared values of the community of moderators:

> I'm independent in that I have complete control and make my own judgements, but I'm also a member of a team of people who are all independent in the same way, and who have all been chosen because we share *common personal values* [my italics] for the community. (Female, moderator survey, Australia, 2019)

These *common personal values* are summed up well in a comment that was typical of quite a few moderators in our sample: 'don't be a complete dickhead on the internet' (male, moderator survey, USA, 2019).

The literature on moderation shows the way in which 'norms' are the product of platform design and affordances, forms of moderation, the interactions between moderators and users, and the cultures these interactions produce (Sternberg, 2012; Matias 2019; Squirrell, 2019; Seering et al., 2019). But what research also shows is that moderators play an active role in shaping these 'norms'. They may see their work as in part founded on an assumption of public consensus about what would be considered appropriate or inappropriate conduct and content (Chandrasekharan et al., 2018), and that instinct is of course what has marked them out for the role. But the evidence suggests that they also use platform affordances to promote the authority of their decision-making, and relish carrying influence within their communities (Squirrell, 2019).

In our own work, we saw in this collective confidence and sense of authority some echoes of Zelizer's (1993) model of the 'interpretive communities' of professional journalists. Of course, no group of social media moderators holds the elevated status of journalists in society (though it is worth noting also that those in the category of 'journalists' in respect of income, security and status now vary almost as much as moderators) – but moderators' social coherence and shared locatedness produce patterns in decision-making which hold authority because they are also the basis of their selection and suitability for the role.

From this position of authority and status (see also Squirrell, 2019) we found that some moderators aimed to actively shape their communities in line with their values:

> Everyone, as individuals, have personal values. We're human. Not robots. [...] we actively try to make our community a better place. We've active. Not passive. (Male, moderator survey, UK, 2019)

For many in our study, the stated aim was to construct a community that was 'welcoming' and 'inclusive'; however, the ways in which that translated into moderation practice varied a great deal. There did seem to be a heightened sense of 'social justice issues', though sexism was noted far less frequently as a topic to intervene on than, say, racism or transgender rights, a pattern which it is difficult not to associate with the gender profile of Reddit moderators. Mostly, however, a welcoming (or *not unwelcoming*) community was understood to be constructed through intervention in relation to questions of conduct rather than content, with a particular emphasis on direct attacks and personal abuse. We found that inclusivity was interpreted primarily as openness to the widest range of views and users feeling sufficiently protected to express them.

This broadly reflects the Habermasian conceptualisation of the public sphere, in which online communities provide a space for citizens to freely debate issues of social importance (Habermas, 1992; Papacharissi, 2002). As this moderator articulated:

> In my opinion, everybody should have the right to be able to discuss their viewpoints on the internet. If somebody ... I mean, there's a lot of viewpoints you might not agree with, but people should have the right to discuss theirs in a polite manner. (Male, moderator, UK, 2019–20)

Underpinning this is a fairly traditional approach to freedom of speech: the principle that all opinions should be allowed unless they are harmful to others. However, the way in which rule-breaking on conduct was understood often forced moderators to use their own judgement as to whether comments were or were not posted in 'good faith' – that is, without intent to offend or be harmful. These are of course extremely difficult judgements to make where many users are anonymous and/or manipulate other users to make a point. The comment below shows how subjective – and perhaps surprising – decisions made on that basis could be:

> I think a lot of people who post, we don't see it that often, but Holocaust denial, I think they genuinely do believe that, they genuinely think the Holocaust didn't happen, but it's not really for me to educate them, I'm not going to ban them because they're denying the Holocaust. (Male, moderator, UK, 2019–20)

Holocaust denial is of course highly offensive to most people (as well as illegal in some states) and can also be defined as targeted hate. The comment should also be understood in the context of the interventions that moderators told us they regularly implemented, which included deleting comments and banning and suspending user accounts – and the irony of the example above of a moderator disciplining a discussion of the Israel–Palestine conflict in order to limit anti-Semitism. As I will go on to discuss, for those users who are confused as to why an exposed female nipple might lead to a deletion or even a ban, these decision-making processes are indefensible or confused at best. But fundamentally, in spite of the apparent autonomy in respect of collective or individual moderator decision-making, in their promotion of provocative or extreme discourse and the inevitable generation of user engagement, these are firmly in line with the objectives of the content moderators' Big Tech overseers.

But in other areas, decision-making is not so clearly aligned, and, on the basis of our data, I'd also argue that through these practices, moderators can, to differing degrees, be seen to represent a new and distinct form of cultural power. It is a power that operates in the parameters set by platforms and the 'new gatekeepers', and in negotiation with users, as I will discuss next. However, in the volume and diversity of interventions made by moderators there is space and opportunity to manage opinion of thought and expression. Even within our sample, moderators varied a great deal in the degree to which they were interventionist. Some were highly proactive in their attempts to steer a conversation by way of adding in-post warnings or counter-information and requesting users to adjust their posts before getting approval. But these moderators need to be seen alongside those who intervene very little – even on issues such as the Israel–Palestine conflict if the framing allows it – and cases where the content that remains unmarked or unchanged becomes highly significant to those who absorb the symbolic meanings of those decisions.

Certainly moderators believe that they have influence, and in our study some claimed they had actively shifted people's views with their interventions. The following moderator comments, though, might be a better indicator of how the influence is felt: 'they [users] start to echo your language, so you can have influence' (female, moderator, UK, 2019–20); 'so over time, people will get used to the rules, and then they'll start moderating themselves to a certain extent' (male, moderator, UK, 2019–20). Of course, the moderation workers of Facebook may not see themselves as having this level of influence, but this kind of moderation does make a difference – as things always do when they are led by humans and not machines.

Moderating bots

This leads us to another new form of influence which inputs into the shaping of our social media landscape – and which moderators are often on the front line of managing – and that is the use of bots. Bots are algorithmically programmed to produce posts, tweets, comments and so on, posing as authentic users, and they are a central aspect of what is sometimes called 'the digital propaganda machine' (Briant, 2018; see also Bastos and Farkas, 2019). Bots are used by groups such as domestic and foreign state actors, major brands and celebrities seeking influence for political, commercial and reputational gains, and can be strategically placed to amplify narratives or to flood and silence opponents and marginalise perspectives.

At the most resourced and strategic end, bots can play a role alongside activities such as data mining in the campaigns of political groups to manage opinion and engineer social media outcomes, the Cambridge Analytica scandal remaining the most talked-about example. Accusations of interference in Western elections from hostile states such as Russia more generally often rest on the question of where bots originate (Silverstein, 2018). But bots can be produced by ordinary users too. It's not easy to estimate the volume of bot activity, but for example during the 2016 Brexit debate, it was estimated that 13,493 Twitter accounts comprised automated content in some form (Bastos and Mercea, 2016).

These strategic communications, unique to the digital environment in their ability to tailor messaging and construct a false sense of consensus, are a key factor in the construction of the social media information environment. But they should be seen in interaction with the agents and mechanisms which seek to limit their spread. There are all sorts of tools for detecting bots or inauthentic users on social media platforms, most of which rely on automation, such as botwatch for Reddit, but many of them can evade detection. Human moderators often pick up those that automated monitors miss, and social media users themselves sometimes detect those missed by both, again in illustration of the dynamic and complex interactions which produce the content we see. Of course, social media users also use the mechanisms available to them as both individuals and collectives – including developing their own bots – to exert influence. It is to the users themselves, who used to be considered to be residing at the other end of the communications circuit but are now intricately entangled with all other aspects of it, that I will now turn.

The (digital) public

The third element in the original circuit was the public, stratified by class, gender, ethnicity and so on and in receipt of selected media content which shapes ideas and opinion in different ways. These processes now take place mostly in the digital arena, where the public engage with news content via social media, search engines or mobile aggregators, as consumption of traditional media continues to decline (Newman et al., 2023). Here I will focus particularly on social media, in part because they were the subject of much focus group discussion (even when not prompted) in my research, and in part because the form of engagement made possible on social media platforms, and their interactions with the newer elements of the circuit already documented, are arguably the most transformative in respect of the kinds of media reception which came before.

What role then do ordinary people play in the construction of this new communications system and how do they perceive, understand and then respond to what they read, hear and engage with in their own carefully crafted corners of it? In my revised notion of the circuit, social media users should not be seen to simply occupy two positions (as consumers and receivers) simultaneously. I would also resist the notion that users are active participatory agents in this new public sphere, as much as I would resist the alternative notion that they are passive dupes of all powerful new forms of digital propaganda. Instead, users should be seen as integral to how power and influence are produced and reproduced, acting in service of and in resistance to power in a range of new and often contradictory ways.

Perceptions of trust and transparency

A good place to start is with the main theme of the first chapter: questions of trust and transparency. In our focus groups with social media users there was a lack of clarity about the management of social media content: most participants were not familiar with the term 'moderation' or had not thought much about these processes or the people and/or mechanisms involved. There was only a general awareness of the existence of guidelines governing the types of content and conduct prohibited on different platforms, and an even vaguer understanding of how content came to be amplified – which is not surprising, as rules and policies are well hidden as well as 'purposefully ambiguous', and algorithms often 'secret' (Suzor et al., 2019).

That moderation – often seen as a form of discipline – was primarily triggered in response to user reports was broadly understood, but there was a sense that decision-making was often a law unto itself, not following any pattern and often unjust. Users were often surprised at the inconsistency in decisions to delete content and ban or suspend users. For example, one participant, a young male social media user, described having a comment, in which he had called someone making racist comments a 'moron', removed for violating Facebook rules while the racist comments remained. Several others described scenarios where men were seen to be allowed to get away with the same behaviour that women were penalised for. In another group there was a consensus that women 'standing up for themselves' would receive abuse, but the abuse itself was something that moderation 'wouldn't touch'. Because of these assumptions, users found themselves offering posts and likes which didn't rock the boat in the communities within which they existed.

The perception that moderation was passive co-existed with a feeling that it could be overly punitive. In some ways, participants felt, it did too much, but in others it did too little. Across this data, there was a strong theme of a lack of transparency and a cynicism about the motives of platforms and their moderation. There was certainly an awareness that platforms operate as businesses first and that ethical standards or maintenance of healthy online communities come a poor second. Some users in our groups were very aware that extreme content or hate speech was amplified – or at least not removed – because ultimately it brings more users in. There was also a sense that there would be more leniency towards powerful voices such as politicians, celebrities and public figures than towards those in marginalised groups, again because of basic market imperatives. Similarly, a small number noted that social media is 'full of bots' that are often amplified by the platforms.

A contradictory consciousness

However, a perhaps surprising finding in this respect is that almost all of the social media users we talked to expressed a desire for *more* moderation rather than less:

> Free speech is very vocal, like you can use free speech on Twitter and it's like … Maybe we should be moderated a little bit because people are being a little bit racist and anti-Semitic. (Female, young social media user, UK, 2019–20)

I return here to a point I made in Chapter 2 – that most people believe there is no alternative to having a digital presence, something which is both structurally and ideologically well established. So some people resign themselves to finding compromises rather than removing themselves from platform cultures altogether.

But there is also a very stark contradiction here. There is an awareness that social media platforms are designed to distort public discourse and opinion, and to amplify the very worst of them in ways which encourage people to behave in more toxic, attention-seeking or uncivil ways than they would IRL (in real life). On the other hand, as the previous comment illustrates, people still desire increasing intervention by the influence mechanisms and agents in order to resolve the very problem they have created. This is further complicated by the perception that platform cultures also represent something authentic: that people are 'a little bit racist' and need moderating.

This contradictory consciousness – that this culture is constructed but is in some ways real – is a crucial point in respect of how influence operates in the digital media environment. This is because, while people might have a broad impression of how these processes work at the structural level to shape what content they are exposed to, they cannot unpick what is 'authentic' and what is not at the level of the collective and individual exchanges they see. If racist content is amplified and encouraged by platform affordances, how can users unpick what is an expression of genuine sentiment and what is not? If users are exposed to racist content every day, is racism a product of the everyday and so perceived as 'normal' behaviour even where it is seen as offensive?

And crucially for the purposes of this book – what can be seen as representing 'public opinion', in the sense of what other people really think, and what then comes to impact on how we think ourselves? On the basis of my own research, I'd say that even where, as one user noted, it 'sometimes feels that there's almost two completely dual cultures', most felt that online discourse was representative of societal tendencies and that pervasive racism and sexism, for example, were digital manifestations of deep-rooted beliefs. As a moderator in our study himself noted, online discourse could distort perceptions:

> People start to think, well, maybe everybody else is like … maybe I'm not the only racist homophobe in the country. (Male, moderator, UK, 2019–20)

Collective resistance and cancel culture

Of course, people react to this kind of exposure in different ways, and some will find their own opposition to prejudice or hateful rhetoric even more cemented and will actively and vocally resist. This is a likelier outcome in those cases where users are immersed in communities which prioritise social justice, often rooted in media, professional or activist discourses, and which are emboldened by a sense of collective support. As discussed in Chapter 3, there may be generational and educational distinctions in this respect which are not necessarily just a reflection of actual opinions and attitudes. Our moderators were also clear that collective user activity could direct the narrative (which could work both ways). While they largely agreed that digital opinion usually plays out within the parameters set by moderation, here they referred to techniques used to resist moderation practice, including users opening multiple accounts, user bots and the strategic organisation of upvoting and downvoting.

At the furthest extreme of strategic organising is the now very divisive concept of 'cancel culture'. Again in reflection of the importance of media and communications in shaping public opinion, when we conducted this work with social media users in 2019–20, the debate on the degree to which cancel culture was seen to exist or not exist, and the communities organising themselves around one position or the other, was not yet well established. That framing – and, I would argue, fairly effective management of opinion for the liberal groups targeted – came later. In the light of this, people discussed what cancel culture might mean and how it might look.

A key opinion, raised in a number of groups, was that the impact of 'cancelling' was felt in financial terms:

> To me, cancel culture seems to be something like showing general outrage at someone doing something bad doesn't have anything happen, whereas cancel culture hits them where it hurts in the money … in the monetary area, and it's more likely to cause change. (Male, young social media user, UK, 2019–20)

Opinion was divided, however, over whether cancel culture was a positive cultural phenomenon or a negative one. Some felt that cancel culture represented 'mob mentality', and it was noted that anonymity emboldened users to contribute. In line with this, some saw cancel culture purely as a product of digital communications: one said that 'social media basically created cancel culture' (female, young social media user, UK, 2019–20). On the basis of the nuances and inequities of platform cultures, some felt that cancel culture could lead to fairly unjust outcomes in response to minor offences:

If anyone does anything slightly controversial, I mean, sometimes it's worth it, sometimes it's not, but people will just jump on the bandwagon and be like, okay, cancelled, like your career's over. (Female, young social media user, UK, 2019–20)

But others felt it was a valid mechanism for social justice, targeting people who deserved consequences for their actions and offering a counter to a mainstream culture which would allow them to express vile views or exhibit abhorrent behaviours. Some felt that it was a positive thing to be part of and offered a form of validation of their own views as acceptable or desirable. The professional British troll Katie Hopkins, who 'built a living out of being horribly offensive and racist' (male, moderator, UK, 2019–20), was seen as a good example of this, as was Kevin Spacey, who was charged with a number of sexual assaults in the UK context (and later cleared).

However, it was not always clear-cut. In one group, for example, there was a discussion of the Canadian rapper Drake, who was said to have been 'grooming a [under-aged] girl from *Stranger Things*' (male, moderator, UK, 2019–20). In this case, the question of wrongdoing and level of evidence were seen to be uncertain, as was the question of whether he was even properly 'cancelled'. This of course raises a key issue with cancel culture, however loosely defined: that the evidence, information and judgement usually rest on unreliable media sources, as well as the amplification of disproportionate responses. This can allow genuine injustice to go unnoticed and minor transgressions to be heavily punished (which of course operates to discourage transgressing 'acceptable' thought and opinion). I will now explore the way in which collective social media responses might reproduce other injustices and inequalities.

Strategies of silencing

Across our empirical work on social media, there was a broad recognition that expressing oneself online is associated with a range of impacts and consequences. These vary in degree of severity and intensity as well as their proportionality, and the outcomes are differentiated across different groups. Here we can look at the way in which what might seem to be individual responses and strategies are aligned with structural forces in respect of who gets to speak and what can be spoken about in society more generally.

In a study of the influence of platform culture and moderator decision-making on how people engage online, Gibson (2019) found that moderation can have a significant impact on individuals' tendencies to self-censor. In my own work, a key aspect of this is the way in which active users moved between different platform cultures, internalising the values of each with ease and at speed. What is interesting is that not only did users self-censor to conform, but they mirrored the moderators' framing of what was acceptable:

> I will swear but I won't aim like a horrible insult. Not for the fact that I don't want this to be taken down but more like I don't want to be a dickhead. (Male, young social media user, 2019–20)

In this respect, in relation to previous observations of moderators, those moderating and those being moderated are aligned.

Most people in our groups, though, were less concerned about the moderation of their own conduct and content (though there may have been a degree of social desirability bias in this attitude). The real concern was the responses they might receive, particularly on platforms which were public-facing, such as Twitter (X), or on public accounts on Facebook or Instagram. Again, it is difficult to distinguish whether online abuse is digitally produced or digitally revealed. But either way, such abuse can be related to expectations of moderation and the knowledge that abusive or negative responses to a user's own posts are less likely to be disciplined (and might even be amplified).

One particular issue was the level of abuse targeting women and other marginalised groups. A key aspect of this was a tendency to focus on appearance and the volume of attacks on women who diverged from narrow beauty standards. As one female social media user noted: 'There is definitely a total hatred or this deep-rooted misogyny, especially with plus size women particularly' (UK, young social media user, UK, 2019–20). But this was one part of what was recognised as the fairly routine nature of misogyny on the major platforms such as Twitter (X): 'you're typically going on to something that's like women deserve to like burn in hell for being whores' (female, young social media user, 2019–20). A number noted how harmful this can be to those in direct or indirect receipt of it:

> It is damaging, especially if like whenever you're seeing this sort of … these comments, these posts, like you're part of the demographic that it's kind of attacking. (Female, young social media user, 2019–20)

As a result, many users self-censor to avoid such toxic comment and abuse. Women and transgender people in our groups were most likely to self-censor, and there was a tendency for the men in the groups to see platform culture as a playful arena rather than one which could induce anxiety. Again, the role of moderation was significant, as people recognised how other users might work around a moderation policy aimed at disciplining directly harmful material, as this comment indicates:

> But if they write it in a certain way where it's not directly what Instagram view as hateful, you can't really deal with it so I just delete it. (Female, young social media user, 2019–20)

However, it is also worth noting that for some of those who did find online engagement stressful, the more they were immersed in it, the less it impacted them, as one noted: 'I'm more worried that I've got used to it, that it doesn't bother me' (male, young social media user, 2019–20). The cumulative effect of this gradual acceptance of online toxicity is to promote the normalisation of abuse, hate and discriminatory discourse.

Female voices in the public sphere

The tendency for women to self-censor has very real structural impacts on who gets to speak and, in consequence, on the range of perspectives available to the public. An illustrative case is that of female journalists, who are confronted with the same processes and forms of abuse as the women in our sample, but in a public-facing role in an industry which increasingly sees social media as an extension of the workplace. A report on the online experiences of female journalists by Claire Kish (2022) has shown that women journalists receive three times more abuse on Twitter (X) than men, and women from marginalised groups (those identifying as Black, Asian, LGBT and so on) are targeted more than white women journalists. Again in line with our research, Kish found that this abuse is often focused on their identity as women and often highly sexualised and misogynistic. Perhaps unsurprisingly, these patterns of abuse have very real personal and professional impacts for journalists, with a significant number responding by either opting to leave journalism or self-censoring on social media. Many simply avoid writing about contentious issues (Ferrier, 2018; Kish, 2022).

Of course, women have historically struggled to be heard in the highly masculine workplaces of news and journalism, but the extent and targeted nature of this kind of abuse can be seen to represent something distinct in the structural barriers to female progression. If much of this abuse takes the form of 'trolling', which in at least some of my groups was seen – mostly by male participants – as an activity which was playful or entertaining, this does raise serious questions about how we've allowed platform cultures to develop and indeed to thrive. However, in respect of our focus on the processes and mechanisms which shape this new media environment, and the kinds of content the public can access, this has significance too. Removing from view the perspectives, stories and experiences of women and marginalised groups of course simply amplifies the perspectives, stories and experience of those not in these groups.

If the promotion of male, pale and stale voices sounds just like the old journalism, of course, in some ways, it does represent continuity. The progress that women have made in respect of entering that elite space in the culture is not supported – and indeed may be challenged – by these processes. This is a much bigger issue in relation to other female voices in the public sphere.

Research has shown, for example, that women at the chalk face of politics face almost daily abuse online, with many no longer willing to express their opinions on social media (Morgan, 2020). The departing First Minister of Scotland, Nicola Sturgeon, noted in 2023 that she was deeply concerned that misogynistic social media abuse was putting young women off entering politics at all, describing the current climate as harsher and more hostile than at any time in the previous thirty years in which she had been in politics (Ferguson, 2023). If Sturgeon is correct – and she should know – this climate can only further promote the attitudes, experiences and ideas that are held by men in society as normal and expected of us all.

Conclusion

In this chapter I have mapped out a new range of elements and processes which expand the circuit of media and communications in Western digital cultures. In this, the aim is not to replace the original elements but to develop the model. Of course, some elements have changed more than others, but the model continues to rotate around the axis of state and corporate power.

I have introduced the new gatekeepers of Big Tech, who control access to an information society and are driven by generating user engagement and revenue, but these interact directly and indirectly with the first element, social and political institutions, including government, business, lobby groups and so on, which continue to influence the nature of information in important ways (especially where political or commercial interests are threatened). Similarly, the second element, professional media content and the key agents such as journalists who produce it, remains prominent in the circuit, but is increasingly reliant on the new gatekeepers of platforms to host it. Media content is also subject to a range of processes, including human moderation and algorithms, which deliver it to users in ways which journalists cannot always control and put it in competition with other persuasive communications including AI, user-generated content and bots. The public, the third element, now largely digitised, interact more directly with content than before and produce it themselves in ways which are differentiated by their own characteristics and contexts, but also by the affordances and learned behaviours of the platforms they inhabit. This is an environment in which social media users begin to 'moderate themselves' as well as others in ways which are likely to limit the spread of any genuinely radical or challenging ideas.

Through the interaction of these different elements, and old and new forms of power, we can see how particular opinions and ideas and the groups expressing them can be marginalised, silenced or deemed to be unacceptable while others are amplified, and the societal outcomes these processes might produce. This brings us to decision-making, the fourth element, which still largely resides in the same groups drawn from our social, political and corporate elites, but with all elements influencing outcomes in different ways and resistance to the narratives we are exposed to a crucial tool in driving social change.

Importantly, the practices of media influence have diversified. If traditional media set the agenda on the issues which are seen as important and determine where people focus their attention, in platform cultures instead the content which circulates identifies perceptions, thoughts and experiences that are common, normal or frequent. The agenda is seen as one which authentically emerges, and as representing what ordinary people think is important (even where there is a contradictory consciousness in respect of how this works). This may be a distinct form of influence, but it is becoming increasingly important. The evidence here suggests it operates mostly in ways which cohere with conventional power, though there is the space for mis-management of opinion in the interactions between the different elements.

5

Climate, COVID-19 and the cost of living: getting up close to global crises

This chapter will take the analysis beyond the period of data collection to examine how three inter-related global crises – climate change, COVID-19 and the cost-of-living crisis – are constructed through different media cultures in ways which produce expectations about the nature and urgency of action to be taken. Here we can see the overall arguments of the book illustrated in a more empirical way. I begin with the ideological practices of the mainstream media which shape the narratives of crisis (or non-crisis) around these issues. In spite of falling levels of public trust, mainstream media remain particularly important in driving decision-making because of their privileged position in respect of political access and influence: when they name a crisis, they create a need to respond. As previously discussed, there is also evidence that people, albeit briefly perhaps, re-orientate themselves to a mainstream culture in times of recognised crisis (Newman et al., 2021).

I will then examine how these media narratives interact with lived experience – the final filter as set out in Chapter 2 – looking at the differential degrees of experiential evidence around climate change, the pandemic and the cost of living to examine how journalistic constructions of proximity and threat impact on public perception and opinion. Here I'll show the way in which media constructions can overwhelm other filters.

I will further discuss the way in which the cost-of-living crisis has come into public discourse at a pivotal moment in which the need for real systemic change is being reinforced across public life – though one which, as current evidence suggests, may turn out to be another non-crisis (at least in respect of the level of response) as power consolidates to ensure the economic system remains intact. It is from these moments, I argue, *in which the possibility of decisive change is missed*, that the disconnect grows and resistance is likely to emerge.

Taking up this theme of eroded trust, the disconnect from mainstream political rhetoric and frustration over the lack of meaningful action, in the second part of the chapter I will focus on the production of alternative forms of political communication around climate change. Here I examine the way in which youth climate activists engaged in their own decentred media cultures have managed to construct very different impressions of proximity and crisis through creative articulations on highly visual social media platforms. Finally, I will argue that political communications on social media more generally can be far removed from the conventional politics of policy and action, even removed from questions of reality itself, and I will examine the challenges this presents for the development of a movement for change.

Crisis in context

A key argument of this book is that any media culture, including its focus, priorities and concerns, both reflects and shapes the political and social system within which it is located, maintaining its own particularities even in an increasingly globalised digital landscape where perspectives, elite speakers and questions that are identified as salient are increasingly shared. Issues must be elevated and prioritised before they are seen as problems to be addressed, and what become seen as problems to be addressed will dictate the kinds of action society takes and the direction it moves in. The elevation of an issue or event to a 'crisis' specifically is a highly ideological act, and here I draw on a definition offered by Laffan:

> A crisis is a decisive moment that pressurises political actors to develop understandings of the events they encounter and the nature and extent of the challenges they face. (Laffan, 2014: 267)

Crucially it is a moment in which the range of actors who hold power to shape public discourse create an expectation, even a demand, for decisive and pressing action to be taken (Blyth, 2007; Widmaier et al., 2007). As the range of studies examining the discursive effort around what is sometimes called the 'migrant crisis' show, broad political consensus can emerge where a body of evidence or even clarity around what that evidence might be is lacking: in this case, that Britain has been subject to an 'uncontrollable mass influx' of migrants, finding solutions to which politicians must prioritise (Danewid, 2022). In other cases, even where evidence is clear and largely consensual among recognised experts, there may be significant resistance to naming a crisis. Similarly, situations that are named as war, conflict, disaster or emergency, with the attendant crises and victims associated with them, are a product of the geo-political and media landscape they inhabit.

Naming the climate crisis

As Donald (2020) notes, climate change has historically been a highly malleable concept; as it is the product of centuries of exploitation of people and resources, just naming it can be an act of resistance which is bound up with demands for social change to different degrees. In 2014 Naomi Klein talked of what she called our 'climate change mismatch' in that 'the climate crisis hatched in our laps at a moment in history when political and social conditions were uniquely hostile to a problem of this nature and magnitude' (Klein, 2014: unpaginated). In Chapter 1, I offered an overview of the structural changes brought on by neoliberalism over the last three decades in the West, which have redirected power and resources to the corporate class, starved the public sphere and ideologically dismantled a commitment to collective endeavour in which media and political decision-making are mutually reinforcing. In this context it is easy to see how taking decisive action on climate change has been at odds with the economic and cultural trajectory of the recent era.

Notably in this article of 2014, Klein uses the term 'crisis', but at that time, the word was very rarely heard in relation to climate change in mainstream political or media discourse in the UK, or anywhere else. Media coverage of climate change in recent decades has been a contested and dynamic space running in parallel to the political trajectory. I have charted at length, across a body of work (see, in particular, Philo and Happer, 2013, and Happer, 2017a), the peaks and troughs of public attention and positive policy action, and I have added to the literature identifying the tendency to construct climate change as a matter of scientific (dis)belief (Boykoff, 2011; Painter, 2013). Here we have seen climate action constructed as conflict – by which I mean in discursive terms rather than the actuality of how it may play out on the ground (though certainly in the more recent context of the 'culture wars' this conflict has become ever more polarised and hostile).

In response to the efforts of NGOs, activist groups and the work of the Intergovernmental Panel on Climate Change (IPCC) on the release of their reports, there has been an increased tendency in some media outlets to position climate as an urgent problem or 'crisis' (Parks, 2020). However, climate change has consistently struggled to assert itself as a sustained priority in public discourse, and even where some local and national governmental bodies have referred to a climate 'crisis' or 'emergency' (BBC News Online, 2019b), it largely does not hold the status or political characteristics of a crisis.

One reason for this may be that climate change has not yet seen, in the West at least, the culmination of a period of 'intensifying struggles and unrest' and/or one in which the internal contradictions of the system are laid bare (Hall, 2019a) – and so the 'decisive moment' is lacking (though it is of course already beginning right across the world and is certainly brewing in many Western nations). But to return to the process of naming, the narrative of crisis has hardly been one which has been rarely or cautiously invoked or one which has operated on a consensual or prescriptive set of understandings. As far back as 1987, Holton noted that:

> Crisis has become such an all-pervasive rhetorical metaphor that its analytical utility for contemporary social thought has become devalued and confused. (Holton, 1987: 502)

The mainstream media in particular happily adopt a narrative frame of crisis, and the decisive moment in which political actors are pressured to respond is in part constructed by a media and political class who have already identified the problem to be addressed (and which actions might lead to a resolution of the crisis). To return to Klein's argument, a key reason why there is such resistance to defining climate change as a crisis is the expectation it creates of urgency of response with radical structural change, for which there is no political appetite. A second cause is what researchers often describe as its relative remoteness as an issue for people in the West (Whitmarsh et al., 2013); however serious, it is easier than others to ignore in the short term. I will return to these obstacles, along with the particular linguistic and visual strategies communicators and journalists have used to positive effect, later in the chapter. But fundamentally media and communications as part of a political system in the West have played a key role in constructing climate change as a non-crisis, as a conflict of scientific belief, as a preoccupation of an elite environmental class, rather than what it essentially is: a struggle between the powerful and the powerless over the future of humanity (Huber, 2022).

Last-minute pandemic planning

If climate change is easy to ignore, the pandemic was in many ways its polar opposite: impossible to ignore, and anything but remote. It certainly didn't struggle to define itself as a 'crisis' (or 'disaster', 'emergency' or 'fight') which almost inherently demanded an urgent response. But Covid as crisis and response – or to be more accurate, as a set of crises and their responses – is every bit as much a product of the political and media systems within which it sits. Covid was experienced very differently in China, for example, which took a highly authoritarian approach to managing the virus through extreme lockdowns (Yerushalmy, 2022), from in Sweden, which took a much more libertarian approach built on public health guidance about social distancing (Frans, 2022). These countries assessed the threats and possible responses through the lens of their own political cultures.

In respect of naming 'the decisive moment' – at which point action becomes inevitable – as an event unfolding across the world of which initially only a minority may have been fully informed and greater public knowledge grew gradually, in the UK at least this was very much a political choice. There has been much discussion about the slowness of the UK government's response. As the death toll escalated across the world and a range of governments were taking decisive action, a meeting of Cobra, the UK's crisis management committee, on 24 January 2020 which raised the alarm, arguing on the basis of consolidating scientific evidence, was largely ignored (Calvert et al., 2020). Similarly, the British mainstream media, including the BBC, positioned Covid at first as a slow-moving global story featuring mainly voices from the scientific community. As one scientist said later, it was perhaps the BBC's moderate language – not shouting 'you lot ought to be petrified because this is going to be a pandemic that will kill hundreds of thousands of people' – that kept the virus off the front page (Helm et al., 2020).

But scientists are not – except perhaps for a short period during the pandemic – primary definers. For Covid to hit the front pages at that point would have needed a politician to be talking of thousands of deaths, and for that to be taken as credible, there would have had to be a cross-media body of evidence identifying and making salient the growing threat, with an expectation of response. It would also have had to battle through the never-ending story of Brexit still dominating the media at the time (Helm et al., 2020). In the event, media coverage began to rise rapidly from early March, prompted by the first major spike in Covid cases globally (Pearman et al., 2021). The UK government responded at what might be described as the very latest possible point. It has been estimated that had the lockdown been initiated even one week earlier, the number of deaths in the first wave of the pandemic would have been cut by half (Johns, 2020).

The government's reluctance to call the lockdown in the UK was also paralleled by the reluctance of the BBC, whose public service role became of utmost importance in respect of communicating public health guidance, to use this term in the early days of the pandemic. It was later revealed that the government had put pressure on the broadcaster to avoid using the term, which led to a rather absurd set of headlines referring to the 'curbs' and 'restrictions' imposed on daily life while the rest of the media emphasised the new grim reality of 'LOCKDOWN' life in the UK (Mason and Elgot, 2023). While they are seemingly contradictory, both tendencies are representative of the ideological underpinning of the UK's media: on one hand a refusal to acknowledge a policy solution antagonistic to prevailing assumptions about what is best for a system focused on freedom of markets and relentless economic growth, and at the other, an indignant condemnation of it (what the *Daily Telegraph* described as the 'end of freedom' and the *Sun* called 'house arrest') (BBC News Online, 2020c).

For the BBC, the background was a weakened corporation in the face of successive governmental interventions to reduce independence, and for the wider media an increasingly narrow set of speakers and perspectives to whom a platform was given to open up discussions about what might be for the public good, in this case containing the virus and saving lives (Philo and Berry, 2023). There is certainly something to be said also for Klein's 'mismatch', in this case a 'COVID mismatch', evidenced by how quickly the normal priorities of the media and political class were resumed – the largely uncritical media promotion of the government's 'eat out to help out' scheme only months later being a good illustration. As the pandemic progressed, we also saw lockdown scepticism become more pronounced, and the critique of government coming from the World Health Organization and the wider international scientific community largely absent, particularly where they suggested strategies involving greater intervention. While the question of the pandemic as 'crisis' was largely undisputed, questions of the appropriateness of the degree and nature of response became highly contested over time.

Defining the cost-of-living crisis

The use of the term 'crisis' in relation to the soaring cost of living has become fairly established practice in the post-pandemic period: it is referred to by people across all layers and spheres of society, from nurses and charities to politicians and celebrities, and of course the media. This is in spite of there being no consensus on what the crisis is, what caused it or the pressing problems it presents to be addressed. It is a global crisis, but it is also highly local. It has roots in the two global crises already covered in this chapter, as well as the war in Ukraine which began in February 2022, when Russia launched its invasion in a major escalation of an ongoing conflict. Indeed, the impact of the war in terms of soaring global energy prices was initially identified by the UK government in early 2022 as the main cause of what was widely referred to in the media at that point as simply the 'energy crisis'. As a result, it was the 'energy crisis' that early 2022 policy solutions – such as offering people help to pay their energy bills – were designed to directly address (HM Treasury, 2022). But as the crisis developed, the way in which local elements, and in particular the Conservative government in power in the UK at the time, dictated the way it was understood, experienced and in consequence responded to, and the idea of proximity became ever more apparent.

In a highly complex set of integrated impacts, including rising energy prices related to the war in Europe, rising food prices caused partly by disrupted supply chains during Covid, stagnation in incomes and acute inflation, it is exceptionally difficult to attribute degrees of causality. In 2023, however, the UK government identified the latter as the number one priority (HM Treasury, 2023). Chancellor Jeremy Hunt set out his annual 'budget for growth' spearheaded by massive tax cuts for business to drive investment and drive down inflation directly (HM Treasury, 2023). Setting a political priority inevitably offers a measure by which governments can be assessed in the media and public opinion (in this case a fairly risky enterprise, as most of the fiscal levers which can be utilised to bring down inflation lie with the Bank of England). On the basis of predictions in March 2023 by the Office for Budget Responsibility that inflation had peaked, the government was already expressing restrained optimism (Weldon, 2023), a few months later it was once again on the back foot (Isaac, 2023).

Either way, this optimism was not widely shared in the media, even among the Conservatives' strongest supporters (though which may, more than anything, signal a media falling out of love with a government in place for far too long). A continuing narrative has been one of the increasingly extreme challenges faced by ordinary people across all sectors of society, and it has often been accompanied by advice on how they might manage their finances (see for example, Chiorando, 2022). Food banks, which have in recent years been used by record numbers, and by families with children in particular (Butler, 2022), are part of this broad pattern of coverage. Perhaps most notable here is the way in which food banks are normalised as an almost inevitable or necessary component of contemporary British society (Beck and Gwilym, 2022). In a depressing illustration, CBBC describes food banks to young viewers as 'a bit like supermarkets, but everything is free' (CBBC *Newsround*, 2019). A significant absence, though, is any analysis of the range of policy solutions, beyond those offered by government, that might address the complex set of causes. This brings us back to the question of how a crisis is constructed and its causes understood, and the attendant and pressing problems it demands a response to, as well as the way in which the media open up or close down possibilities for consideration.

In fact, food poverty, fuel poverty and the inability to afford essentials such as clothes or decent housing are, as the Independent Food Aid Network highlights:

the result of a complex set of structural issues relating but not restricted to problems of insecure, inadequate and expensive housing, insecure and low paid employment, insufficient social welfare provision, poor health, and environmentally unsustainable and socially unjust food production and distribution system. (The Public Purse, 2019: unpaginated)

So while the cost-of-living crisis must be located in the global political context of the COVID-19 recovery, the war in Ukraine and indeed the ongoing economic impacts of Brexit, we should apply a longer lens to understand how we have arrived at this juncture. Further, that we see it as a consequence not of one area of political decision-making but of the intersection of key sectors of public provision and need including food, housing, energy and employment. Satnam Virdee (2023), for example, offers a historical account of a crisis which lies in the neoliberal settlement from the 1970s, the financial crash of 2008 and resultant austerity, and a series of political measures that have produced inequalities which are geographical (the north–south divide), racialised, gendered and generational in nature. Some groups have benefitted from the hardships: Britain's richest 1 per cent have gained over £21 trillion in new wealth since 2020 when the pandemic hit (Christensen et al., 2023), and the top 1 per cent of households possess wealth 230 times greater than the least wealthy 10 per cent (Bancroft, 2022).

A key point is that the current 'crisis' impacts differentially – so it's a question not just of a crisis of what but also of a crisis for whom. For example, the problem of food banks had been growing since 2012, but was only elevated in importance once it impacted on teachers and nurses and not just those relying on welfare (Butler, 2022; Sosenko et al., 2022). That the growth in food banks is not sustained front-page news in a developed twenty-first-century economy is itself strong evidence of the crisis we are in – and it's one of representation as much as economic inequality. Why are we not speaking of this reality which surely itself is concrete evidence of a failed society?

Proximity to the crises

While crises are constructed in particular ways through the processes I have discussed, of course, the ways in which they are understood and responded to and the degree to which media accounts are accepted or resisted as the preferred ways of thinking about them will vary and are not always predictable. The reasons why they may differ are the focus of Chapter 2, in which I offered a model integrating six different filters which underpin or shape these responses: ideology, priorities and established value systems, opinion communities, identity and alignment, assessments of credibility and lived experience. Here I will explore the final filter, lived experience, in a more focused way.

Research, as I argued in Chapter 2, shows that audiences draw on their own experiences, including close involvement or observation of events in their own lives, to assess the credibility of media accounts that are presented to them. But these assessments battle with what is to some degree an oppositional force, because journalism is at the same time in the business of identifying and promoting issues and experiences as close to or of direct relevance to audiences through their own selections and framings. In this, as I noted in Chapter 2, audiences take what is already there in terms of frames of reference, understanding and knowledge and shape it into positions which resonate with them.

In theories of journalism, this closeness relates to the concept of 'proximity' (which, though related, is distinct from lived experience in important ways and should not be conflated directly with it). Various phenomena are associated with the idea of proximity in journalism studies, though generally it is accepted as a key criterion in respect of assessing 'newsworthiness', the quality which determines what will and will not be published and when (Mast and Temmerman, 2021). It is rooted in the sense that audiences will be most interested in a story which they perceive to be close or relevant to them, and this can extend beyond questions of geography and everyday experience to cultural commonalities and values (Amigo, 2023).

For the normative model of journalism, of equal importance is the principle of operating in the 'public interest', which includes informing audiences of what is close or of relevance to them even if they don't recognise it. A critical media perspective would critique these normative – what we might call idealistic – models of journalistic practice, which produce proximity as part of a system of 'news values'. A key point of contention is how much the public are told what reporting they *should* be interested in, as opposed to what they are *actually* interested in, what they care about and what impacts them directly. In a highly politicised and commercialised media environment, journalists construct a sense of closeness or 'belonging' – to geographical spaces, to identity-based communities, etc. – to serve political objectives which can operate to marginalise particular groups (Philo et al., 2013). Digital news in particular is 'saturated with markers of "personalization" and "proximity"' which have helped to promote populist narratives in recent years (Mast and Temmerman, 2021: 695).

So we have to understand the role of experience with this conundrum in mind: direct experience, observation and closeness play an important role in shaping opinion and belief, but media, increasingly in an immersive digital world, personalise and draw in individuals though identity categories and a constructed sense of closeness and what is or should be relevant to them. This is symbolic of the battle for public opinion more generally: to construct a crisis which people recognise as being *for them* and to make people feel that the explanations and solutions offered are beneficial to the group to which they belong. With this in mind we can return to the question of the perceived closeness or remoteness of the crises and related questions of the need for urgent and/or appropriate action.

Researchers have found that historically the perception of climate change as a remote issue, as a question of geography or temporality, can be a barrier in respect of public engagement, where engagement is understood as including at least some element of personal or emotional connection to the issue (Lorenzoni and Pidgeon, 2006; Moser and Dilling, 2007; Whitmarsh, 2008). On the other hand, studies have shown – perhaps unsurprisingly – that direct experience of environmental impacts such as air pollution and climate-related events such as flooding have a clear correlation with perceptions of risk and related levels of concern (Whitmarsh, 2008; Lujala at al., 2015). In my own research, I have similarly heard people talk about the importance of experiencing or seeing something in order to believe it. Inarguably, direct and unambiguous experience or observation is one of the most, if not *the* most, convincing forms of evidence. That quality of being direct and unambiguous in respect of the subject of media reporting is, however, relatively rare. People aren't usually asked to skip rope with a plank of wood (see Chapter 2). What might seem like an obvious statement – that Covid is distinct from climate change in that the threat of people contracting and dying of the virus is direct and unambiguous in a way that climate change isn't – is worth examining in more depth.

COVID-19: timeline of media and public response

In this section I will draw on a range of sources which provide a timeline of Covid deaths, media coverage and public concern in the early months of the pandemic (Mach et al., 2021; National Records of Scotland, 2021; Pearman et al., 2021; Sample, 2021; ONS, 2022; YouGov, 2022a). With any analysis of this nature a note of caution must be built in which relates not only to the interpretation of statistics but also the question of what information is and isn't publicly available. As a media researcher, the one question that I'd want to ask of people is: what was it that first made you aware of the pandemic and crucially what sparked genuine concern of the kind that would make you change your behaviour or demand action from government? We don't currently have an answer to that. What is immediately apparent, however, is the way the growth in media coverage paralleled the growth of fear of contracting the virus (Pearman at al., 2021; YouGov, 2022a). Media attention was very sparse in February 2020 and built in March towards a peak at the end of the month, while public concern grew from approximately a quarter of the British population at the beginning of March to over 60 per cent at the end of it.

The correlation between media coverage and the trajectory of the pandemic is a much more complex and difficult to assess, but by a range of measures is far weaker. As noted, the spike in global cases was aligned to some degree with the initial spike in coverage in the UK and indeed the rest of the world to a greater or lesser degree (Pearman et al., 2021). In their measurement of the ratio of media coverage to weekly Covid cases, however, researchers for *The Lancet* found a very poor correlation, with media coverage consistently behind the curve (and that misalignment becoming even more pronounced as the pandemic progressed, something I will return to).

But, of course, the number of cases is not the only thing which will signal importance or demand attention. On the grounds of both newsworthiness and what is important or of value to people, the priority will be the number of deaths and indeed the threat of death to oneself and one's friends and family, as noted in Chapter 2. This hasn't been charted in the same systematic way. We do however have access to timelines which highlight key moments of significance. China reported its first death and called a lockdown in January 2020, and by the end of the month cases were confirmed in the UK, with the first death in the country at the beginning of March (Sample, 2021). The media coverage was by this point on a significant upward trajectory (Mach et al., 2021; Pearman et al., 2021). The points at which recorded 10,000 deaths, with half in Europe (20 March), and 100,000 deaths with lockdowns right across the European continent (9 April) (BBC News Online, 2020b; Sample, 2021), broadly aligned with media attention globally and locally.

In respect of public concern, polling also suggests a peak in respect of escalating fear of contracting the virus in the last week of March 2020, rising to as high as 78 per cent in one Ipsos poll (Skinner, 2020; YouGov, 2022a). This is to be expected given the combination of growing global cases, increased media coverage and decisive government action in the form of the lockdown on 24 March in that week. But what is perhaps more surprising is that, according to the evidence, this peak in late March was the highest that public fear of the virus ever reached (YouGov, 2022a) – and on the basis of the numbers in the UK in late March, it is likely that most people still wouldn't have known anyone who had contracted or died from the virus (with only 68.5 deaths per 100,000 persons according to the Office for National Statistics, Campbell and Saul, 2020). As deaths increased exponentially, and the likelihood of death impacting people directly grew, public concern did not follow suit.

As I note, this is likely to have been due to a complex set of reasons, not least people's limited capacity for what may at first have been highly intensive anxiety about a phenomenon unprecedented in living memory. But what is interesting is that the trajectory of public concern did continue to show a correlation with media attention, and this was related to both its volume and its nature. In fact, research conducted by *The Lancet* showed that coverage waned clearly after the initial media frenzy (Pearman et al., 2021) – something which might seem quite surprising to those living at the time when Covid seemed to be a story that was all-encompassing.

Perhaps more significant than the volume of coverage, however – still huge in relation to all contemporaneous issues – was the shift in emphasis. In both the UK and the US, there was from around that point in late March to early April a notable politicisation in media coverage (Hart et al., 2020). Further, while initially reporting was framed around scientific updates, healthcare workers and national and global case numbers, the focus shifted significantly to questions of economic impacts (Colarossi, 2020). Again this was mirrored in public opinion polls. While, as discussed in the Introduction, concerns over health were initially intense and were prioritised by a majority over anything else (Happer, 2020), fear of the virus gave way over these months to a return to a more normal situation in which the economy was returned to its place as a primary concern (Smith, 2020). Subsequent spikes in death rates did not shift this very much (Pearman et al., 2021). In fact, as the pandemic progressed, levels of fear and concern about the virus and expectations of societal response became more atomised around already existing communities of opinion and belief (which both reflect and are shaped by media consumption habits, as discussed in Chapter 2).

The secondary analysis I've conducted infers that the way in which the 'crises' of Covid were made salient by peaks and troughs in media coverage and framed in respect of relevance and/or threat to particular groups at particular times played a significant role in how people responded. Of course, this has to be seen in the context of the range of filters we apply when looking at how media might influence how people feel or think about any subject. Direct experience undoubtedly played a role in shaping people's judgements on priority levels and on what should happen at different points during the pandemic, in all sorts of ways – from feelings of vulnerability in relation to health conditions to feelings of injustice as relatives died alone in care homes. But perceptions of closeness or relevance are to some degree a construct. The issues of Covid and climate change are not as different in this respect as they might appear.

The role of words and images in constructing fear and urgency

With Covid, the fear of death grew as it was perceived to get closer, and peaked in the UK when it spread to Europe. Much of this was rooted in regular reporting of deaths with causality clearly attributed to Covid, and predictions of what these would mean for Britain by showing raw footage from countries such as Italy, which was ahead in respect of its Covid trajectory. Photos showing the Italian army transporting coffins by the load (BBC World Service, 2020), supplemented by fake and more extreme images circulating on social media (Reuters, 2020), made a huge visual impression in those final weeks of March 2020. On a personal note, I found these images haunting, and they were the trigger for a significant shift in my own approach, including a move to home working (which I appreciate I was lucky enough to be in a position to make).

Imagery is crucial in media framing of issues and can be especially powerful in provoking emotional responses such as the one I had. There is a whole body of work on the role of imagery in climate communication by NGOs and researchers, premised on the assumption that effective imagery can play a key role in promoting a collective commitment to climate action (O'Neill, 2017; Climate Outreach, 2019; O'Neill, 2020). Journalistic framing using imagery can also be particularly powerful in making salient – or rendering invisible – particular categories of people, countries and regions, as well as the scientific or other explanations of what we see and experience (Rebich-Hespanha at al., 2015). As that implies, owing to its polysemic nature, imagery can also be the most manipulative of communication tools and plays a key role in propaganda and misinformation (Barthes, 1964). Digital imagery, which circulates at speed and is often divorced from text-based narrative or explanations, is particularly susceptible to manipulation and distortion.

One of the things that research in the field of climate communications uncovered initially was that the imagery conventionally used in reporting, such as polar bears, smoke stacks and political actors, contributed to a framing of the issue as distant, (O'Neill, 2017; Climate Outreach, 2019; O'Neill, 2020), and I found in my own research that was this was replicated in the words and phrases used by audience members when they talked it through. Recognising this evidence, the IPCC, NGOs, climate activists and campaigning journalists made a concerted effort to shift the language and imagery of climate: to bring it a little closer and to give it proximity.

By 2019 in the UK, we had witnessed something that, I would argue, represented a genuine shift – a growth in momentum which can be traced variously to the discursive skill of a unique Swedish schoolgirl (whom I will come back to), the public disruption of Extinction Rebellion and other protest groups across Britain's biggest cities, and a distinct shift in media and political attention, all building on the decades of work done by the IPCC, NGOs, academics and activists. One factor in this was a concerted shift in language, in which journalists, political bodies and communicators sought collectively to emphasise the urgency and proximity of climate. For example, in May 2019, the *Guardian* changed its style guide to replace 'climate change' with terms such as 'climate emergency' or 'climate breakdown' in its reporting, as did the *Independent* (Carrington, 2019b; Gabbatiss et al., 2021), while the BBC issued a new editorial policy on climate to reduce 'false bias' alongside increasing its coverage (Hickman, 2018; The Gdelt Project, 2020a). At the same time stronger terms including 'climate crisis' began to be used by the Met Office, paralleling shifts in the language used by the UN (Carrington, 2019b). In the same year, a number of UK councils and then the Scottish and UK governments called a 'climate emergency'. Though it might be argued the latter represented an emergency in name only, this linguistic shift made an impact: public concern over climate in the UK reached an all-time high at that point in June 2019 (Carrington, 2019a).

Either through concerted effort – such as an explicitly stated rethinking by the *Guardian* underpinned by the work of NGOs on climate engagement (Shields, 2019) – or in reflection of the interdependency of journalistic practice, political priorities and levels of public interest and knowledge, there was also a parallel shift in imagery. In the context of the US news landscape, the trajectory has been one away from polar bears (too gentle to illustrate catastrophe or emergency if nothing else) towards depictions of droughts and desert lands (The Gdelt Project, 2020b). In both the US and the UK, there has been a rise in reporting of heatwaves and wildfires more generally in comparison with other aspects of climate reporting (Hopke, 2020). However, researchers have questioned the degree to which the imagery has been consistent with the message. For example, O'Neill has noted that as temperature records were broken in the summer of 2019 across Europe – which analysis suggests was made 100 times more likely by climate change – reports were often accompanied by images of people sunbathing, having fun on the beach and generally having a jolly old time in the heat of the sun (O'Neill, 2019).

Constructions of (un)certainty

There are also of course images of global wildfires and burning seas of red in the broad landscape of reporting, but this tendency towards unclear and ambiguous messaging is indicative of a broader and long-standing phenomenon. As most of my own work on climate and public opinion has shown, a key barrier to disengagement is the sense of uncertainty that operates as a persistent doubt about whether to take action on this issue *relative to other things*. The final part is important because it relates to the key theme here of the construction of an issue as closest, most relevant and directly impactful, something which people are convinced is a priority because of clear and unambiguous evidence. This has never been tested with climate as people are immersed in centred and decentred media cultures which never allow the crisis of climate to be amplified without a wave of alternative noise to confuse, obfuscate and often directly counter the message. In the early days of Covid, long before most people were likely to the effects of it directly, the nature of the threat to people's lives and well-being at least was clear, if not the degree and appropriate response to it. It could be argued it was the one moment in recent history in which there was a shared orientation point and consensual understanding. Once the message about threats, impacts and action became less clear, and people moved away from the mainstream, public opinion was less consistent.

We can look at this in another way if we imagine an alternative news environment in which headline after headline provides a running toll throughout a summer, culminating in a terrifying total of 11,000 deaths. This is in a neighbouring country where many of our friends and family, including young children, are currently on holiday. And worse, this killer is predicted by the World Health Organization to cause a quarter of a million deaths every year between 2030 and 2050 (WHO, 2021). This, of course, relates to the summer of 2022, in which intense heatwaves spread across Europe, with France seeing record temperatures reach a peak in one small town of 45.9°C, more than 1.5°C above the previous record set in 2003, which climate scientists concluded was made at least five times more likely by human-caused climate change (Dunne, 2019). It is France's national statistics institute (INSEE) which calculated the figure of 11,000 excess deaths in relation to a recent comparable period which were most likely explained by the heatwave (Roucaute, 2022).

Now, of course, the counterargument would be that the causal link proposed for the deaths through Covid is much more concrete than that for the deaths from climate change through heatwaves or other impacts. Certainly, one aspect of this is the great care taken by climate scientists themselves to be precise in respect of the likelihood of causation and the importance of the scientific model of uncertainty. But there are also uncertainties about the methodology used to assess the likelihood that Covid is a contributory factor to a death in those cases where a positive test result has been obtained (Department of Health and Social Care, 2020). There is no fixed methodology, and recording techniques vary wildly across different countries, making international comparisons of numbers of deaths difficult(Morris and Reuben,

2020). However, at least in the early days of the reporting of Covid, a sense of scientific uncertainty was not identified as a key consideration – quite rightly, as it would have been hugely problematic for the public health guidance that was so crucial to saving lives.

A more general point is that most of the mainstream media don't concern themselves unduly with scientific certainty. It might even be said that some elements of the mainstream media – some tabloids come to mind! – don't always concern themselves with evidence and facts. This is not an argument that Covid and climate are equivalents in this respect, but serves more to illustrate that proximity, levels of threat and priority are not necessarily constructed in ways that reflect certainty.

Solutions and priorities

I return to the third crisis, the one that is made to feel most present as I write this now: the cost-of-living crisis. This is a term which began to enter the media as the dominant lens through which the current set of conditions, and attendant problems, were understood more or less as Covid left the centre stage in early 2022. As already noted, while complex, in many ways it is a crisis of the gradual neoliberal shrinking of the welfare state, and in particular in the UK, of the programme of austerity from 2010 that was imposed in response to the failings of that very same system. If the way in which a crisis is usually described is by reference to its cause – Covid crisis, financial crisis, migration crisis – rather than its impacts, it is arguably more accurate to describe this as the austerity crisis. Indeed, research has shown that austerity is implicated in over 300,000 deaths in the UK since 2012 (Butler, 2022). However, the use of 'austerity' as a term lessened in public discourse just as the cost-of-living crisis increased. One might cynically argue that this was to avoid the ridiculousness of explicitly stating that the austerity crisis should be solved by more austerity.

However, the range of measures prescribed by politicians and media to address the cost-of-living crisis must, we are told, rest on fiscal measures which limit the spending power of the state yet again. The think tanks which play such a key role in shaping the political culture – including the Institute of Economic Affairs and the Adam Smith Institute – both highlight the decarbonisation agenda as contributing to the crisis through regulations, fracking bans and expenditure on renewables (Lesh and Nie, 2022; MacDonald et al., 2022;). Evidence from polling which would be entirely predictable on the basis of my own empirical work – the belief that we should be not be 'fiddling while Rome burns' – suggests the majority agree at the time of writing. Fifty-one per cent support a temporary increase in the amount of energy the UK generates from high carbon sources like coal if it would reduce energy bills, while nearly three-quarters of Britons (73 per cent) prioritise the cost of living over the environment and climate change, with only 15 per cent taking the opposing view (Smith, 2022). Once again climate change, when pitted against economic challenges, loses its proximity and its priority status (at least for certain groups) very quickly.

Whether the cost-of-living crisis might lead to that 'decisive moment' which leads to genuine social change, or is another crisis that isn't really a crisis, like the financial crash of 2008, remains to be seen. Certainly the UK state seems to be in a period of collapse across healthcare, education, local government and transport after decades of being progressively dismantled by neoliberal policies. Currently the solutions being proposed look like more of the same. On 21 June 2023 an economic advisor to Chancellor Jeremy Hunt openly stated on Radio 4's *Today* programme that the Bank of England should 'force' a recession to curb inflation (currently positioned as the cause of the cost-of-living crisis). In such a case of what we might call 'saying the quiet part out loud', it's not unreasonable to conclude that at least some members of the political class believe that the public should undergo a period of hardship and pain in order to stabilise the economy and benefit their own class, who coincidentally also caused the (austerity) crisis.

That these measures might be accepted as the only way for the country to recover, with the possibility of any meaningful social change removed, offers a clear guide as to why so many people feel a disconnect from our mainstream media culture. As the financial crash showed, it is often the missed moment to take action that is the key to longer-term public opinion and resistance. If Covid indicated that people may become more likely to turn to the mainstream media in a recognised crisis, it might also be that it is in these important moments they are most disappointed with what they see there and hence their investment in alternative sources is exacerbated. In these social media spaces, proximity is constructed in very different ways, and I will examine this issue in the remainder of the chapter.

Alternative constructions of proximity and crisis

In Chapter 3, I discussed in detail the way in which social media cultures often align with more traditional categories and divisions to shape very different ways of articulating and responding to social issues. This also relates to discussions in Chapter 2 about the different modes of assessing trust and credibility of information – from those who align broadly with a centred culture to those who exist almost completely in a decentred culture of their own composition. Young people tend to exist in more decentred cultures than other age groups, albeit not exclusively, and have many very different conversations where different concerns, priorities and values circulate. Here what is seen as a 'crisis', and the way in which a sense of proximity is understood and its relation to experience, also varies greatly.

A good illustration of how this operates can be seen in the media coverage of and engagement with the UN Climate Change Conference of the Parties (COP26), which took place in Glasgow in November 2021. As this was an international event with real political importance, with much of the mainstream media including the BBC committed to increasing attention to climate change, there was a significant volume of coverage of the talks. As a physical and virtual event which brought global activists and campaigners together as a community to bond over their deep concern about climate change, it was an unrivalled period of engagement. In spite of the shared orientation, what emerged was two very separate and distinct conferences – what we might call the official COP and the unofficial COP (or 'the people's COP' as it is sometimes known). This was not as simple as two opposed groups protesting (or partying) in different places, but was the product of two very separate media environments which construct climate change as an issue in distinct ways (Painter et al., 2018).

On the BBC and in the newspapers, there was extensive coverage of the delegates' talks, analysis of the pledges being made and reporting following the convention of centring the primary definers of politicians and official speakers (Painter et al., 2018). A key moment was the arrival of President Obama (who mistook Scotland for the 'Emerald Isles'). Mostly the pledges made to invest enormous amounts of money to meet the goal of Net Zero – including one from a coalition of global financial institutions – directed the news beats (Plumer, 2021). The tone was one of serious business. Activists and campaigners weren't ignored – indeed their colourful imagery decorated many of the news articles and broadcast items – but the understanding of climate as a political issue to be solved by those already in power was the dominant framing. In contrast, the unofficial COP was a global gathering of a different kind of change-maker, emphasising the power of the collective over individual power agents, often exposing the hypocrisy and failures of the latter, and full of informal moments, inspiring talks and chants, and people from all over the world having a bit of fun while simultaneously showing quite a lot of anger.

And if it felt as though there were two separate COPs in 2021, this separation become one of two increasingly antagonistic sides at COP28, held in Dubai in 2023. Presided over by the oil executive Dr Sultan Al Jaber, the conference was from the outset dogged by allegations that the United Arab Emirates, which he represented, intended to use COP28 to strike oil and gas deals (Carbon Brief, 2023). During the conference, activists reported a culture of harassment, surveillance and intimidation by representatives of the industry and claimed that they were not allowed to add their voices to many events, so that their dissenting narrative was stifled (Green, 2023). The distance between these groups supposedly committed to the same political objective had begun to look increasingly difficult to reconcile.

The unofficial COP should be seen as the product of a mass movement, initiated by climate activists, which has mobilised global protests to shift opinion, increase concern and demand political action using a range of social media platforms to communicate and connect (Anderson, 2017). It is a movement in which youth voices have become dominant, in part because of their being social media natives, and in part because of the tendency to centre climate change as an issue of concern bound up with their relatively long lens on the future. As youth have come to dominate, the movement has increasingly been located in the cultural spaces they inhabit, with platforms such as Instagram and TikTok being prominent (Hautea et al., 2021; Molder et al., 2021). While the affordances of these two platforms are very different, what unites them is their emphasis on the visual: Instagram promotes high-engagement individuals who visualise their everyday lives and encourage others to do the same, while TikTok enables the customisation of short-form video content which is informal, meme-based and transient (Hautea et al., 2021; Molder et al., 2021). These are also spaces which centre the voices of influencers and celebrities over politicians or journalists. It is a whole new way of communicating, away from the sombre evidence and analysis of traditional media to a highly emotive, entertaining, impressionistic way of planting a message. The conventional model looks staged and inauthentic – and perhaps most importantly overly negative – to frequent users of the new one.

If Obama's arrival at COP26 merited significant attention from professional journalists, the arrival of another figure at these conferences galvanises the online climate world (though notably she is now significant enough to garner attention across both environments). This is, of course, the Swedish activist Greta Thunberg, who began her school strike for climate in 2018 and encouraged millions of young people to follow her. It is inarguable that the affordances of the new social media ecosystem allowed her to emerge and increase her following, but her skills as a communicator – totally at ease with the tools and strategies of the contemporary era – shouldn't be underestimated. Notably in an environment made up of selfies, she smiles a lot – again in a direct contrast to journalists and politicians, who rarely smile and certainly not while on television. The viral TikTok video of her dancing to the now iconic Rick Astley song looks spontaneous and authentic, while the idea of a politician doing the same provokes an immediate recoil.

Molder et al. (2021) have charted the framings Thunberg uses on Instagram, where her use of positive and motivational language directed at the collective (using 'we' and 'us') is central and visuals of large groups protesting have gradually overtaken the lonely pictures from her early days. Blame and anger are directed at the older generations and those in power. In my own focus groups in 2019, young people described her as a figure who divided the age groups. In line with the themes in Chapter 3, these discussions also evidenced young people's perception of older people more generally as lacking sophistication in respect of both climate scepticism and their way of expressing themselves online, as this comment indicates:

> Obviously, it's not everybody's cup of tea and everything, but I mean she's a kid. And she is a kid who has Asperger's as well, and you get like people, older people in their forties and their fifties like messaging her saying, I'm on a plane. It's like, grow up! You're bullying a child, like? (Male, young social media user, 2019–20)

Greta's approach is not the only one in respect of climate activism online, though her framings of both collective action and hope, and of blame and anger against those in power, are widely spread, negotiated and reworked. A comprehensive understanding of what the whole youth climate ecosystem looks like is not yet in place. But the one thing that can be said with some confidence is that it is an environment that operates on new principles in respect of modes of both communication and persuasion. As someone who has worked in this field for a while, I have been struck by the way the insights of sustained research showing the role of media in engaging people on climate are sometimes turned on their heads.

For example, in the past there was an accepted wisdom among climate communicators – which was repeated at conferences and in published papers many times – that the disaster framing, the instilling of fear about the impacts of climate change, would most likely lead to disengagement. However, when looking at the videos which circulate and gain traction on TikTok, for example, I'm no longer convinced this is the case. In fact, dystopian visions of a future in which climate has destroyed life on earth are something of a currency on the platform. But the key is the way in which the platform's affordances allow personalisation and immediacy in this kind of content. Hautea et al. (2021) describe how this works:

> [I]ndividual TikToks become vehicles for personal narratives, which are then connected through features such as hashtags and viral sounds. [...] TikTok creators connect disparate ideas through memetic themes while maintaining individualistic identities, sustain message persistence in cyberspace without explicit tethering to on-the-ground events, deploy humor and juxtaposition to disrupt dominant climate discourses, and deploy communicative power in swiftly shifting discursive environments. (Hautea et al., 2021)

In other words, where professional media messaging about climate impacts was science-led, remote and unrelatable, these young climate communicators, who may not be rooted directly in the science or policy questions, have managed to tether this global issue to their own anxiety, anger and frustrations and crucially their own personal stakes. Greta Thunberg is the exemplar; emerging as a pigtailed schoolgirl with home-made signs, she made the concerns of the world her concerns. Climate change wasn't about other people's experiences: it was about her own and everyone's. Collectively, though their engagement, social media activists have managed to do something that has proved elusive to professional journalists (even those who were really trying): they have constructed a sense of proximity to climate change, and through a sense of belonging to a global online community, they have shrunk the globe. As evidenced by the levels of anxiety, anger and engagement, for many young people, climate change is unquestionably a crisis.

The disconnect, crisis and political action

However, as I explained in Chapter 1, these developments must be seen as a product of an intricately connected set of social, political and technological changes, and of the juncture we find ourselves currently in. I'd certainly argue that online climate activism is a positive development and that it has played an important role in shifting public opinion, albeit particularly among the young, and that this generation is going to lead the demand for action in the years to come. However, it is important to see this online activism in the context of a highly polarised political environment in which people turn to atomised communities of alternative information and opinion further and further removed from a shared public sphere in which trust has collapsed. They are part of a series of decentred cultures which are moving further away from the 'core communicative institution of democracy' (Kreiss, 2017: 445).

As I noted earlier in this chapter, the naming of a crisis in the traditional media is in part embraced or resisted because it implies a need for urgent prescribed solutions, which creates an expectation of political action. While the collective voices of individual platforms are heard – indeed politicians monitor the platforms routinely – because these platforms do not have the same relationship of interdependency with the political class as the mainstream media, the expectations raised are also not the same. The greater likelihood of young people not voting – and the reliability of the older middle classes in doing so – must also be seen as a factor in which platforms politicians listen and respond to.

That problem doesn't seem insurmountable, as social media narratives are increasingly influential in how people think and speak, and this influence spreads across different offline and online environments. I also wouldn't want to claim that conventional politics is the only way to make social change happen! But I would argue that meaningful change is much more challenging to deliver when media messaging circulates in 'cyberspace without explicit tethering to on-the-ground events' (Hautea et al., 2021). What does seem to be true is that because climate change is constructed as having proximity and is seen to carry everyday relevance for young people, the kinds of solutions that are needed, and even knowledge of what is currently being done, remain distant for many. TikTok videos don't leave much space for policy analysis, and that's in part what young people like about these platforms. I'm conscious that a fair response to that might be: neither do tabloid newspapers or even broadcast media, and so what's new? However, there is something distinct about a video showing a barren earth in fifty years' time cut through with shots of the clock of doom from *Stranger Things* as a mode of political communications (Happer and Åberg, 2024), compared with the press reporting of politics, which has at least some engagement with political objectives and policy choices, albeit highly simplified and aimed at steering the public in particular directions.

Of course, there is lots of substantial content too in this new climate media ecosystem – for example, countless very informative explanatory videos on the UN conferences for those who are new to them – and the imagery of dystopia is at the other end of the spectrum. But the climate media ecosystem needs to be seen in the context of a new decentring of our media environment in which alternative speakers and sources of evidence and persuasion circulate online, and which if left unchecked can move away from facts and lived experience. As I discussed in Chapter 1 in relation to Covid, a decentring of the communications across the different media environments has led to negative impacts such as reduced vaccination take-up and a growing resistance to public health guidance. I also noted that one of the characteristics of populism was a tendency to act as a free-floating signifier, which has allowed it to attach itself to and justify any policy programme. Here, the danger is that political actors can gain support through rhetoric rather than action on the ground, and we lose the foregrounding of what kinds of action make a difference to people's actual lives.

Conclusion

Throughout this chapter I have examined the ways in which climate change, Covid and the cost of living are constructed as crises, and the way in which those constructions relate to the possibility of decisive political action and social change. A key argument is that mainstream media play a central role in shaping what society should consider important problems to be addressed, and in creating expectations of responses in a complex interplay of power, communications, public opinion and decision-making. In decentred cultures, very different constructions of what is important, who is to blame and what is to be done circulate, but there is no question that the collective voice expressed there, however loud, currently finds it more difficult to create expectations of those in power. This may be one of the reasons why people turn to the mainstream media more during crises such as Covid; in spite of the erosion of trust, they know it is the one arena in which real political action may be determined (which bolsters the influence of the mainstream media in a circular way even when it is losing audiences).

In this chapter we can also see the broader arguments of the book illustrated in a more empirical way. In respect of the filter model of opinion formation, while lived experience plays a significant role in how media constructions are negotiated and understood – and this is particularly the case when understandings are formed through engagement with our opinion communities – where media narratives reflect the dominant ideology, these can often overwhelm the former. It was notable during Covid that the original priority of personal and collective health gave way over time to the usual economic priorities as the media shifted emphasis. Social media cultures around climate change, shaped by immersion in opinion communities and decentred modes of media engagement, illustrate the way in which frustration with a lack of political action, and a distrust of those who have failed to lead it, push people towards alternatives. If this is one area in which we see the disconnect very clearly, even those more rooted to a mainstream culture are likely to disengage when moments of change are missed. The cost-of-living crisis is happening as I write and may be different, but the mechanisms in place to deliver continuing hegemony look pretty robust, and once again those who are at the sharp end of the crisis are likely to be those who are most disconnected.

Conclusion

I began this book by posing the question set by Walter Lippmann in 1922: is public opinion simply the product of persuasive communications or propaganda – and, if not, to what degree might it represent thought independent of media influence? I presented a model informed by a large of body of empirical research which identified six filters that media messaging interacts with to construct people's ideas, opinion and thought. In this I moved beyond questions of how mainstream media, still relatively consistent in respect of the social and political narratives they promote, manage public opinion to an understanding of the new mechanisms for governing thought and opinion in social media environments in which the norms of acceptable public expression and belief are absorbed through constant engagement. Here social media has scaled up the invitation to conformity of expression and belief (Arendt, 2022).

Importantly, this approach located these processes in socio-political systems as well as the interpersonal exchanges and experiences that people confront in their everyday lives. I drew on the concept of a *contradictory consciousness* to explain the way in which people tend to approach the content produced on social media: with an awareness that people say and do things they would never say or do IRL (in real life) but, at the same time, holding a mostly subconscious assumption that as most of this content is collectively produced by *real people* it must represent something that is authentic about the culture as a whole. In some cases, this leads people to talk about online and offline experiences (what they see and hear) interchangeably – 'I know that loads of people are angry about this because I've heard what they're saying.' Of course, this is even more powerful when the content is visual in nature: again, in spite of the knowledge that visuals are more easily manipulated than words, video content leaves most people with an impression of what is going on that they tend to absorb.

If this is a significant and relatively new form of influence, I see it as co-existing with the more traditional forms of media power, in which there tends to be a recognisable communicative core, and in many ways as not so distinct from it. I presented three broad modes of media engagement – *holistic*, *centred* and *decentred* – to show the way in which different groups position themselves in relation to the old core of mainstream media. I have documented the role of age, class, and education in shaping engagement, and argued that low levels of trust and a disconnect from the public narrative are factors in positioning people at a distance from the centre, with some barely engaging with mainstream culture at all. However, those who invest heavily in their own decentred cultures constructed through social media, where these different mechanisms for governing thought and opinion are in operation, are subject to less visible forms of power and influence. These new influence agents – Big Tech, platform owners, forms of moderation, bots, etc. – may prioritise securing engagement over opinion management, but political and commercial interests are often aligned.

Ultimately what we come to believe cannot be disentangled from the dominant narratives circulating in the media cultures we inhabit, but they are not reproduced in simple ways. Even where, as I argue, this model can be applied to anticipate the kinds of patterns of opinion we might see on issues of contemporary significance, there are moments of resistance, rejection and reworking which can, if collectively expressed, force a response from those in power. Here people recognise their own experience and observation as separate from how media present things to be. It is at these points that we can begin to understand how social change happens, and where those who wish to see positive outcomes might intervene. While the media system is designed to limit radical change, there are journalists and communicators who seek to do good work, and we have many examples of where they have achieved this, even when there have been very well-resourced groups seeking to stop them.

Media, public opinion and change

To demonstrate how media and communicators might intervene to steer outcomes, it is helpful to look to some instances in which we've witnessed genuine societal change, and where media, information and shifts in public opinion and belief have facilitated this. If we take the historical case of attitudes and behaviours around smoking, a slow-moving form of progress often in the face of intense lobbying from the tobacco industry, we can see how a concerted effort across science, public health communications and policy initiatives, including bans on advertising and smoking in public, resonated with people's perceptions, experiences and priorities to produce change. In the UK, this culminated in 2023 with the Prime Minister proposing an eventual full ban which would mean that most of today's young people will never be able to buy cigarettes – in response to which, such is the shift in norms and attitudes across fifty years, very few people are putting up a serious objection. Change wasn't simply imposed: consent was won through a battle over public opinion, in part to ideologically rework 'freedom to smoke' as 'freedom from smoke'. But it is important to see this as the product largely of a twentieth-century model of media, with the smoking ban being in place before Facebook even arrived on the UK scene – and while I would argue that there remains real value in this approach, it does need some adaption and revision.

On the ongoing battle to win public consent for climate action, there has been a less linear path – which should again be seen in the context of even more committed resistance from powerful groups to action being taken, and the shifting nature of political will. The period leading up to the passing of the ambitious and popular UK Climate Change Act in 2008 saw the release of Al Gore's globally recognised documentary and the landmark Fourth Assessment Report of the IPCC, which consolidated the relevant science at the time. This opened up a volume of largely positive media and public attention, which aligned with a modernised New Labour government in the UK that positioned climate action as a key objective.

However, the financial crash, the change of government and the imposition of austerity from 2010 shifted media, political and public priorities, and what emerged was the construction of climate action as a barrier to getting out of economic difficulties, both in the media and, as my own research showed, among members of the public (Happer, 2017a). Similarly in the US, a year after he took office, Trump rowed back on the ambitious UN climate agreement made in Paris made by his predecessor. Here I would argue that the stream of scepticism about the science and the motivations of those leading action over many years created a sense of doubt in people's minds that nagged away and made de-prioritisation of the issue much easier.

In the UK in 2019 we again witnessed a significant shift in attitudes and levels of concern in response to further advances in scientific knowledge, a changed journalistic approach and a concerted shift in language and imagery in local and national governments inspired by the work of NGOs and activists. This was a largely effective intervention. Again, however, it also demonstrates how easily climate action can be deprioritised in the face of other challenges. In early 2020 the rapid shift in focus due to Covid did not allow for the growth in climate concern to be manifested in demands for government action. As we learned with smoking, change happens incrementally, and the battle to maintain momentum must be ongoing.

However, in this case, it's also important to factor in the impacts of a new media system, and in particular the moves to more decentred cultures where people align themselves with different opinion communities. If open climate scepticism reduced in the mainstream media right across the globe (Painter, 2023), it moved into online spaces with ease, and grew particularly prominent in the decentred cultures organised around conspiracy theories, many of which have focused on Covid mitigation efforts in the last few years (mask wearing, vaccination and so on).

On the other hand, the decentred cultures of large numbers of young people, often far removed from conventional politics, engage intensely with the issue. In their largely visual cultures on platforms such as Instagram and TikTok, climate change is an issue of proximity and urgency in which people feel they are seeing the impacts in real time. While we should not speak of young people as a monolith all holding the same opinions, the fact that 70 per cent of young people around the world feel some level of climate anxiety suggests that the issue is unlikely to ever be a secondary consideration when voting preferences come up for the next generation (Buchholz, 2022). I like to think there will come a point when politicians won't be in a position to ignore this call, but interventions to establish the equitable, fair and progressive nature of policy in the face of ongoing right-wing narratives which pit economics against climate are (always) urgently needed.

On political outcomes more specifically, I charted in Chapter 1 the way in which demands for change in countries across the West emerged from a growing disconnect with a neoliberal political and media system, where people's feelings and opinions had no receptive outlet. In spite of a late attempt by the media to manage public opinion back towards ultimate trust in mainstream narratives, a series of political outcomes including the election of Trump and Brexit could not be derailed. Here application of the six-filter model outlined in Chapter 2 shows how the interaction of experience, interpersonal communications and the investment in social media alternatives produced collective resistance to mainstream media messages – such as those promoting Hillary Clinton for president – resulting in a push for change, albeit not the positive change many hoped for.

In relation to both of these outcomes, we can also see the ways in which the traditional model of media influence might require revision. If the conventional wisdom in the UK was that 'it was the *Sun* wot won it' for successive prime ministers, it seems unlikely that the press alone, in spite of their enduring influence on British life, could ever win an election again. For a start, the political identities that shaped news readership have been disrupted, while other identity categorisations have become established. But a significant number of people literally never see mainstream news, and at best engage with a second-hand version of it via social media communities which present it already interpreted in ways which reflect the values, ideologies and belief systems already there. Here we have seen the way in which such communities can be easily infiltrated by data-mining companies such as

Cambridge Analytica, which use algorithms to target voters and influence voting preferences. These unethical and in some cases illegal interventions show deep knowledge of how opinions now form in the digital environment.

I finally want to discuss another area in which I have observed public opinion shift across the years of my research and which is increasingly manifested in demands for change that might be met in different ways. This is the question of state intervention and the balancing of rights, freedoms and protections. I noted in Chapter 4 that social media users, confronted with online cultures in which racism, homophobia and misogyny were rampant, desired more protection from platforms; here I return to the contradictory consciousness, as this amounts to asking for protection from those forces which produced the culture people want to be protected from in the first place. But it does have a logic to it as social media users, especially women and marginalised groups, often find these cultures difficult places to be, although they don't want to leave them. There is some evidence to suggest that this desire for further controls in respect of free speech is more widely felt than in the past, especially among young people (Bristow, 2015; Duffy et al., 2022). As one focus group participant said, the problem is that 'free speech is very vocal'.

But on the basis of my own research and other evidence I would argue that this desire for more protections, and, specifically for the state and other organisations to do more to protect people, is much more broadly felt than just in the area of social media. Again, if we consider the context this is not surprising. Since 2008, we have had the financial crash, austerity and the more recent cost-of-living crisis, the pandemic and the climate crisis narrated for the first time through our very 'vocal' social media cultures, where everything is felt intensely. These have been exceptionally turbulent and challenging times. The neoliberal myth of 'freedom' has been exposed, as people's collective experiences show them that we need economic security to be free. Of course, there are decentred cultures saying the very opposite, but survey work suggests that these attitudes are quite widespread (Curtice and Scholes, 2023).

It will be interesting to watch how governments and other organisations respond: more censorious policy regarding social media, most certainly, and increasing authoritarian measures are a significant concern. But there is the space to do more positive things. It is only through empirical work of the kind reported in this book that we can identify these spaces to create change and assess the sorts of communications and policy interventions that might be effective. In this, decision-makers must not merely be listening, but must integrate the concerns or desires raised collectively into their response; as I have I mentioned, there is a need to communicate the importance of a just climate transition, but this would work only if the transition *is* actually fair and just, and takes into account the fears people are raising about job losses and so on. It's just more noise otherwise, and will only add to the disconnect. In the final section I will focus specifically on how to practically undertake this work in order to identify and develop interventions which might be effective.

Conceptual contribution

My book aims to contribute to the academic literature across a number of areas of investigation. Firstly, it engages with questions of trust, in public life more generally and in forms of media more specifically. If there is a current acceptance that we have experienced an identifiable collapse in trust, albeit to different degrees in different groups, what can be said about this and what are the opportunities for winning trust back? I drew on sociological perspectives to argue that trust is at the heart of any social contract and that people invest trust over time where they observe and learn to expect consistency in the way in which public institutions act. However, this consistency is rooted in a belief that these institutions will consistently act with *good intent*, and that ultimately is the important part.

Journalism experienced a digital revolution in its business which demystified the professional norm of 'objectivity' or 'truth seeking' as readers and audiences were exposed to a whole range of different versions of what is happening in the world. Readers and audiences have always understood that journalists must piece together an interpretation from the range of materials they select and edit. But if they had held the belief that journalists were acting with good intent in their choosing of the version of events to promote, it wouldn't have mattered if there were various others to choose from. The problem was that the other versions often reflected their own interests more than professional journalism in the neoliberal era did; this is at the heart of the disconnect I identified. It also explains why people might follow someone like Trump even where they don't necessarily believe he tells the 'truth'. It is why the focus on identifying fake news or misinformation to win back trust in professional news outlets without a reckoning with the complicity of journalists in promoting a politics that did not prioritise the public good was always a little pointless.

I also build on the large body of work looking at how people process information differentially through the lens of ideology, partisanship, identity and so on, though I qualify that this is not necessarily an assessment of 'truth'. In this, I see a very serious problem in the division of 'trust' from 'truth', even if 'truth' in journalism was only ever an investment in the best and fairest version of events (which of course should have its foundation in 'truth' via the careful collection of evidence, if not necessarily a raw, unfiltered 'truth' which would be impossible to translate anyway). Where truth is engaged with as a relative quality, which I saw in some of my focus groups, it becomes easier for politicians to build support through rhetoric and emotion without any check on what is actually delivered. At the darkest end, this is how totalitarian states operate (Arendt, 1976). So I do think that the loss of the 'core communicative institution of democracy' is very significant (Kreiss, 2017: 445). Society is a collective endeavour, and there needs to be some consensual understanding of what is going on in the world if we are to engage with what might be best for people collectively.

But journalism has made the mistake of seeing what is going on in decentred cultures as the opposition: as fake, as full of misinformation, as something the elites should want to stamp out. Yes, there are harmful extremes among them, and they operate on different principles from professional journalism, but an engagement with what everyday people are doing on these platforms might be a good starting point for winning back trust. They may not be authentic representations of what people think and believe, but they do represent something about where they position themselves in relation to other people and sources of information. On climate change, for example, it may well be that decentred cultures are much more closely aligned to actual science and evidence than what is published in many outlets of mainstream journalism, and that's not the only example. If many people are seeking out new sources on, say, the Israel–Palestine conflict, professional journalists should ask themselves why. Similarly, if people turned to mainstream journalism in a crisis such as Covid, at a time when communications were paramount, what is there than can be built on?

My work also engages with questions raised in the literature that relate to filter bubbles, echo chambers and the different ways in which media users engage with content online. Most work in this area suggests that the evidence on whether users construct their own media environments to limit exposure to opposing viewpoints is inconclusive, and I would agree. My research indicates that users move through different platforms and cultures at speed and with ease, and that only a proportion isolate themselves in one media opinion community. These people can become very alienated from a mainstream culture. However, even those who do that will exist in workplace, educational and other social contexts where other views will be heard, and my model suggests that people form opinions in the intersection of a range of influences across online and offline life. I would recommend more research in this area to investigate those who may become totally disaffected and/or radicalised in their decentred cultures at the corners of social media.

Finally, I contribute to the literature on identity and media engagement. I mentioned above that the political identities which shaped loyal readership of newspapers have been disrupted by the new digital model of distribution. But of course this is only half of the story. These largely class-based alignments have also been disrupted by the processes of individualisation in the neoliberal era, which fragment people in the workplace as well as online. Here we have seen class as a marker of differentiation eroded as people join temporal (or 'coatpeg') communities of difference that actually leave them fairly disconnected from the collectives to which they might have been seen to traditionally belong (Bauman, 2001).

This atomisation of identity and opinion, supported by the affordances of social media, has, I would argue, made people angrier at each other, making solidarity much more difficult to build. An example that I examined in some depth in Chapter 3 is the construction of a generational divide, of two groups almost inherently conflicted over interests, opinions and perceptions of advantage. As my research has disproportionately involved young people, I have seen evidence of a fairly unpleasant rhetoric around older people, which I have argued could be seen as a proxy for prejudice based on class or education. But I am open to the claim that older generations may express equally unpleasant attitudes about young people as a category (even where they may love their grandchildren!). Other intersecting divisions will be present too – which is why I used the term 'atomisation' rather than polarisation. Here we see the intersection of a mainstream media construction, social media atomisation and the damaging effects of a political individualisation play out.

Negotiating a complex information environment and media literacy

Some very valuable work has been done in the broad area of media literacy in recent years, in acknowledgement of how difficult it has become to interpret and understand events in the world in the face of such a complex and often overwhelming information environment. This work is exceptionally important if we are to avoid a tendency that I have seen from time to time in my own research: of people just giving up in believing anything or avoiding news altogether (though there are a lot of complex reasons as to why that might happen). From my own work, I would offer the following thoughts.

As noted earlier, I found the focus from around 2016 on fact-checking and identifying fake news, disinformation and misinformation in both the media and academia largely unhelpful, both discursively and practically. First, there was often a failure to distinguish the terms. 'Fake news' is conceptually vague. Are we talking about fake news outlets – which would lie in opposition to professional news outlets – or does the term refer to false and inaccurate information that may come from either fake or legitimate news outlets but may also come from authentic social media users? And are we concerned with misinformation, which again is likely to be passed on by everyday users who may not have the resources to assess evidence, but may also be produced by poorly resourced journalism? Or are we mostly concerned with disinformation, which has the intent to persuade or deceive through a distorted framing? The *Daily Mail* as a professional news outlet may present an argument which is broadly evidence-based but is framed in such a way as to manipulate and deceive to particular ends.

Further, the idea that young people (or any group of people) are going to move through our fast-paced multi-media environment by stopping to check all sources of information and assess whether they are credible or have good intent seems a little unlikely. Of course, they will do this in a general sense, and the way in which they do so shapes the holistic, centred and decentred modes of media engagement I identified in Chapter 2. But once these approaches are established, people won't necessarily assess every source. My research shows that if a bomb goes off on the other side of the world, a significant number will have already consulted multiple media sources to piece together an understanding within the first ten minutes of the news breaking. Some people may prioritise professional news outlets among these sources, but others do not stop to check credibility or intent. Recently news outlets and social media platforms have begun to attach a fact-checker to posts as they go out, which to some degree addresses the problem of speed. However, a fundamental issue remains: who is trusted to actually get close to the fairest version of the 'truth' with all the caveats of my discussion above? Those who invest in the BBC as a trusted source will see its fact-checking unit as legitimate, but others will just perceive it as an extended form of bias.

So I find more valuable those approaches that begin with what people should look out for in respect of the techniques that media and communications use to manipulate or manage opinion and emotions, and ask them to check *themselves* instead (for a good example, see Common Sense Media, 2020). I should stress this is not a suggestion that we remove the responsibility of news outlets for producing ethical and evidence-based journalism or of social media platforms for limiting the spread of harmful disinformation and place it on individuals instead. The former remain the priority. However, arming people with critical skills which may then produce a demand for better journalism in a circular way seems to make sense.

My first recommendation would be to approach this in a holistic way rather than address it source by source. That would start with raising awareness of the way in which the digital media environment is managed as a whole, a topic which I covered in depth in Chapter 4. This would involve looking at the structures of management, including Big Tech, platform owners, the algorithms that promote provocative comments and silence others, moderation practices that are designed and directed disproportionally by young men who represent their own values, bots, data-mining companies and so on, which produce content that is every bit as constructed and interest-led as that produced by mainstream media, to show that there is a systematic rationale to this construction and it's not simply full of biased journalists or crazed and/or prejudiced people. Social media users see exactly what the interest groups who shape the platform cultures want them to see. According to my research, when people say they don't trust social media, they mean that it's made up of a random set of sources that aren't verified or operating on the basis of conventional evidence. When looking at the individual sources, in fact, young people are very keen-eyed – they can spot a bot a mile away! But the key point is: *we shouldn't trust social media, because it's an embodiment of coordinated power.*

In respect of checking ourselves, this awareness is the starting point, and, from there, social media users can look at their information environment as a whole, with the understanding that if they are suddenly receiving a volume of information presenting a particular line on any issue, it may be that that coherence is organised by interest groups which are aimed at persuasion. This is particularly the case where users are subject to modes of communication that draw them in as members of particular groups organised around identity or other political beliefs. This involves asking: why am I receiving this? Is there a coherence to the content I'm exposed to? Am I positioned as being threatened or attacked by this in some way? Am I positioned against other groups? Is the content persuasive more because of emotions and powerful rhetoric than because of the evidence which is presented? How am I made to feel and is that likely to cloud my judgement? How prominent are the visuals and is there any way they might have been doctored or misrepresented? Most importantly, people should ask: are these media representations alienating me from my own experience and getting in the way of clear thinking?

Of course, I'd also recommend this alongside a more traditional approach to assessing sources and evidence, and note that this is not as simple as making a distinction between professional media and non-professional media. Here again some of the same questions apply. While outlets like the BBC will fact-check and are editorially and legally obliged not to doctor video content or make up quotes, because of their reliance on elite speakers, political interests will be represented in their reporting. In times of war, domestic interests will be promoted. So it is worth again taking a holistic view of news outlets and the interests they represent, and of where evidence and opinion is rooted.

Finally, while I would not advocate that people take the time to check every source, and know it's not realistic to do so anyway, thinking in a general way about sources and in particular where experts are coming from can be useful. For example, scientists largely produce work from peer review, and so there is a solid basis for what is said in their work, and there are reputable and credible institutions which can be researched online. Among the whole range of topics that are the subject of discussion in different media forms, it seems to me a good strategy to select those that are important: if each and every source cannot be verified and investigated, and intuition is a pretty poor guide, it may be better to devote more research time to claims about the economy than to whether celebrities are having affairs (though the latter might be more entertaining). In making these recommendations I largely have young people, and the younger the better, in mind, but I'd add the very important caveat that I don't believe they are the only group who need guidance. I think we all do, and I do aim to constantly check sources myself.

Application of the model

The real-world value of this research lies both in its contribution to understandings of how things are in the world, and in its insights into how we might apply those understandings to changing the world. More specifically, I present this work for use as (a) a general model for anticipating and identifying patterns of opinion in relation to specific examples where the filters for a sample population are known (or can come to be known), and (b) as a methodological tool which allows researchers and practitioners to identify the points at which interventions can be made to steer opinions and/ or behaviours towards those which might lead to outcomes for the public good. Of course, these two are inevitably inter-connected – and certainly it would be very difficult to successfully develop strategies for (b) without having done the work of (a) – but public opinion is routinely monitored for a whole variety of other reasons.

I want to offer here a more practical guide to doing empirical research which draws on the six filters (ideology, values and priorities, interpersonal communities, identity, modes of media engagement and experience) to anticipate and understand patterns in media engagement and opinion, and to identify the points at which opinions might be open to change and how media and communications interventions can respond to them. This builds on the methodological approach developed by members of the Glasgow

University Media Group over many years (see especially Philo and Happer, 2013). I see this as having value for researchers, communicators and practitioners in health, climate and other policy areas, and I would like to encourage its application in a range of different research contexts.

1 Anticipating patterns of opinion

In Chapter 2, I took two specific examples – immigration and Covid mitigation measures – to show how patterns of opinion may emerge where the filters are known. Here I drew on knowledge already available. However, as it is an inductive model which has been developed through qualitative research, and will therefore evolve and be refined through application, the more accurate and up-to-date the data used to do this the better. In order to anticipate patterns of opinion in relation to a range of issues, researchers can gather generalised information from participants in the following way.

Questionnaires

Data collected in questionnaires would include:

- Demographics including age, gender, geography and markers of social class such as income, education and occupation;
- Main mode of accessing information (options: news aggregator, individual news website, social media platform, etc.);
- Intensity of social media use;
- Main activity on social platforms (options: engaging with friends, following sources of information; professional or personal branding, etc.);
- Media outlets typically engaged with (options: professional news outlets, independent outlets, local news outlets, podcasts, blogs, etc.);
- Most trusted sources (scientists, politicians, journalists, campaigners, people known to me, etc.);
- Least trusted sources (options: scientists, politicians, journalists, campaigners, people known to me, etc.)
- Topics of particular interest (options: climate, LGBTQ rights, human rights, socialist politics, etc.);
- Responses to a number of statements organised about ideologies, priorities and values (e.g. 'the economy is more important than anything else', 'people should look out for themselves and their families first', 'people should feel a sense of national pride', 'morality is very important in public life', etc.).

This information provides an insight into the positioning of individuals in relation to demographics and identifications, modes of media engagement (holistic, centred and decentred), sources of trust, interpersonal and online contexts and broad ideological and belief systems. On the basis of this developed survey work, patterns of opinion across different groups may be anticipated in relation to issues of concern, and these can also be cross-verified with traditional survey data. This data can also be used to organise focus groups in order to explore these patterns in more depth as part of a mixed-methods approach, as described below.

2 Investigating patterns of opinion and their relation to media in more depth

If the aim is to identify and understand patterns of opinion in more depth, including their relation to the six filters, researchers can build on the questionnaire work as set out above to categorise participants into centred, decentred and holistic media users on the basis of their dominant mode of engagement (as they may not sit exclusively in one), which may intersect with other demographic or occupation categories to compose focus groups, e.g. 'students/decentred' or 'manual workers/holistic' and so on.

Focus groups

Focus group discussions can then investigate how opinions are actually produced through media messaging in interaction with the other filters in these pre-categorised groups. So, for example, if the issue is the obesity epidemic (as named by the World Health Organization), a suggested set of questions for discussion is as follows:

- What is the first thing that comes into your mind when you hear the phrase 'obesity epidemic'?
- Where have you read or heard about it? What evidence and sources have you engaged with? Have you read or heard a lot about it?
- Do you talk to your friends and family about this in real life? On social media? Do you engage with other people on this topic on social media? What have you heard said there and by whom?
- How important do you think the obesity epidemic is in relation to other things going on at the moment and why?
- Do you think what you read in the media about the obesity epidemic chimes with your own experience or observation of it? Do you think all the important elements of it are being covered?
- Do you think everyone is broadly experiencing the obesity epidemic in the same way? Are there groups that are impacted more than others? Where do you place yourself and the people you know in this?
- Who or what do you think is responsible for the obesity epidemic? What should be done about it?

With these questions, researchers can assess understandings of and opinions on the obesity epidemic and identify the sources and other forms of evidence shaping these and their relation to the six filters. These discussions can stand alone to provide an in-depth understanding or can lay the foundation for a second stage within the same groups focused on developing effective communications interventions.

Notable about this approach is its reliance on participants' own accounts of the information they have been exposed to and the sources accessed. In the past, media researchers would begin with media content analysis to assess the patterns in language, sources and framings which participants would be likely to be exposed to and which would influence and shape their own ideas. But identifying what any individual is routinely exposed is much more difficult now, and so in some ways this approach allows us to work backwards: to let participants indicate which sources and ideas they are exposed to, which then can be contextualised in the wider media environment to understand how media influence might operate.

3 Developing effective media and communications interventions

Once the first stage of the focus groups has established the nature of the patterns of opinion in relation to the issue in question, the aim would be to identify points at which new or alternative media messaging may interact with the filters to produce shifts in these patterns. I have given examples of shifts in opinion which we can learn from throughout the book: the construction of proximity and threat combined with consistency of messaging delivered a broad consensus on early Covid action overriding ideology and direct experience; attitudes towards the criminal justice system shifted when communications were consistent with people's direct experience of it; and immigration became far less of a priority for people when it was no longer on the front pages and other priorities took over. People accepted recommendations for policy and behaviour change when these took into account the concerns they had and the obstacles they faced.

In all of these cases, opinions were not fixed; however, most people do also have lines that are more difficult to cross, and these are usually related to what we might call the primary filters of ideology – understood as the stakes they have invested in the system and their perceptions of threat – identity/social positioning and striking evidence from lived experience. Communications strategies must take these into account in order to be effective. Research can identify where there are openings for change through the presentation of new information alongside potential sources and/or new solutions and ways of thinking about issues. What is presented will vary according to the categorisation of groups and the attitudinal positions they hold, and what is most likely to be persuasive. Here researchers should aim to identify perspectives or information on the issue in question which challenge or redirect how it is already understood but which chime with the primary filters; this might consist of looking at what was said in the first stage and perhaps focusing more on what was neglected in previous discussions.

Focus groups, second stage

New information. Returning to the example of the obesity epidemic, suggestions of new information to present might include:

- An outline of the individual consequences of obesity such as rates of morbidity, serious disease and disability;
- Information which emphasises the public costs of obesity, including public spending and pressures on the NHS;
- Information which emphasises the unequal impacts of obesity and the role of poverty, food pricing and access to sport and exercise;
- Information which emphasises the structural obstacles to eating healthily such as food additives, lack of infrastructure to support sport and exercise such as cycling, and the routines of school and work life which make it more difficult for everyone to manage their own weight.

Questioning following this new information should focus on what strikes participants as important or surprising, and where existing views are challenged or cemented.

Potential solutions. On the basis of the new information, proposed solutions can be presented, though of course researchers are most likely to seek to promote one in particular; for the obesity crisis, this might include taxes on sugar, labelling on ultra-processed foods, subsidies for healthier foods, investment in school or workplace sport and exercise, etc. Questions following this might include the following, using the sugar tax as an example:

- Have you read about the sugar tax?
- What did you read about it and where?
- What did you think?
- If you took a negative/positive view, why did you take that view? Was it because of the way it was framed, the source who presented it, the evidence offered?
- What do you think now? Do you think it might be effective?
- Do you think the sugar tax is fair? Do you think it is fair to you or the people you know? How do you think the people you know would respond to this?
- If no, how might it be made fairer?
- What else might persuade you to change your mind? What sources and evidence would help to persuade you? Are there particular conditions in relation to the policy which might make it acceptable?

- What other solutions might be considered? Where did you hear about this other solution and what was the source? Why would you prefer this solution?
- Do you have an example of a policy in any area that you feel was fair *and* effective?
- What is the key thing people in power never consider when imposing solutions?

As a result of the questioning about new information and proposed solutions, in combination with the previous stage which provides insight into media, the filters and opinion making, it is possible to identify the points at which shifts in opinion may be possible. This provides insight into the sources, evidence and framings which are most likely to be acceptable, as well as the areas of concern or threat which emerge – consideration of which is important in convincing people that they are listened to when proposals are made. People's perceptions that they aren't listened to and their interests are not considered are a key reason for rejecting new proposals, and this relates also to perceptions of fairness and what is at stake. From this body of evidence, media and communications interventions can be developed which aim to work with or slightly shift the filters which are already in place for any population group.

However, as I have argued throughout this book, driving any significant change involves a combination of media and communications and policy which is orientated around public opinion and experience. As such, interventions that only rely on the former will not be as effective as those which have political support and involve policy or structural change. The research above identifies those points at which people may be open to change, but the change must be in itself fair, effective and workable. You can't persuade people that a plank of wood is a skipping rope, and great communications are pointless if policy is bad.

For those researchers like myself who are often most concerned with communications which aim to produce collective demands for change rather than support for new proposals, hopefully it goes without saying that these techniques and everything in this book are aimed at producing positive change and not manipulating people to believe things that are not in their interests. This is where media and communications can do good work, and sometimes even succeed.

Appendix: empirical studies and datasets, 2011–2020

The data referred to directly and indirectly and which underpins the main arguments in the book is drawn from a series of empirical studies involving focus groups undertaken by the Glasgow University Media Group. For an overview of the Glasgow University Media Group's methodological approach to audience focus groups, see chapter 3 of Philo and Happer (2013), *Communicating Climate Change and Energy Security: New Methods in Understanding Audiences*'. I was the lead and/or main researcher in all of these studies and worked in collaboration with a range of colleagues across different institutions and independent organisations to identify and recruit participants and code and analyse the data. I have referred to 'my research' throughout this book to mean my whole body of work and to avoid the confusion of using 'our', which would have to be qualified each time. The studies were funded by different bodies, and were recruited and sampled in different ways, though always organised geographically. Consequently, to contextualise the data quoted as clearly as possible, the labelling is consistent across studies (rather than across the book).

The focus groups were each made up of between four and six participants and, for most studies, were recruited on the basis of the participants being from the same socio-economic group and being naturally occurring. By this, I mean people who would normally congregate and speak to one another in the regular course of their lives and would therefore have a pre-existing rapport which could be tapped into in the groups. So the groups were drawn from people who worked together, such as cleaners and janitors, call centre workers, students on the same course or those who interacted via their local communities. The groups were recruited to represent a range of socio-demographic criteria. Because of a particular interest in social media engagement, which developed across these studies, young people are particularly well represented. Participants located in Glasgow and/or Scotland are over-represented as a result of the researchers' location.

For the international study in 2015, market researchers screened and recruited the samples and used conventional classifiers of age, income and occupation (as markers of social class). For the international survey of

Reddit moderators, which is drawn on in Chapter 4, the sampling strategy is explained below. Groups were not organised around gender and were therefore largely mixed-gender in composition. The data comments are labelled by gender, as in the transcriptions. Similarly groups were largely not organised around ethnicity, and comments are not labelled in this way; however, I have highlighted ethnicity where it is known and may be relevant to the discussion. Most of the data was collected before GDPR regulations were introduced and so was not made publicly available, but I have indicated sharing and data repositories where relevant. All research projects were approved by Glasgow University's College of Social Sciences ethics committee and adhered to strict ethical guidelines in respect of informed consent and data management.

2011–2012 sample

Climate change and energy security: assessing the impact of information and its delivery on attitudes and behaviour

This research was undertaken by the Glasgow University Media Group in collaboration with colleagues at Chatham House and received funding from the UK Energy Research Centre (UKERC). The groups were UK-wide and organised around occupational or social groupings which were naturally occurring. The project was conducted in two waves, with a first sample of eighteen distinct groups and a total of 100 participants in 2011, and a second wave, following up with six of the original groups six months later in 2012, to assess the longitudinal impacts of the information and discussion. The groups were composed as follows:

1. Middle income, mix of Asian and white, Glasgow
2. Low income, cleaners, Glasgow
3. Students, Oxford
4. Students, Oxford
5. High income, Sussex
6. Professionals, Sussex
7. Low income, mix of Afro-Caribbean and Asian, London
8. Low income, Bradford
9. Middle income, residents, Norfolk
10. Middle income, residents, Norfolk
11. Students, Glasgow
12. Students, Glasgow

In the text, participants from these groups are labelled e.g. '(Male, middle income, UK, 2011–12)'.

Key reference
Philo, G. and Happer, C. (2013) *Communicating Climate Change and Energy Security: New Methods in Understanding Audiences*. New York: Routledge.

2013 sample

Public attitudes, beliefs and engagement with energy behaviours, and the role of social media

This research was undertaken by the Glasgow University Media Group and funded by Glasgow City Council. The research included eight distinct groups and a total of fifty participants. The groups were recruited to represent the range of socio-economic groups across the city of Glasgow, as well as other comparable UK cities. The students were drawn from a range of higher education institutions across the city. The groups were composed as follows:

1. Small business owners
2. Part-time and shop workers
3. Office workers
4. Middle income/professionals
5. Service sector workers
6. Cleaners and janitors
7. Students
8. Students

In the text, participants from these groups are labelled e.g. '(Female, office workers, Glasgow, 2013)'.

Key reference
Happer, C. and Philo, G. (2016) 'New approaches to understanding the role of the news media in the formation of public attitudes and behaviours on climate change', *European Journal of Communication*, 31(2), 136–51.

2014 sample

Probation, media representations and public understanding of justice

This research was undertaken by the Glasgow University Media Group in collaboration with colleagues in Criminology in the Sociology Department at the University of Glasgow and was funded by the British Academy/ Leverhulme Small Research Grant. The research included four distinct groups and an overall sample of twenty-seven people all living within travelling distance of Glasgow, though group 4 was nationally diverse, with most having travelled to Scotland for work or study. The groups were composed as follows:

1. Manual workers
2. Manual workers
3. Students
4. Middle income, web designers

In the text, participants from these groups are labelled e.g. '(Female, manual workers, Glasgow, 2014)'.

Key reference
Happer, C., McGuinness, P., McNeill, F. and Tiripelli, G. (2019) 'Punishment, legitimacy and taste: the role and limits of mainstream and social media in constructing attitudes towards community sanctions', *Crime, Media, Culture*, 15(2), 301–21.

2015 sample

Public understanding and behaviour, and the impact of diet for climate change and food security policies: case studies in Brazil, China, UK and US

This research was undertaken by the Glasgow University Media Group in collaboration with colleagues at Chatham House and was funded by the Avatar Alliance Foundation. The sampling procedure was mirrored across the UK, the US, China and Brazil, although in this book I have drawn only on the first two sample groups. In each country, nine focus groups were held in three regions, with participants drawn from three socio-economic groups in each: low income, middle income/professional, and students (each with three participants). All respondents were drawn from geographically diverse but urban areas. The groups were recruited by Ipsos-MORI to represent normal socio-demographic criteria, and were selected on the basis of age, gender and income levels. Participants were also screened prior to participating in the groups for levels of concern about climate change, meat consumption and environmental issues in order to obtain a spread of views on these issues. The total sample sizes were seventy-two in the US and fifty-five in the UK. The groups were composed as follows:

UK

1. Low income, London
2. Middle income/professional, London
3. Students, London
4. Low income, Manchester
5. Middle income/professional, Manchester
6. Students, Manchester
7. Low income, Glasgow
8. Middle income/professional, Glasgow
9. Students, Glasgow

US

1. Low income, Washington DC
2. Middle income/professional, Washington DC
3. Students, Washington DC
4. Low income, San Francisco
5. Middle income/professional, San Francisco
6. Students, San Francisco
7. Low income, Dallas
8. Middle income/professional, Dallas
9. Students, Dallas

In the text, participants from these groups are labelled e.g. '(Male, low income, US, 2015)'.

Key references

Wellesley, L., Happer, C. and Froggatt, A. (2015) *Changing Climate, Changing Diets: Pathways to Lower Meat Consumption*. London: Chatham House.

Happer, C. and Wellesley, L. (2019) 'Meat consumption, behaviour and the media environment: a focus group analysis across four countries', *Food Security*, 11, 123–39.

2018 sample

Public trust and understanding of online content moderation, and its impacts on public discourse

This research was undertaken by Glasgow University Media Group in collaboration with colleagues in the School of Social and Political Sciences at the University of Glasgow and was an internally funded project. The research included five distinct groups and an overall sample of twenty-seven. Participants were aged between eighteen and twenty-five were very active on social media platforms and were based in Glasgow, with international students over-represented in the sample. The groups were composed as follows:

1. Young, intensive social media users
2. Young, intensive social media users
3. Young, intensive social media users
4. Young, intensive social media users
5. Young, intensive social media users

In the text, participants from these groups are labelled e.g. '(Male, young social media user, 2018)'.

Key reference
Happer, C. and Hoskins, A. (2019) 'Trolling the everyday: the shifting norms of public discourse', British Sociological Association.

2019–20 sample

Public trust and understanding of online content moderation, and its impacts on public discourse

This research was conducted by the Glasgow University Media Group in collaboration with colleagues from the School of Social and Political Sciences and the Department of Computing Science at the University of Glasgow. The study was supported by the Engineering and Physical Sciences Research Council (EPSRC), which indirectly funded the research through the Human Data Interaction Network administered at the university. The research had two dimensions, survey and focus group data collection, both of which are reported in Chapter 4.

Survey of Reddit moderators

A survey of Reddit moderators was open from July to October 2019. Respondents were recruited using three different methods. First, the Subreddit List service was used to identify 500 of the most popular subreddits, and then the unique identifier for each moderator listed was recorded. The research team then messaged the moderator group for each subreddit, inviting them to participate. Later, to strengthen the sample size, the team went back to each individual moderator and sent them a direct message via

Reddit, again encouraging participation. Finally, the survey link was posted to the specific subreddits r/samplesize and r/needamod. These methods delivered a sample of 218, of whom more than 80 per cent identified as male, 60 per cent were aged twenty-nine or younger, and more than 50 per cent were based in the US, with another 19 per cent drawn from the UK. The sample is in line with existing demographic data on Reddit moderators and users (Barthel et al., 2016).

In the text, survey respondents are labelled e.g. '(Male, moderator survey, Australia, 2019)'.

Focus groups

The focus group research included five groups, with the final group bringing together participants from previous groups and an overall sample of seventeen. The groups were each made up of either social media content moderators or social media users. The moderator groups were recruited via the international survey of Reddit moderators and through a large organisation which hosts social media communities via the major platforms (primarily Facebook). In the text, data comments are labelled 'moderator', and where the distinction between the two categories of moderators is important, this is highlighted. These groups included both online and face-to-face participants. For the user groups, we used local recruiters to compose naturally occurring groups where participants were aged between eighteen and twenty-five and active on social media platforms. The final group was composed of participants from the Reddit moderator group and representatives from one of the user groups, and in those groups labelling is in accordance with the original groups participants took part in (groups 1–4 as below):

1. Moderators, Reddit
2. Moderators, large UK organisation
3. Female, young social media users, Glasgow
4. Male, young social media users, Glasgow
5. Reddit moderators and social media users, Glasgow

In the text, participants from these groups are labelled e.g. '(Male, moderator, 2019–20)'.

Dataset: Happer, C., Storer, T., Hoskins, A. and Alkharashi, A. (2021) 'Public trust and understanding of online content moderation, and its impacts on public discourse'. The data is deposited in a repository at the University of Glasgow at DOI: https://doi.org/10.5525/gla.researchdata.1177.

Bibliography

Adams, R. (2017) 'British universities employ no black academics in top roles, figures show', *Guardian*, 19 January. www.theguardian.com/education/2017/jan/19/british-universities-employ-no-black-academics-in-top-roles-figures-show (accessed 23 September 2023)

Adorno, T. (1991) *The Culture Industry: Selected Essays on Mass Culture*. London: Routledge.

Airey, L., Lain D., Jandrić J. and Loretto, W. (2021) 'A selfish generation? "Baby Boomers", values, and the provision of childcare for grandchildren', *Sociological Review*, 69(4): 812–29. DOI: https://doi.org/10.1177/0038026120916104

Anderson A. A. (2017) 'Effects of social media use on climate change opinion, knowledge, and behavior'. In: *Oxford Research Encyclopedia of Climate Science*. New York: Oxford University Press. DOI: https://doi.org/10.1093/acrefore/9780190228620.013.369

Amigo, L. (2023) '"Apart but together". proximity to audiences in times of pandemic. The case of the Italian daily *L'Eco di Bergamo*', *Journalism Studies*, 24(14): 1797–818. DOI: https://doi.org/10.1080/1461670X.2023.2193657

Ang, I. (1985) *Watching Dallas: Soap Opera and the Melodramatic Imagination*. London: Routledge.

Ang, I. (1991) *Desperately Seeking the Audience*. London: Routledge.

Arendt, H. (1976) *The Origins of Totalitarianism*. New York: A Harvest Book.

Arendt, H. (2022) *On Lying and Politics*, introduction by David Bromwich. Library of America. New York: Penguin Random House.

Bachmann, R. (1998) 'Trust – conceptual aspects of a complex phenomenon'. In: Lane, C. and Bachmann, R. (eds), *Trust Within and Between Organizations: Conceptual Issues and Empirical Applications*. Oxford: Oxford University Press, pp. 298–322.

Bak-Coleman, J. B., Alfano, M., Barfuss W., Bergstrom, C. T. et al. (2021) 'Stewardship of global collective behavior', *Proceedings of the National Academy of Sciences*, 118(27). DOI: https://doi.org/10.1073/pnas.2025764118

Bancroft, H. (2022) 'Wealth of the richest one per cent in UK more than 230 times that of the poorest ten per cent, ONS says', *Independent*, 8 January. www.independent.co.uk/news/business/household-wealth-richest-one-percent-poorest-ons-b1989181.html (accessed 7 October 2023)

Baraka, A. (2021) 'Build back better legislation: new Keynesianism or neoliberal public relations stunt?', *Common Dreams*, 11 October. www.commondreams.org/views/2021/10/11/build-back-better-legislation-new-keynesianism-or-neoliberal-public-relations-stunt (accessed 19 September 2023)

Barrie, C., Hanhrie, H. and McGinty B. (2020) 'Trust in science and COVID-19', Johns Hopkins Bloomberg School of Public Health. publichealth.jhu.edu/2020/trust-in-science-and-covid-19 (accessed 19 September 2023)

Barthel, M., Stocking, G., Holcomb, J. and Mitchell, A. (2016) 'Reddit news users more likely to be male, young and digitalin their news preferences', Pew Research Center, 25 February. www.journalism.org/2016/02/25/reddit-news-users-more-likely-to-be-male-young-and-digital-in-their-news-preferences/ (accessed 6 October 2023)

Barthes, R. (1964) 'Rhetoric of the image', *Communications*, 4: 40–51. DOI: https://doi.org/10.3406/comm.1964.1027

Bartlett, B. (2015) 'How Fox News changed American media and political dynamics', *SSRN*, 3 June. DOI: https://doi.org/10.2139/ssrn.2604679

Bastos, M. and Farkas, J. (2019) '"Donald Trump is my president!": the Internet Research Agency propaganda machine', *Social Media + Society*, 5(3). DOI: https://doi.org/10.1177/2056305119865466

Bastos, M. T. and Mercea, D. (2016) 'Serial activists: political Twitter beyond influentials and the Twittertariat', *New Media & Society*, 18(10): 2359–78. DOI: https://doi.org/10.1177/1461444815584764

Bauman, Z (2001) *The Individualised Society*. Cambridge: Polity.

BBC News Online (2019a) 'Boris Johnson: first speech as PM in full', Politics, 24 July. www.bbc.co.uk/news/uk-politics-49102495 (accessed 16 September 2023)

BBC News Online (2019b) 'UK Parliament declares climate change emergency', 1 May. www.bbc.co.uk/news/uk-politics48126677 (accessed 7 October 2023)

BBC News Online (2020a) 'Coronavirus: White House targets US disease chief Dr Anthony Fauci', 14 July. www.bbc.co.uk/news/world-us-canada-53392817 (accessed 7 October 2023)

BBC News Online (2020b) 'Covid-19: milestones of the global pandemic', 29 September. www.bbc.co.uk/news/world-54337098 (accessed 7 October 2023)

BBC News Online (2020c) 'Newspaper headlines: UK "under house arrest" as coronavirus measures "end freedom"', 24 March. www.bbc.co.uk/news/blogs-the-papers-52013243 (accessed 7 October 2023)

BBC News Online (2022) 'Covid vaccine: how many people are vaccinated in the UK?', 4 March. www.bbc.co.uk/news/health-55274833 (accessed 8 October 2023)

BBC World Service (2020) 'Italian army takes coffins as virus deaths mount', Newsday, 19 March. www.bbc.co.uk/programmes/p0872zh9 (accessed 7 October 2023)

Beck, D. J. and Gwilym, H. (2022) 'The food bank: a safety-net in place of welfare security in times of austerity and the Covid-19 crisis', *Social Policy and Society*, 22: 545–61. DOI: https://doi.org/10.1017/S1474746421000907

Benton, J. (2019) 'Why do some people avoid news? Because they don't trust us – or because they don't think we add value to their lives?', Nieman Lab. www.niemanlab.org/2019/06/why-do-some-people-avoid-news-because-they-dont-trust-us-or-because-they-dont-think-we-add-value-to-their-lives/ (accessed 15 September 2023)

Berry, M. (2012) 'The *Today* programme and the banking crisis', *Journalism*, 1 (18): 253–70. DOI: https://doi.org/10.1177/1464884912458654

Binder, S. and Richards, L. (2020) 'UK Public opinion toward immigration: overall attitudes and level of concern', The Migration Observatory. https://migrationobservatory.ox.ac.uk/resources/briefings/uk-public-opinion-toward-immigration-overall-attitudes-and-level-of-concern/ (accessed 22 May 2024)

Blackmore, P. (2016) 'Universities vie for the metric that cannot be measured: prestige', *Guardian*, 29 March. www.theguardian.com/higher-education-network/2016/mar/29/universities-vie-for-the-metric-that-cannot-be-measured-prestige (accessed 23 September 2023)

Blyth, M. (2007) 'Powering puzzling or persuading? The mechanisms of building institutional orders', *International Studies Quarterly*, 51(4): 761–77. DOI: https://doi.org/10.1111/j.1468-2478.2007.00475.x

Bobo, J. (1995) *Black Women as Cultural Readers*. New York: Columbia University Press.

Bond, P. (2016) 'Leslie Moonves on Donald Trump: "It may not be good for America, but it's damn good for CBS"', *Hollywood Reporter*, 29 February. www.hollywoodreporter.com/news/general-news/leslie-moonves-donald-trump-may-871464/ (accessed 17 September 2023)

Bonikowski, B. and Gidron, N. (2016) 'The populist style in American Politics: presidential campaign discourse, 1952–1996', *Social Forces*, 94(4), 1593–621. DOI: https://doi.org/10.1093/sf/sov120

Bonilla-Silva, E. (1997) 'Rethinking racism: toward a structural interpretation', *American Sociological Review*, 62(3): 465–80. DOI: https://doi.org/10.2307/2657316

Bonilla-Silva, E. (2012) 'The invisible weight of whiteness: the racial grammar of everyday life in contemporary America', *Ethnic and Racial Studies*, 35(2): 173–94. DOI: https://doi.org/10.1080/01419870.2011.613997

Borenstein, S. and Fingerhut, H. (2020) 'AP-NORC/USAFacts poll: US trust in COVID-19 information down', Associated Press News, 20 October. apnews.com/article/virus-outbreak-donald-trump-pandemics-media-social-media-d3c50f-0479f8ac123c8cf548c33282be (accessed 19 September 2023)

Borrett, A. (2022) 'One third of households already struggling to pay energy bills even without next price cap hike', Sky News, 24 August. www.msn.com/en-gb/news/uknews/one-third-of-households-already-struggling-to-pay-energy-bills-even-without-next-price-cap-hike/ar-AA115m5A (accessed 26 September 2023)

Bourdieu, P. (1993a) Public opinion does not exist. In *Sociology in Question*, trans. Richard Nice. London: Sage, pp. 149–57.

Bourdieu, P. (1993b) '"Youth" is just a word'. In *Sociology in Question*, trans. Richard Nice. London: Sage, pp. 94–102.

Bourdieu, P. (1998) *On Television*, translated by Priscilla Pankhurst Ferguson. New York: New Press.

boyd, d. (2017) 'Why America is self-segregating', *Zephoria*, 10 January. www.zephoria.org/thoughts/archives/2017/01/10/why-america-is-self-segregating.html (accessed 23 September 2023)

Bibliography

Boykoff, M. T. (2011) *Who Speaks for the Climate? Making Sense of Media Reporting on Climate Change*. Cambridge: Cambridge University Press.

Boykoff, M. T. and Boykoff, J. M. (2004) 'Balance as bias: global warming and the US prestige press', *Global Environmental Change*, 14: 125–36. DOI: https://doi.org/10.1016/j.gloenvcha.2003.10.001

Boykoff, M. T. and Boykoff, J. M. (2007) 'Climate change and journalistic norms: a case-study of US mass-media coverage', *Geoforum*, 38: 1190–204. DOI: https://doi.org/10.1016/j.geoforum.2007.01.008

Brey, P., Gauttier, S. and Milam, P. (2019) 'Harmful internet use Part II: impact on culture and society'. European Parliamentary Research Service, January. www.europarl.europa.eu/RegData/etudes/STUD/2019/624269/EPRS_STU(2019)624269_EN.pdf (accessed 23 September 2023)

Briant, E. (2018) 'I've seen inside the digital propaganda machine. And it's dark in there', *Guardian*, 20 April. www.theguardian.com/commentisfree/2018/apr/20/cambridge-analytica-propaganda-machine (accessed 6 October 2023)

Briant, E., Watson, N. and Philo, G. (2013) 'Bad news for disabled people: how the newspapers are reporting disability', Strathclyde Centre for Disability Research and Glasgow Media Unit. www.gla.ac.uk/media/Media_214917_smxx.pdf (accessed 23 September 2023)

Brignall, M. (2019) 'Young Britons believe dream of owning home is over, survey says', *Guardian*, 31 July. www.theguardian.com/money/2019/jul/31/young-britons-believe-dream-of-owning-home-is-over-survey-says (accessed 22 September 2023)

Bristow, J. (2015) 'How fear of offending has trumped freedom of speech among today's young people', The Conversation, 21 January. https://theconversation.com/how-fear-of-offending-has-trumped-freedom-of-speech-among-todays-young-people-36392 (accessed 7 June 2024)

Brodeur, A., Baccini, L. and Weymouth, S. (2020) 'How COVID-19 led to Donald Trump's defeat', *Conversation*, 7 December. https://theconversation.com/how-covid-19-led-to-donald-trumps-defeat-150110 (accessed 19 September 2023)

Bruns, A. (2019) *Are Filter Bubbles Real?* Cambridge: Polity Press.

Bryant, M. (2020) 'US voter demographics: election 2020 ended up looking a lot like 2016', *Guardian*, 5 November. www.theguardian.com/us-news/2020/nov/05/us-election-demographics-race-gender-age-biden-trump (accessed 23 September 2023)

Buchholz, K. (2022) 'This chart shows global youth perspectives on climate change', *World Economic Forum*, 26 October. www.weforum.org/agenda/2022/10/chart-shows-global-youth-perspectives-on-climate-change/ (accessed 23 October 2023)

Buckingham, D. (2000) *After the Death of Childhood: Growing Up in the Age of Electronic Media*. Cambridge: Polity Press.

Burki, T. (2020) 'The online anti-vaccine movement in the age of COVID-19', *The Lancet Digital Health*, 2(10), October, E504–E505. DOI: https://doi.org/10.1016/S2589-7500(20)30227-2

Butler, P. (2022) 'Over 330,000 excess deaths in Great Britain linked to austerity, finds study', *Guardian*, 5 October. www.theguardian.com/business/2022/oct/05/

over-330000-excess-deaths-in-great-britain-linked-to-austerity-finds-study (accessed 7 October 2023).

Byers, D. (2016) 'How the media missed Bernie Sanders', *CNN*, 18 January. edition.cnn.com/2016/01/18/politics/bernie-sanders-media/index.html (accessed 7 October 2023).

Cadwalladr, C. and Graham-Harrison, E. (2018) 'Revealed: 50 million Facebook profiles harvested for Cambridge Analytica in major data breach', *Guardian*, 17 March. www.theguardian.com/news/2018/mar/17/cambridge-analytica-facebook-influence-us-election (accessed 6 October 2023).

Calvert, J., Arbuthnott, G. and Leake, J. (2020) 'Coronavirus: 38 days when Britain sleepwalked into disaster', *The Times*, 18 April. https://www.thetimes.com/uk/politics/article/coronavirus-38-days-when-britain-sleepwalked-into-disaster-hq3b9tlgh (accessed 5 June 2024).

Cameron, N. (2018) 'How liberal bias created Fox News', *Unherd*, 25 June. unherd.com/2018/06/liberal-bias-created-fox-news/ (accessed 17 September 2023).

Cammaerts, B. et al. (2016) 'Journalistic representations of Jeremy Corbyn in the British press: from watchdog to attackdog', London School of Economics and Political Science report, 1 July. https://eprints.lse.ac.uk/67211/1/CAmmaerts_Journalistic%20representations%20of%20Jeremy%20Corbyn_Author_2016.pdf (accessed 19 September 2023).

Campbell, A. and Caul, S. (2020) 'Deaths involving COVID-19, England and Wales: deaths occurring in March 2020', Office for National Statistics, 16 April. www.ons.gov.uk/peoplepopulationandcommunity/birthsdeathsandmarriages/deaths/bulletins/deathsinvolvingcovid19englandandwales/deathsoccurringinmarch2020 (accessed 7 October 2023).

Caplan, R. (2018) 'Content or context moderation? Artisanal, community-reliant, and industrial approaches', *Data & Society*, 14 November. datasociety.net/library/content-or-context-moderation/ (accessed 6 October 2023).

Carbon Brief (2023) (multiple authors) 'COP28: Key outcomes agreed at the UN climate talks in Dubai', 13 December. www.carbonbrief.org/cop28-key-outcomes-agreed-at-the-un-climate-talks-in-dubai/ (accessed 29 January 2024).

Carrington, D. (2019a) 'Public concern over environment reaches record high in UK', *Guardian*, 5 June. www.theguardian.com/environment/2019/jun/05/greta-thunberg-effect-public-concern-over-environment-reaches-record-high (accessed 7 October 2023).

Carrington, D. (2019b) 'Why the *Guardian* is changing the language it uses about the environment', *Guardian*, 17 May. www.theguardian.com/environment/2019/may/17/why-the-guardian-is-changing-the-language-it-uses-about-the-environment (accessed 7 October 2023).

CBBC *Newsround* (2019) 'What are food banks and why do people use them?', 12 November. www.bbc.co.uk/newsround/av/54887135 (accessed 7 October 2023).

Chandrasekharan, E., Samory, M., Jhaver, S. et al. (2018) 'The internet's hidden rules: an empirical study of Reddit norm violations at micro, meso, and macro scales', *Proceedings of the ACM on Human-Computer Interaction*, 2 (Computer-Supported Cooperative Work and Social Computing), art. 32, 1–25.

Chang, C. (2019) 'The media can take Bernie Sanders a little seriously, as a treat', *Esquire*, 20 December. www.esquire.com/news-politics/a30299555/bernie-sanders-blackout-media-bias-coverage-campaign-2020/ (accessed 19 September 2023)

Chiorando, M. (2022) 'Money-saving tips that REALLY work: parents share their tried-and-tested advice amid the cost of living crisis – including freezing milk, ditching birthday cards and cutting dishwasher tablets in half', *Mail Online*, 30 August. www.dailymail.co.uk/femail/article-11157177/UK-cost-living-crisis-save-money-home.html (accessed 7 October 2023)

Christensen, M.-B., Hallum, C., Maitland, A., Parrinello, Q. and Putaturo, C. (2023) 'Survival of the richest: how we must tax the super-rich now to fight inequality', Oxfam, January 2023. oxfamilibrary.openrepository.com/bitstream/handle/10546/621477/bp-survival-of-the-richest-160123-en.pdf (accessed 7 October 2023)

Cineas, F. and North, A. (2020) 'We need to talk about the white people who voted for Donald Trump', *Vox*, 7 November. www.vox.com/2020/11/7/21551364/white-trump-voters-2020 (accessed 26 September 2023)

Clarence-Smith, L. (2022) 'Free speech law to stop university cancel culture watered down by No 10', *Telegraph*, 1 December. www.telegraph.co.uk/news/2022/12/01/free-speech-law-stop-university-cancel-culture-watered-no-10/ (accessed 6 September 2023)

Clark, D. (2023) 'Higher education in the UK – statistics & facts', Statista, 20 December. www.statista.com/topics/6938/higher-education-in-the-uk/#topicOverview (accessed 2 February 2024)

Clark, G., Thrift, N. and Tickell, A. (2004) 'Performing finance: the industry, the media and its image', *Review of International Political Economy*, 11(2): 289–310. DOI: https://doi.org/10.1080/09692290420001672813

Climate Outreach (2019) *Climate Visuals: A Climate Outreach Project*. climatevisuals.org/ (accessed 7 October 2023)

Coe, K. and Griffin, R. A. (2020) 'Marginalized identity invocation online: the case of President Donald Trump on Twitter', *Social Media + Society*, 6(1). DOI: https://doi.org/10.1177/2056305120913979

Colarossi, J. (2020) 'Comparing how media around the world frames coronavirus news', *The Brink*, 25 June. www.bu.edu/articles/2020/comparing-how-media-around-the-world-frames-coronavirus-news/ (accessed 7 October 2023)

Common Sense Media (2020) 'What is media literacy, and why is it important?', 4 June. https://www.commonsensemedia.org/articles/what-is-media-literacy-and-why-is-it-important#:~:text=Media%20literacy%20is%20the%20ability%20to%20identify%20different,radio%2C%20newspapers%2C%20and%20magazines%29%20of%20most%20parents%27%20youth. (accessed 7 June 2024)

Crawford, C. et al. (2016) *Family Background and University Success; Differences in Higher Education Access and Outcomes in England*. Oxford: Oxford University Press.

Curtice, J. and Scholes, A. (2023) 'Role and responsibilities of government', National Centre for Social Research. https://natcen.ac.uk/sites/default/files/2023-09/BSA%20

40%20Role%20and%20responsibilities%20of%20government.pdf (accessed 7 June 2024)

Curtis, C. (2017) 'Forget the flat caps – this is what Labour voters really look like', *New Statesman*, 25 April. www.newstatesman.com/politics/the-staggers/2017/04/forget-flat-caps-what-labour-voters-really-look (accessed 23 September 2023)

Danewid, I. (2022) 'Policing the (migrant) crisis: Stuart Hall and the defence of whiteness', *Security Dialogue*, 53(1): 21–37. DOI: https://doi.org/10.1177/0967010621994074

Davidson, N. (2016) 'Crisis neoliberalism and regimes of permanent exception', *Critical Sociology*, 43(4–5): 615–34. DOI: https://doi.org/10.1177/0896920516655386

Davies, R. and Rushe, D. (2019) 'Facebook to pay $5bn fine as regulator settles Cambridge Analytica complaint', *Guardian*, 24 July. www.theguardian.com/technology/2019/jul/24/facebook-to-pay-5bn-fine-as-regulator-files-cambridge-analytica-complaint (accessed 6 October 2023)

Dawson, M. (2012) 'Reviewing the critique of individualization: the disembedded and embedded theses', *Acta Sociologica*, 55(4): 305–19. DOI: https://doi.org/10.1177/0001699312447634

Department for Digital, Culture, Media & Sport (2012) 'Leveson Inquiry: report into the culture, practices and ethics of the press', 29 November. www.gov.uk/government/publications/leveson-inquiry-report-into-the-culture-practices-and-ethics-of-the-press (accessed 19 September 2023)

Department of Health and Social Care (2020) 'New UK-wide methodology agreed to record COVID-19 deaths', UK Government, 12 August. www.gov.uk/government/news/new-uk-wide-methodology-agreed-to-record-covid-19-deaths (accessed 10 October 2023)

Deneen, P. J. (2018) *Why Liberalism Failed*. New Haven, CT: Yale University Press.

Deuze, M. (2005) 'What is journalism? Professional identity and ideology of journalists reconsidered', *Journalism*, 6(4): 442–64.

De Vreese, C. H., Esser, F. and Stanyer, J. (2018) 'Populism as an expression of political communication content and style: a new perspective', *The International Journal of Press/Politics*, 23(4), 423–38. DOI: https://doi.org/10.1177/19401612187900

Dinan, W. and Miller, D. (2012) 'Sledgehammers, nuts and rotten apples: reassessing the case for lobbying self-regulation in the United Kingdom', *Interest Groups and Advocacy*, 1(1): 105–14. DOI: https://doi.org/10.1057/iga.2012.5

Doherty, C., Kiley, J. and O'Hea, O. (2018) 'The generation gap in American politics', Pew Research Center. www.pewresearch.org/politics/2018/03/01/the-generation-gap-in-american-politics/ (accessed 23 October 2023)

Donald, R. (2020) 'Greenlining segregation and environmental policies from the New Deal to the climate crisis', PhD thesis University of Columbia.

Donovan, J. (2020) 'Deconstructing disinformation's threat to democracy', *The Fletcher Forum of World Affairs*, 44(1): 153–60, JSTOR. www.jstor.org/stable/48599286 (accessed 23 October 2023)

Dubois, E. and Blank G. (2018) 'The echo chamber is overstated: the moderating effect of political interest and diverse media', *Information, Communication & Society*, 21(5): 729–45. DOI: https://doi.org/10.1080/1369118X.2018.1428656

Duffy, B. (2021) 'Younger generations are the most fatalistic about climate change', *New Scientist*, 15 September. https://www.newscientist.com/article/2290232-younger-generations-are-the-most-fatalistic-about-climate-change/ (accessed 3 June 2024)

Duffy, B., Glenn Gottfried, G., Skinner, G. et al. (2022) 'Freedom of speech in the UK's "culture war"', The Policy Institute, King's College London, and Ipsos. https://www.kcl.ac.uk/news/free-speech-in-the-uks-culture-war-attitudes-to-causing-offence-or-harm (accessed 7 June 2024)

Dunne, D. (2019) 'France's record-breaking heatwave made "at least five times" more likely by climate change', Carbon Brief, 2 July. www.carbonbrief.org/frances-record-breaking-heatwave-made-at-least-five-times-more-likely-by-climate-change/ (accessed 7 October 2023)

Dzhanera, Y. (2020) 'Trump approval rating rises as he responds to the coronavirus outbreak', *CNBC*, 25 March. www.cnbc.com/2020/03/24/trump-approval-rating-rises-amid-response-to-coronavirus.html (accessed 10 September 2023)

Eavis, P. and Lohr, S. (2020) 'Big Tech's domination of business reaches new heights', *New York Times*, 19 August. www.nytimes.com/2020/08/19/technology/big-tech-business-domination.html (accessed 6 October 2023)

Edelman (2018) Edelman Trust Barometer 2018. www.edelman.com/sites/g/files/aatuss191/files/2018-10/2018_Edelman_Trust_Barometer_Global_Report_FEB.pdf (accessed 28 August 2023)

Edelman (2020) Edelman Trust Barometer 2020. https://www.edelman.com/trust/2020-trust-barometer (accessed 28 August 2023)

Edgerly, S. (2017) 'Seeking out and avoiding the news media: young adults' proposed strategies for obtaining current events information', *Mass Communication and Society*, 20(3): 358–77. DOI: https://doi.org/10.1080/15205436.2016.1262424

Edgerly, S. (2022) 'The head and heart of news avoidance: how attitudes about the news media relate to levels of news consumption', *Journalism*, 23(9): 1828–45. DOI: https://doi.org/10.1177/14648849211012922

Ehrenreich, B. and Ehrenreich, J. (2013) 'Barbara and John Ehrenreich: the real story behind the crash and burn of America's managerial class', *AlterNet*, 20 February. www.alternet.org/2013/02/barbara-and-john-ehrenreich-real-story-behind-crash-and-burn-americas-managerial-class (accessed 26 September 2023)

Ehrenreich, J. and Ehrenreich, B. (1979) 'The professional/managerial class': In: Walker, P. (ed.), *Between Labor and Capital*, 1st ed. Boston: South End Press, pp. 5–48.

Elliott, R. (2021) 'Generationalism: understanding the difference between what generations are and what generations do', *The Sociological Review Magazine*, 5 October. DOI: https://doi.org/10.51428/tsr.fmel4859

Erickson, J., Yan, B. and Huang, J. (2023) 'Bridging echo chambers? Understanding political partisanship through semantic network analysis', *Social Media + Society*, 9(3). DOI: https://doi.org/10.1177/20563051231186368

Farage, N. (2013) 'Nigel Farage: the bloated BBC bullies those who disagree with its liberal bias', *Telegraph*, 4 July. www.telegraph.co.uk/news/politics/ukip/

10159310/Nigel-Farage-The-bloated-BBC-bullies-those-who-disagree-with-its-liberal-bias.html (accessed 15 September 2023)

Ferguson, K. (2022) 'STILL IN THE STEAM AGE. National rail strike: teachers and binmen threaten to join railway workers on strike causing chaos not seen since 1970s', *Sun*, 19 June. www.thesun.co.uk/news/18938968/national-rail-strike-teachers-binmen-posties-join/ (accessed 23 September 2023)

Ferguson, B. (2023) 'Nicola Sturgeon admits she is "deeply worried" social media abuse will put women off entering politics', *Scotsman*, 16 February. www.scotsman.com/whats-on/arts-and-entertainment/nicola-sturgeon-admits-she-is-deeply-worried-social-media-abuse-will-put-women-off-entering-politics-4029051 (accessed 6 October 2023)

Ferrier, M. (2018) 'Attacks and harassment: the impact on female journalists and their reporting', International Women's Media Foundation. www.iwmf.org/wp-content/uploads/2018/09/Attacks-and-Harassment.pdf (accessed 6 October 2023)

Fine, B. (2010) 'Neoliberalism as Financialisation'. In: Saad-Filho, A. and Yalman, G. (eds), *Transitions to Neoliberalism in Middle-Income Countries: Policy Dilemmas, Economic Crises, Mass Resistance*. London: Routledge, pp. 11–23.

Fisher, M. (2009) *Capitalist Realism: Is There No Alternative?* Winchester: Zero Books.

Flaxman, S., Goel, S. and Rao, J. M. (2016) 'Filter bubbles, echo chambers, and online news consumption', *Public Opinion Quarterly*, 80(S1), 298–320. DOI: https://doi.org/10.1093/poq/nfw006

Ford, M. and Hoskins, A. (2022) *Radical War: Data, Attention & Control in the Twenty-First Century*. Oxford: Hurst/Oxford University Press.

Frans, E. (2022) 'Did Sweden's controversial Covid strategy pay off? In many ways it did – but it let the elderly down', *Conversation*, 12 August. theconversation.com/did-swedens-controversial-covid-strategy-pay-off-in-many-ways-it-did-but-it-let-the-elderly-down-188338 (accessed 7 October 2023)

Fraser, N. (1990) 'Rethinking the public sphere: a contribution to the critique of actually existing democracy', *Social Text*, 25/26, 56–80. DOI: https://doi.org/10.2307/466240

Fraser, N. (2000) 'Rethinking recognition', *New Left Review*, 3 (May–June): 107–20. https://newleftreview.org/issues/ii3/articles/nancy-fraser-rethinking-recognition (accessed 25 October 2023)

Friedman, S. (2020) *The Class Ceiling: Why it Pays to be Privileged*. London: Polity Press.

Gabbatiss, J. Hayes, S. Goodman, J. and Prater, T. (2021) 'Analysis: how UK newspapers changed their minds about climate change', Carbon Brief. interactive.carbonbrief.org/how-uk-newspapers-changed-minds-climate-change/ (accessed 7 October 2023)

The Gdelt Project (2020a) 'Climate change coverage steadily increases on BBC compared with CNN/MSNBC/Fox News', 23 January. blog.gdeltproject.org/climate-change-coverage-steadily-increases-on-bbc-compared-with-cnn-msnbc-fox-news/ (accessed 7 October 2023)

The Gdelt Project (2020b) 'Climate change through imagery: global warming's polar bears giving way to climate crisis deserts', 7 March. https://blog.gdeltproject.org/

climate-change-through-imagery-global-warmings-polar-bears-giving-way-to-climate-crisis-deserts/ (accessed 7 October 2023)
Gerbaudo, P. (2021) *The Great Recoil: Politics after Populism and the Pandemic*. London and New York: Verso Books.
Gibson, A. (2019) 'Free speech and safe spaces: how moderation policies shape online discussion spaces', *Social Media +Society*, 5(1). DOI: https://doi.org/10.1177/2056305119832588
Giddens, A. (1991) *Modernity and self-identity: Self and society in the late modern age*. Cambridge: Polity Press.
Gillespie, T. (2018) *Custodians of the Internet: Platforms, Content Moderation, and the Hidden Decisions that Shape Social Media*. New Haven, CT: Yale University Press.
Gimpel, J. G. (2017) 'Immigration policy opinion and the 2016 presidential vote issue relevance in the Trump-Clinton election', Center for Immigration Studies. https://cis.org/sites/default/files/2017-12/gimpel-2016-vote.pdf (accessed 12 September 2023)
Glasgow University Media Group (1985) *War and Peace News*. Milton Keynes: Open University Press.
Gould, S. and Harrington, R. (2016) '7 charts show who propelled Trump to victory', *Insider*, 11 November. www.businessinsider.com/exit-polls-who-voted-for-trump-clinton-2016–11?r=US&IR=T (accessed 26 September 2023)
Gramsci, A. (1971) *Selections from the Prison Notebooks*. London: Lawrence and Wishart.
Gray, E., Ormiston, R. and Coyle, T. (2022) 'Concern about cost of living, views on energy sources, and preferred date for IndyRef2: findings from new Ipsos Scotland polling', Ipsos, 20 August. www.ipsos.com/en-uk/concern-about-cost-of-living-views-energy-sources-and-preferred-date-indyref2-ipsos-scotland (accessed 23 September 2023)
Green, G. (2023) 'Environmental campaigners filmed, threatened and harassed at Cop28', *Guardian*, 20 December. www.theguardian.com/environment/2023/dec/20/threats-intimidation-creating-climate-of-fear-un-cop-events (accessed 29 January 2024)
Greve, J. E. (2019) 'Are Bernie Sanders' attacks on the media fair – or Trumpian?', *Guardian*, 27 August. /www.theguardian.com/us-news/2019/aug/27/bernie-sanders-attacks-media-press-fair-or-trump-2020-democrats (accessed 17 September 2023)
Grynbaum, M. M. (2017) 'Fox News drops "fair and balanced" slogan as right-wing broadcaster scrambles to avert ratings slump', *Independent*, 15 June. www.independent.co.uk/news/world/americas/fox-news-fair-balanced-slogan-roger-ailes-bill-o-reilly-sexual-harassment-rebrand-a7791216.html (accessed 15 September 2023)
Guo, E. (2020) 'Facebook is now officially too powerful, says the US government', *MIT Technology Review*, 9 December. www.technologyreview.com/2020/12/09/1013641/facebook-should-be-broken-up-says-us-government/ (accessed 6 October 2023)
Habermas, J. (1992) *The Structural Transformation of the Public Sphere*. Cambridge: Polity Press.

Hall, S. (1973) *Encoding and Decoding in the Television Discourse.* Birmingham: University of Birmingham, Centre for Contemporary Cultural Studies.

Hall, S. (2019a) *Essential Essays,* vol. 1. *Foundations of Cultural Studies,* ed. D. Morley. Durham, NC: Duke University Press.

Hall, S. (2019b) *Essential Essays,* vol. 2. *Identity and Disapora,* ed. D. Morley. Durham, NC: Duke University Press.

Hall, S. and Jefferson, T. (eds) (2006) *Resistance through Rituals: Youth Subcultures in Post-War Britain.* 2nd ed. London and New York: Routledge.

Hart, P. S., Chinn, S. and Soroka, S. (2020) 'Politicization and polarization in COVID-19 news coverage', *Science Communication,* 42(5): 679–97. DOI: https://doi.org/10.1177/1075547020950735

Happer, C. (2017a) 'Belief in change: the role of media and communications in driving action on climate change'. In: Elliott, A., Cullis, J. and Damodaran, V. (eds), *Climate Change and the Humanities: Historical, Philosophical and Interdisciplinary Approaches to the Contemporary Environmental Crisis.* London: Palgrave Macmillan, pp. 177–97.

Happer, C. (2017b) 'Financialisation, media and social change', *New Political Economy,* 22(4): 437–49. DOI: https://doi.org/10.1080/13563467.2017.1259301

Happer, C. (2020) 'Coronavirus: calls from journalists for an end to the lockdown are out of step with public opinion', *Conversation,* 15 April. theconversation.com/coronavirus-calls-from-journalists-for-an-end-to-the-lockdown-are-out-of-step-with-public-opinion-136279 (accessed 6 September 2023)

Happer, C. and Hoskins, A. (2019) 'Trolling the everyday: the shifting norms of public discourse', British Sociological Association. www.britsoc.co.uk/media/24958/ac2019_all_abstracts_by_session.pdf (accessed 25 October 2023)

Happer, C., Hoskins, A. and Merrin, W. (eds) (2018) *Trump's Media War.* Cham, Switzerland: Palgrave Macmillan.

Happer, C., McGuinness, P., McNeill, F. and Tiripelli, G. (2019) 'Punishment, legitimacy and taste: the role and limits of mainstream and social media in constructing attitudes towards community sanctions', *Crime, Media, Culture,* 15(2): 301–21. DOI: https://doi.org/10.1177/1741659018773848

Happer, C. and Philo, G. (2013) 'The role of the media in the construction of public belief and social change', *Journal of Social and Political Psychology,* 1(1): 321–36. DOI: https://doi.org/10.5964/jspp.v1i1.96

Happer, C. and Philo, G. (2016) 'New approaches to understanding the role of the news media in the formation of public attitudes and behaviours on climate change', *European Journal of Communication,* 31(2): 136–51. DOI: https://doi.org/10.1177/0267323115612213

Happer, C., Philo, G. and Froggatt, A. (2012) 'Climate change and energy security: assessing the impact of information and its delivery on attitudes and behaviour', project report, UK Energy Research Centre. London: UK Energy Research Centre.

Happer, C., Schlesinger, P., Langer, A. I., Mabweazara, H. and Hinde, D. (2022) 'Scotland's sustainable media future: challenges and opportunities: a stakeholder analysis', project report, Glasgow University Media Group and Centre for Cultural Policy Research. https://eprints.gla.ac.uk/276125/1/276125.pdf (accessed 6 October 2023)

Happer, C., Storer, T., Hoskins, A. and Alkharashi, A. (2021) 'Public trust and understanding of online content moderation, and its impacts on public discourse'. Database in a repository at the University of Glasgow, DOI: https://doi.org/10.5525/gla.researchdata.1177

Happer, C. and Wellesley, L. (2019) 'Meat consumption, behaviour and the media environment: a focus group analysis across four countries', *Food Security*, 11: 123–39. DOI: https://doi.org/10.1007/s12571-018-0877-1

Happer, C. and Åberg, A. (2024) 'Stranger things on TikTok: young people, climate change and upside down political communication', *HumaNetten*, 52: 9–26. ISSN: 1403-2279

Harvey, D. (2016) 'Neoliberalism is a political project: an interview with David Harvey' (with B. S. Risager), *Jacobin*, 23 July. https://jacobin.com/2016/07/david-harvey-neoliberalism-capitalism-labor-crisis-resistance/ (accessed 23 September 2023)

Harvey, D. (2018) *The Limits to Capital*. London and New York: Verso Books.

Hautea, S., Parks, P., Takahashi, B. and Zeng, J. (2021) 'Showing they care (or don't): affective publics and ambivalent climate activism on TikTok', *Social Media + Society*, 7(2). DOI: https://doi.org/10.1177/20563051211012344

Heath, A. Jowell, R. and Curtice, J. (1988) 'Class dealignment and the explanation of political change: a reply to Dunleavy', *West European Politics*, 11(1): 146–8. DOI: https://10.1080/01402388808424674

Helm, T., Graham-Harrison, E. and McKie, R. (2020) 'How did Britain get its coronavirus response so wrong?', *Guardian*, 19 April. www.theguardian.com/world/2020/apr/18/how-did-britain-get-its-response-to-coronavirus-so-wrong (accessed 7 October 2023)

Herman, E. and Chomsky, N. (1988) *Manufacturing Consent*. New York: Pantheon Books.

Hickey, S. (2022) 'Mick Lynch: I never believed in the European Union', LBC, 19 August. www.lbc.co.uk/radio/presenters/james-obrien/mick-lynch-i-never-believed-in-european-union-rmt-strikes/ (accessed 23 October 2023)

Hickman, L. (2018) 'Exclusive: BBC issues internal guidance on how to report climate change', Carbon Brief, 7 September. www.carbonbrief.org/exclusive-bbc-issues-internal-guidance-on-how-to-report-climate-change/ (accessed 7 October 2023)

HM Treasury (2022) 'Millions to receive £350 boost to help with rising energy costs', 3 February. www.gov.uk/government/news/millions-to-receive-350–boost-to-help-with-rising-energy-costs (accessed 7 October 2023)

HM Treasury (2023) 'Chancellor unveils a budget for growth', 15 March. www.gov.uk/government/news/chancellor-unveils-a-budget-for-growth (accessed 7 October 2023)

Hochuli, A., Hoare, G. and Cunliffe, P. (2021) *The End of the End of History: Politics in the Twenty-First Century*. Alresford: Zero Books.

Hoggart, R. (2009) *The Uses of Literacy: Aspects of Working Class Life*. London: Penguin Books.

Holton, R. J. (1987) 'The idea of crisis in modern society', *The British Journal of Sociology*, 38(4): 502–20. DOI: https://doi.org/10.2307/590914

Hopke, J. E. (2020) 'Connecting extreme heat events to climate change: media coverage of heat waves and wildfires', *Environmental Communication*, 14(4): 492–508. DOI: https://doi.org/10.1080/17524032.2019.1687537

Huber, M. (2022) *Climate Change as Class War*. London and New York: Verso.

Hussain A., Ali, S., Ahmed M. and Hussain S. (2018) 'The anti-vaccination movement: a regression in modern medicine', *Cureus*, 10(7), 3 July: e2919. www.ncbi.nlm.nih.gov/pmc/articles/PMC6122668/ (accessed 6 September 2023)

Ibbotsen, C. (2022) 'Which professions would Britons back going on strike?', YouGov, 21 July. https://yougov.co.uk/topics/economy/articles-reports/2022/07/21/which-professions-would-britons-back-going-strike (accessed 23 September 2023)

Isaac, A. (2023) 'Governments advised to cut public spending or raise taxes to curb inflation', *Guardian*, 25 June. www.theguardian.com/business/2023/jun/25/governments-advised-to-cut-public-spending-or-raise-taxes-to-curb-inflation (accessed 7 October 2023)

Ives, P. (2018) 'Gramsci's common sense: inequality and its narratives', *Contemporary Political Theory*, 17 (1): 22–25. DOI: https://doi.org/10.1057/s41296-017-0107-1

Jackson, D. and Moloney, K. (2016) 'Inside churnalism: PR, journalism and power relations in flux', *Journalism Studies*, 17(6): 763–80. DOI: https://doi.org/10.1080/1461670X.2015.1017597

Jaspers, E. (2018) 'Values', *Oxford Bibliographies*, 27 October. www.oxfordbibliographies.com/view/document/obo-9780199756384/obo-9780199756384-0182.xml (accessed 27 May 2024)

Jackson, H. and Ormerod, P. (2017) 'Was Michael Gove right? Have we had enough of experts?', *Prospect*, 14 July. www.prospectmagazine.co.uk/essays/44655/was-michael-gove-right-have-we-had-enough-of-experts (accessed 19 September 2023)

Jayakumar, S., Ang, B. and Anwar. N. D. (eds) (2021) *Disinformation and Fake News*. Singapore: Palgrave Macmillan.

Jenson, T. and Tyler, I. (2015) 'Benefits broods: the cultural and political crafting of anti-welfare commonsense', *Critical Social Policy*, 4(35): 470–91. DOI: https://doi.org/10.1177/02610183156008

Johns, S. (2020) 'Neil Ferguson talks modelling, lockdown and scientific advice with MPs', Imperial College London, 10 June. www.imperial.ac.uk/news/198155/neil-ferguson-talks-modelling-lockdown-scientific/ (accessed 7 October 2023)

Johnson, J. (2019) 'Analysis of primetime MSNBC programs finds Sanders received "least" and "most negative" coverage of top 2020 Democrats', *Common Dreams*, 14 November. www.commondreams.org/news/2019/11/14/analysis-primetime-msnbc-programs-finds-sanders-received-least-and-most-negative (accessed 19 September)

Johnston, I. (2017) 'Donald Trump stopping US government scientists from speaking out publicly is "chilling"', *Independent*, 25 January. www.independent.co.uk/climate-change/news/donald-trump-gag-us-government-scientists-environment-stop-speaking-public-tweeting-twitter-climate-change-a7544971.html (accessed 19 September 2023)

Jorge, A. (2019) 'Social media, interrupted: users recounting temporary disconnection on Instagram', *Social Media + Society*, 5(4). DOI: https://doi.org/10.1177/2056305119881691

The Jouker (2019) 'BBC has explaining to do over record Farage Question Time appearance', *National*, 10 May. www.thenational.scot/news/17631396.bbc-explaining-record-farage-question-time-appearance/ (accessed 17 September 2023)

Jowit, J. (2013) 'Strivers v shirkers: the language of the welfare debate', *Guardian*, 8 January. www.theguardian.com/politics/2013/jan/08/strivers-shirkers-language-welfare (accessed 18 September 2023)

Jurkowitz, M. et al. (2020) 'U.S. media polarization and the 2020 election: a nation divided', Pew Research Center, 24 January. www.pewresearch.org/journalism/2020/01/24/u-s-media-polarization-and-the-2020-election-a-nation-divided/ (accessed 6 September 2023)

Kahan, D. M. (2015) 'What is the "science of science communication?"', *Journal of Science Communication*, 14(3): 1–12. Yale Law School, Public Law Research Paper no. 539. DOI: https://doi.org/10.2139/ssrn.2562025

Khamis, S., Lawrence, A. and Welling, R. (2017) 'Self-branding, "micro-celebrity" and the rise of social media influencers', *Celebrity Studies*, 2(8): 191–208. DOI: https://doi.org/10.1080/19392397.2016.1218292 www.engender.org.uk/content/publications/Gendered-online-harassment-of-women-journalists.pdf (accessed 6 October 2023)

Kirk, I. (2022) 'Non-dom scandal and COVID fines send Johnson and Sunak favourability scores tumbling', YouGov, 19 April. yougov.co.uk/politics/articles/42164-non-dom-scandal-and-covid-fines-send-johnson-and-s (accessed 23 September 2023)

Kish, C. (2022) 'Gendered online harassment of women journalists: a review of research, employment laws and gender equality policies for Scotland', Engender report.

Klein, N. (2014) 'Climate change is the fight of our lives – yet we can hardly bear to look at it', *Guardian*, 23 April. www.theguardian.com/commentisfree/2014/apr/23/climate-change-fight-of-our-lives-naomi-klein (accessed 7 October 2023)

Klein, N. (2019) *On Fire: The Burning Case for a Green New Deal*. UK: Allen Lane.

Kreiss, D. (2015) 'The problem of citizens: E-democracy for actually existing democracy', *Social Media + Society*, 1(2). DOI: https://doi.org/10.1177/2056305115616151

Kreiss, D. (2017) 'The fragmenting of the civil sphere: how partisan identity shapes the moral evaluation of candidates and epistemology', *American Journal of Cultural Sociology*, 5: 443–59. DOI: https://doi.org/10.1057/s41290-017-0039-5

Kwan Wei, K. T. (2024) '"Free speech absolutist" Elon Musk explains his decision to ban Hamas' X account: "This was a tough call"', Business Insider Africa, 9 January. https://africa.businessinsider.com/politics/free-speech-absolutist-elon-musk-explains-his-decision-to-ban-hamas-x-account-this/6j9f1d5 (accessed 4 June 2024)

Laffan, B. (2014) 'Framing the crisis, defining the problems: decoding the Euro area crisis', *Perspectives on European Politics and Society*, 15(3): 266–80. DOI: https://doi.org/10.1080/15705854.2014.912395

Langer, G. (2020) '64% distrust Trump on coronavirus pandemic; approval declines as cases grow: POLL', ABC, 17 July. abcnews.go.com/Politics/64-distrust-trump-coronavirus-pandemic-approval-declines-cases/story?id=71779279 (accessed 17 September 2023)

Larana, E. (1994) *New Social Movements: From Ideology to Identity*. Philadelphia: Temple University Press.

Lawton, C. and Ackrill, R. (2016) 'Hard evidence: how areas with low immigration voted mainly for Brexit', *Conversation*, 8 July. theconversation.com/

hard-evidence-how-areas-with-low-immigration-voted-mainly-for-brexit-62138 (accessed 23 September 2023)

Lazarsfeld, P., Berelson, B. and Gaudet, H. (1968) *The People's Choice*. New York: Columbia University Press.

Lazarsfeld, P. F. and Merton, R. K. (1971) 'Mass communication, popular taste, and organized social action'. In W. Schramm, W. and Roberts, D. F. (eds), *The Process and Effects of Mass Communication*. Urbana and Chicago, IL: University of Illinois Press, pp. 554–78.

Lee, J. and Hyunjoo L (2010) 'The computer-mediated communication network: exploring the linkage between the online community and social capital', *New Media and Society*, 12(5): 711–27. DOI: https://doi.org/10.1177/1461444809343568

Leong, A. D. and Ho, S. S. (2021) 'Perceiving online public opinion: the impact of Facebook opinion cues, opinion climate congruency, and source credibility on speaking out', *New Media & Society*;23(9): 2495–515. DOI: https://doi.org/10.1177/1461444820931054

Lesh, M. and Nie, K. (2022) 'Cutting through: how to address the cost of living crisis', Institute for Economic Affairs, June. iea.org.uk/wp-content/uploads/2022/07/DP111_Cutting-Through_web17389-1.pdf (accessed 7 October 2023)

Levitz, E. (2020) 'This one chart explains why the kids back Bernie', *Intelligencer*, 15 February. nymag.com/intelligencer/2020/02/this-one-chart-explains-why-young-voters-back-bernie-sanders.html (accessed 26 September 2023)

Lewis, J., Wahl-Jorgensen, K. and Inthorn, S. (2004) 'Images of citizenship on television news: constructing a passive public', *Journalism Studies*, 5(2): 153–64. DOI: https://doi.org/10.1080/1461670042000211140

Lippmann, W. (2010) *Public Opinion*. US: Greenbook Publications, LLC.

Liu, C. (2021) *Virtue Hoarders: The Case against the Professional Managerial Class*. Minneapolis: University of Minnesota Press.

Livingstone, S. (2013) 'The participation paradigm in audience research'. *The Communication Review*, 16(1–2), 21–30. DOI: https://doi.org/10.1080/10714421.2013.757174

Lorenzoni, I. and Pidgeon, N. F. (2006) 'Public views on climate change: European and USA perspectives', *Climatic Change*, 77: 73–95. DOI: https://doi.org/10.1007/s10584-006-9072-z

Luhmann, N. (2000) 'Familiarity, confidence, trust: problems and alternatives'. In: Gambetta, D. (ed.) *Trust: Making and Breaking Cooperative Relations*. Oxford: Department of Sociology, University of Oxford, pp. 94–107.

Lujala, P. Lein, H. and Ketil Rød, J. (2015) 'Climate change, natural hazards, and risk perception: the role of proximity and personal experience', *Local Environment*, 20(4): 489–509. DOI: https://doi.org/10.1080/13549839.2014.887666

Lukes, S. (2005) *Power: A Radical View*. 2nd edition. Hampshire: Palgrave Macmillan.

Macdonald, J., Marlow, M. and Bromley-Davenport, C. (2022) 'Pulling out all the stops: how the government can go for growth and cut the cost of living', The Adam Smith Institute. static1.squarespace.com/static/56eddde762cd9413e151ac92/t/62a7453d88b95723b67b7ad2/1655129406133/Pulling+Out+All+the+Stops+Version+5.pdf (accessed 7 October 2023)

Mach, K. J., Salas Reyes, R., Pentz, B. et al. (2021) 'News media coverage of COVID-19 public health and policy information', *Humanities and Social Sciences Communicationsi* 8: 220. DOI: https://doi.org/10.1057/s41599-021-00900-z

Marcuse, H. (2002) *One-Dimensional Man: Studies in the Ideology of Advanced Industrial Societyi*, Routledge Classics. Abingdon: Routledge.

Martin, G. and Roberts, S. (2012) 'Exploring legacies of the baby boomers in the twenty-first century', *The Sociological Review*, 69(4): 727–42. DOI: https://doi.org/10.1177/00380261211006326

Mason, R. and Elgot, J. (2023) 'BBC came under No 10 pressure to avoid using "lockdown" in early pandemic, leak shows', *Guardian*, 14 March. www.theguardian.com/media/2023/mar/14/bbc-editors-asked-journalists-to-avoid-using-lockdown-at-start-of-pandemic (accessed 7 October 2023)

Mast, J. and Temmerman, M. (2021) 'What's (the) news? Reassessing "news values" as a concept and methodology in the digital age', *Journalism Studies*, 22(6): 689–701. DOI: https://doi.org/10.1080/1461670X.2021.1917445

Matias, J. N. (2019) 'The civic labor of volunteer moderators online', *Social Media+ Society*, 5(2). DOI: https://doi.org/10.1177/2056305119836778

Mavron, N. (2021) Coronavirus and compliance with government guidance, UK: April 2021', Office for National Statistics. www.ons.gov.uk/peoplepopulationandcommunity/healthandsocialcare/conditionsanddiseases/bulletins/coronavirusandcompliancewithgovernmentguidanceuk/april2021 (accessed 23 September 2023)

McCombs, M. (2004) *Setting the Agenda: The Mass Media and Public Opinion*. Cambridge: Polity Press.

McDonnell, A. and Curtis, C. (2019) 'How Britain voted in the 2019 general election', YouGov, 17 December. yougov.co.uk/politics/articles/26925-how-britain-voted-2019-general-election?goal=0_494ca252da-415a00bd20–312673957&redirect_from=%2Ftopics%2Fpolitics%2Farticles-reports%2F2019%2F12%2F17%2Fhow-britain-voted-2019–general-election (accessed 26 September 2023)

McDonnell, J. (2020) 'Majority support new lockdown measures, but it's not helping the government', YouGov, 24 September. https://yougov.co.uk/topics/politics/articles-reports/2020/09/24/majority-support-new-lockdown-measures-its-not-hel (accessed 6 September 2023)

McLaren, L., Neundorf, A. and Paterson, I. (2020) 'Anti-immigration attitudes are disappearing among younger generations in Britain', *Conversation*, 27 August. https://theconversation.com/anti-immigration-attitudes-are-disappearing-among-younger-generations-in-britain-119856 (accessed 23 October 2023)

McVeigh, R. and Estep, K. (2019) *The Politics of Losing*. New York: Columbia University Press.

McVeigh, R., Cunningham, D. and Farrell, J. (2014) 'Political polarization as a social movement outcome: 1960s Klan activism and its enduring impact on political realignment in southern counties, 1960 to 2000', *American Sociological Review*, 79(6): 1144–71. DOI: https://doi.org/10.1177/0003122414555885

Meade, A. (2021) 'Rupert Murdoch's News Corp strikes deal as Facebook agrees to pay for Australian content', *Guardian*, 21 March. www.theguardian.com/

media/2021/mar/16/rupert-murdochs-news-corp-strikes-deal-as-facebook-agrees-to-pay-for-australian-content (accessed 6 October 2023)

Merrin, W. (2014) *Media Studies 2.0*. London: Routledge.

Merrin, W. (2021) 'Hyporeality, the society of the selfie and identification politics', *The Journal of Media Art Study and Theory*, 2(1), 16–39. DOI: https://doi.org/10.59547/26911566.2.1.02

Mills, T. (2016) *The BBC: Myth of a Public Service*. London and New York: Verso Books.

Mills, T. (2017) 'Media bias against Jeremy Corbyn shows how politicised reporting has become', *Conversation*, 26 January. https://theconversation.com/media-bias-against-jeremy-corbyn-shows-how-politicised-reporting-has-become-71593

Misra, T. (2016) 'Racial segregation, not economic hardship, explains Trump', Bloomberg, 16 August. www.bloomberg.com/news/articles/2016-08-16/gallup-economist-jonathan-rothwell-finds-trump-support-linked-to-lack-of-racial-diversity-not-economic-distress (accessed 23 September 2023)

Misztal, B. A. (1992) 'The notion of trust in social theory', *Policy, Organisation and Society*, 5(1), 6–15. DOI: https://doi.org/10.1080/10349952.1992.11876774

Molder, A. L., Lakind, A., Clemmons, Z. E. and Chen, K. (2021) 'Framing the global youth climate movement: a qualitative content analysis of Greta Thunberg's moral, hopeful, and motivational framing on Instagram', *The International Journal of Press/Politics*, 27(3), 668–95. DOI: https://doi.org/10.1177/19401612211055691

Möllering, G. (2001) 'The nature of trust: from Georg Simmel to a theory of expectation, interpretation and suspension', *Sociology*, 35(2): 403–20. DOI: https://doi.org/10.1177/S0038038501000190

Montanaro, D., Kurtzleben, D. Horsley, S. et al. (2016) 'Fact check: Donald Trump's speech on immigration', NPR. 31 August. https://www.npr.org/2016/08/31/492096565/fact-check-donald-trumps-speech-on-immigration (accessed 27 May 2024)

Morgan, D. (2020) 'Women in politics face "daily" abuse on social media', BBC Online, 24 May. www.bbc.co.uk/news/uk-wales-politics-52785157 (accessed 6 October 2023)

Morley, D. (1980) *The Nationwide Audience*. London: BFI.

Morozov, E. (2019) 'Capitalism's New Clothes', *The Baffler*, 4 February. thebaffler.com/latest/capitalisms-new-clothes-morozov (accessed 6 October 2023)

Morris, C. and Reuben, A. (2020) 'Coronavirus: why are international comparisons difficult?', *BBC News*, 17 June. bbc.co.uk/news/52311014 (accessed 6 October 2023)

Moser, S. C., and Dilling, L. (2007) *Creating a Climate for Change: Communicating Climate Change and Facilitating Social Change*. Cambridge: Cambridge University Press.

Mudde, C., and Kaltwasser, C. R. (2017) *Populism: A Very Short Introduction*. New York: Oxford University Press.

Mudge, S. L. (2008) 'What is neo-liberalism?', *Socio-Economic Review*, 6(4): 703–31. DOI: https://doi.org/10.1093/ser/mwn016

Muntaner C. (2018) 'Digital platforms, gig economy, precarious employment, and the invisible hand of social class', *International Journal of Health Services*, 48(4): 597–600. DOI: https://doi.org/10.1177/0020731418801413

National Records of Scotland (2021) 'Deaths involving coronavirus (COVID-19) in Scotland'. www.nrscotland.gov.uk/statistics-and-data/statistics/statistics-by-theme/vital-events/general-publications/deaths-involving-coronavirus-covid-19-in-scotland/archive (accessed 7 October 2023)

Newman, N. et al. (2021) Reuters Institute Digital News Report 2021, Reuters Institute for the Study of Journalism, 23 June. https://ssrn.com/abstract=3873260

Newman, N. with Fletcher, R., Eddy, K. et al. (2023) 'Reuters Institute digital news report 2023', Reuters Institute for the Study of Journalism. https://reutersinstitute.politics.ox.ac.uk/sites/default/files/2023-06/Digital_News_Report_2023.pdf (accessed 9 September 2023)

NPR Staff (2016) 'Fact check and full transcript of the final 2016 presidential debate', NPR, 19 October. www.npr.org/2016/10/19/498293478/fact-check-trump-and-clinton-s-final-presidential-debate (accessed 15 September 2023)

Oborne, P. (2021) *The Assault on Truth*. London: Simon and Schuster.

O'Carroll, L. (2023) 'EU warns Elon Musk over "disinformation" on X about Hamas attack', *Guardian*, 10 October. https://www.theguardian.com/technology/2023/oct/10/eu-warns-elon-musk-over-disinformation-about-hamas-attack-on-x (accessed 4 June 2024)

Office for National Statistics (ONS) (2022) 'Deaths due to COVID-19, registered in England and Wales', 1 July. www.ons.gov.uk/peoplepopulationandcommunity/birthsdeathsandmarriages/deaths/datasets/deathsduetocovid19registeredinenglandandwales2020 (accessed 7 October 2023)

Oldroyd, R. (2016) 'Donald Trump and the media's "epic fail"', *Bureau of Investigative Journalism*, 9 November. www.thebureauinvestigates.com/blog/2016-11-09/donald-trump-and-the-medias-epic-fail (accessed 9 September 2023)

O'Neill, S. (2017) 'Engaging people with climate change imagery'. In: *The Oxford Encyclopedia of Climate Change Communication*, Oxford Research Encyclopedia (Climate Science). Oxford University Press. DOI: https://doi.org/10.1093/acrefore/9780190228620.013.371

O'Neill, S. J. (2019) 'Guest post: how heatwave images in the media can better represent climate risks', Carbon Brief, 29 August. /www.carbonbrief.org/guest-post-how-heatwave-images-in-the-media-can-better-represent-climate-risks/ (accessed 7 October 2023)

O'Neill, S. (2020) 'More than meets the eye: a longitudinal analysis of climate change imagery in the print media', *Climatic Change*, 163: 9–26. DOI: https://doi.org/10.1007/s10584-019-02504-8

Oreskes, M. and Conway, E. M. (2010) *Merchants of Doubt: How a Handful of Scientists Obscured the Truth on Issues from Tobacco Smoke to Global Warming*. New York: Bloomsbury Press,

Owen, G. (2022) 'Tories accuse Angela Rayner of Basic Instinct ploy to distract Boris: MPs claim Labour deputy leader likes to put PM "off his stride" by crossing and uncrossing her legs at PMQs', *Daily Mail*, 23 April. www.dailymail.co.uk/

news/article-10746873/Tories-accuse-Angela-Rayner-Basic-Instinct-ploy-crosses-uncrosses-legs-PMQs.html (accessed 23 September 2023)

Painter, J. (2013) *Climate Change in the Media: Reporting Risk and Uncertainty.* London: Bloomsbury Publishing.

Painter, J. (2023) 'Climate change: multi-country media analysis shows scepticism of the basic science is dying out', *Conversation*, 18 April. https://theconversation.com/climate-change-multi-country-media-analysis-shows-scepticism-of-the-basic-science-is-dying-out-198303 (accessed 29 January 2024)

Painter, J. et al. (2018) 'How 'digital-born' media cover climate change in comparison to legacy media: a case study of the COP 21 summit in Paris', *Global Environmental Change*, 48 (1–10). DOI: https://doi.org/10.1016/j.gloenvcha.2017.11.003

Papacharissi, Z. (2002) 'The virtual sphere: the internet as a public sphere', *New Media & Society*, 4(1): 9–27. DOI: https://doi.org/10.1177/14614440222226244

Parks, P. (2020) 'Is climate change a crisis – and who says so? An analysis of climate characterization in major U.S. news media', *Environmental Communication*, 14:1, 82–96, DOI: https://doi.org/10.1080/17524032.2019.1611614

Patterson, T. E. (2016) *News Coverage of the 2016 Presidential Primaries: Horse Race Reporting Has Consequences.* Cambridge: Shorenstein Center on Media, Politics and Public Policy.

Pearman, O. et al (2021) 'COVID-19 media coverage decreasing despite deepening crisis', *The Lancet*, 5(1), January: e6–37. DOI: https://doi.org/10.1016/S2542-5196(20)30303-X

Petley, J. (2015) 'How the Murdoch press has waged a relentless campaign against the BBC (and why it's worked)', *Conversation*, 26 August. /theconversation.com/how-the-murdoch-press-has-waged-a-relentless-campaign-against-the-bbc-and-why-its-worked-45523 (accessed 17 September 2023)

Pew Research Center (2019) 'Millennial life: how young adulthood today compares with prior generation', 14 February. www.pewresearch.org/social-trends/2019/02/14/millennial-life-how-young-adulthood-today-compares-with-prior-generations-2/ (accessed 2 February 2024)

Phelan, S. (2018) 'Neoliberalism and media'. In: Damien, C. Melinda, K. Martijn, M. and Primrose, D. (eds), *The SAGE Handbook of Neoliberalism.* London: SAGE Publications, pp. 539–52.

Philo, G. and Berry, M. (2023) '"We need to start building up what's called herd immunity": scientific dissensus and public broadcasting in the Covid-19 pandemic', *British Journal of Sociology*, 74(3): 453–75. DOI: https://doi.org/10.1111/1468-4446.13010

Philo, G, Briant, E. and Donald, P. (2013) *Bad News for Refugees.* London: Pluto Press.

Philo, G. and Happer, C. (2013) *Communicating Climate Change and Energy Security: New Methods in Understanding Audiences.* New York: Routledge.

Philo, G. and Hewitt, J. (1976) 'Trade unions and the media', *Industrial Relations Journal*, 7(3): 4–19. DOI: https://doi.org/10.1111/j.1468-2338.1976.tb00186.x

Philo, G., Miller, D. and Happer, C. (2015) 'Circuits of communication and structures of power: the sociology of the mass media'. In: Holborn, M. (ed.), *Contemporary Sociology.* Cambridge: Polity Press, pp. 444–70.

Plumer, B. (2016) 'Full transcript of Donald Trump's acceptance speech at the RNC', *Vox*, 22 July. www.vox.com/2016/7/21/12253426/donald-trump-acceptance-speech-transcript-republican-nomination-transcript (accessed 15 September 2023)

Plumer, B. (2021) 'On day 3 of the climate summit, Big Money makes a pledge', *New York Times*, 13 November. www.nytimes.com/live/2021/11/03/world/cop26–glasgow-climate-summit (accessed 7 October 2023)

Public Health England (2021) 'Appendix C: ethnic minority experiences of COVID-19', 3 December. www.gov.uk/government/publications/final-report-on-progress-to-address-covid-19-health-inequalities/appendix-c-ethnic-minority-experiences-of-covid-19#dissemination-and-application (accessed 23 September 2023)

Public Policy Polling (2017 'Americans think Trump will be worst president since Nixon', 26 January. www.publicpolicypolling.com/wpcontent/uploads/2017/09/PPP_Release_National_12617.pdf (accessed 19 September)

The Public Purse (2019) 'UK food bank facts and the challenges they face', 16 October. https://www.thepublicpurse.org.uk/welfare/uk-food-bank-facts-and-the-challenges-they-face/ (accessed 23 September 2023)

Ralph, P. and Relman, E. (2018) 'These are the most and least biased news outlets in the US, according to Americans', *Insider*, 2 September. www.businessinsider.com/most-biased-news-outlets-in-america-cnn-fox-nytimes-2018–8?r=US&IR=T (accessed 19 September 2023)

Rebich-Hespanha, S., Rice, R. E., Montello, D. R. et al. (2015) 'Image themes and frames in US print news stories about climate change', *Environmental Communication*, 9(4): 491–519. DOI: https://doi.org/10.1080/17524032.2014.983534

Reuters (2020) 'False claim: photo shows coffins of coronavirus victims in Italy', Reuters staff, 28 March. www.reuters.com/article/uk-factcheck-italy-coffins-idUSKBN21F0XL (accessed 7 October 2023)

Reynolds, M. (2019) 'The strange story of Section 230, the obscure law that created our flawed, broken internet', *Wired*, 24 March. www.wired.co.uk/article/section-230-communications-decency-act (accessed 6 October 2023)

Riegel, V. (2019) 'Migrants, diasporas and the media', *European Journal of Communication*, 34(6): 682–90. DOI: https://doi.org/10.1177/0267323119887856

Roberts, S. (2019) *Behind the Screen: Content Moderation in the Shadows of Social Media*. New Haven, CT: Yale University Press.

Rodgers, S. (2019) 'Labour's manifesto launch: "It's time for real change"', Labour List, 21 November. https://labourlist.org/2019/11/labours-manifesto-launch-its-time-for-real-change/ (accessed 2 February 2024)

Rosenbaum, M. (2017) 'Local voting figures shed new light on EU referendum', *BBC News*, 6 February. www.bbc.co.uk/news/uk-politics-38762034 (accessed 23 October 2023)

Rothwell, J. T. and Diego-Rosell, P. (2016) 'Explaining nationalist political views: the case of Donald Trump', *SSRN*, 2 November. DOI: https://doi.org/10.2139/ssrn.2822059

Roucaute, D. (2022) 'Heat wave "likely" to have caused over 11,000 additional deaths in France this summer', *Le Monde*, 6 September. www.lemonde.fr/en/

france/article/2022/09/06/heat-wave-likely-to-have-caused-over-11-000-additional-deaths-in-france-this-summer_5996012_7.html (accessed 23 October 2023)

Sample, I. (2021) 'Covid timeline: the weeks leading up to first UK lockdown', *Guardian*, 12 October. www.theguardian.com/world/2021/oct/12/covid-timeline-the-weeks-leading-up-to-first-uk-lockdown (accessed 7 October 2023)

Sample, I. and Walker, P. (2021) 'Covid response "one of UK's worst ever public health failures"', *Guardian*, 12 October. www.theguardian.com/politics/2021/oct/12/covid-response-one-of-uks-worst-ever-public-health-failures (accessed 6 September 2023)

Savage, M. (2015) *Social Class in the 21st Century*. Milton Keynes: Pelican.

Sayer, A. (2004) 'Moral economy'. Department of Sociology, Lancaster University. www.comp.lancs.ac.uk/sociology/papers/sayer-moral-economy.pdf (accessed 23 October 2023)

Schaeffer, K. (2021) 'Despite wide partisan gaps in views of many aspects of the pandemic, some common ground exists', Pew Research Center. www.pewresearch.org/fact-tank/2021/03/24/despite-wide-partisan-gaps-in-views-of-many-aspects-of-the-pandemic-some-common-ground-exists/ (accessed 23 September 2023)

Schertzer, R. and Woods, E. (2021) '#Nationalism: the ethno-nationalist populism of Donald Trump's Twitter communication', *Ethnic and Racial Studies*, 44(7): 1154–73. DOI: https://doi.org/10.1080/01419870.2020.1713390

Schudson, M. (1978) *Discovering the News*. New York: Basic Books.

Scott, M. (2023) 'Hamas hate videos make Elon Musk Europe's digital enemy No. 1', *Político*, 11 October. https://www.politico.eu/article/twitter-x-hamas-images-elon-musk-europe-content-police/ (accessed 4 June 2024)

Seering, J., Wang, T., Yoon, J. et al. (2019) 'Moderator engagement and community development in the age of algorithms', *New Media and Society*, 21(7): 1417–43. DOI: https://doi.org/10.1177/1461444818821316

Shields, F. (2019) 'Why we're rethinking the images we use for our climate journalism', *Guardian*, 18 October. www.theguardian.com/environment/2019/oct/18/guardian-climate-pledge-2019-images-pictures-guidelines (accessed 7 October 2023)

Shoemaker, P. J. (1991) *Gatekeeping*, Communication Concepts 3. Newbury Park, CA: Sage.

Shoemaker, P. J. and Vos, T. P. (2009) *Gatekeeping Theory*. London: Routledge.

Silverstein, J. (2018) 'Russian bots retweeted Trump 500,000 times at end of 2016 campaign, created fake Facebook events seen by thousands', *Newsweek*, 28 January. www.newsweek.com/russian-bots-facebook-twitter-trump-2016-campaign-793122 (accessed 6 October 2023)

Simmel, G. (1978) *The Philosophy of Money*. London: Routledge.

Skeggs, B. (2009) 'The moral economy of person production: the class relations of self-performance on "reality" television', *Sociological Review*, 57(4). DOI: https://doi.org/10.1111/j.1467-954X.2009.01865.x

Skeggs, B. and Yuill, S. (2019) 'Subjects of value and digital personas: reshaping the bourgeois subject, unhinging property from personhood#', *Subjectivity*, 12: 82–99. DOI: https://doi.org/10.1057/s41286-018-00063-4

Skinner, G. (2020) 'More people staying at home as concern about coronavirus increases', Ipsos, 2 April. www.ipsos.com/en-uk/more-people-staying-home-concern-about-coronavirus-increases (accessed 7 October 2023)

Skinner, G. and Mortimore, R. (2017) 'How Britain Voted in the 2017 Election', Ipsos, 21 June. www.ipsos.com/en/how-britain-voted-2017-election (accessed 26 September 2023)

Smith, M. (2020) 'YouGov's "top issues tracker" finds worry over the two concepts marching in lockstep', YouGov, 8 July. yougov.co.uk/topics/politics/articles-reports/2020/07/08/concern-over-health-and-economy-are-now-conjoined- (accessed 7 October 2023)

Smith, M. (2022) 'What impact is the cost of living crisis having on support for tackling climate change?', YouGov, 12 October. https://yougov.co.uk/topics/politics/articles-reports/2022/10/12/what-impact-cost-living-crisis-having-support-tack (accessed 23 October 2023)

Sobolewska, M. and Ford, R. (2020) *Brexitland: Identity, Diversity and the Reshaping of British Politics*. Cambridge: Cambridge University Press.

Solís Arce, J. S., Warren, S. S., Meriggi, N. F. et al. (2021) 'COVID-19 vaccine acceptance and hesitancy in low- and middle-income countries', *Nature Medicine*, 27: 1385–94. DOI: https://doi.org/10.1038/s41591-021-01454-y (accessed 6 September 2023)

Sosenko, F., Bramley, G. and Bhattacharjee, A. (2022) 'Understanding the post-2010 increase in food bank use in England: new quasi-experimental analysis of the role of welfare policy', *BMC Public Health*, 22: 1363. DOI: https://doi.org/10.1186/s12889-022-13738-0

Squirrell, T. (2019) 'Platform dialectics: the relationships between volunteer moderators and end users on reddit', *New Media & Society*, 21(9): 1910–27. DOI: https://doi.org/10.1177/1461444819834317

Stacey, K. and Politi, J. (2021) 'Republicans urge supporters to embrace vaccines in abrupt shift of tone', *Financial Times*, 23 July. www.ft.com/content/fc3db449-b312-4d1d-8acd-58cee1bce594 (accessed 6 October 2023)

Statista (2016) 'Should the United Kingdom remain a member of the European Union or leave the European Union?', June. www.statista.com/statistics/572613/eu-referendum-decision-by-highest-educational-attainment-uk/ (accessed 23 September 2023)

Statista (2023) 'Number of trade union members in the United Kingdom from 1892 to 2021', May. https://www.statista.com/statistics/287241/uk-trade-union-membership/ (accessed 23 September 2023)

Stempeck, M. (2019) 'See Big Tech's terrible diversity record, visualized using its logos. Fast Company', 11 November. www.fastcompany.com/90428465/see-big-techs-terrible-diversity-record-visualized-using-its-logos (accessed 6 October 2023)

Sternberg, J. (2012) *Misbehavior in Cyber Places: The Regulation of Online Conduct in Virtual Communities on the Internet*. Lanham, MD: Rowman & Littlefield.

Stephens, D. (2021) 'Will social distancing end on July 19? The latest Covid rules explained', LBC, 5 July. www.lbc.co.uk/hot-topics/coronavirus/social-distancing-rules-end-july-19/ (accessed 6 September 2023)

Stone, J. (2020) 'Coronavirus: UK lockdown supported by 93 per cent of public, poll finds', *Independent*, 24 March. www.independent.co.uk/news/uk/politics/coronavirus-uk-lockdown-boris-johnson-poll-yougov-latest-a9420526.html (accessed 28 August 2023)

Strandberg, T. (2020) 'Coronavirus: US and UK governments losing public trust', *Conversation*, 6 May. theconversation.com/coronavirus-us-and-uk-governments-losing-public-trust-137713 (accessed 19 September 2023)

Strauss, C. (2014) *Making Sense of Public Opinion: American Discourses about Immigration and Social Programs*. Cambridge: Cambridge University Press.

Sullivan, M. (2016) 'The media didn't want to believe Donald Trump could win. So they looked the other way', *National Post*, 9 November. nationalpost.com/news/world/the-media-didnt-want-to-believe-donald-trump-could-win-so-they-looked-the-other-way (accessed 17 September 2023)

Sulzberger, A. and Baquet, B. (2016) 'To our readers, from the publisher and executive editor', *New York Times*, 13 November. www.nytimes.com/2016/11/13/us/elections/to-our-readers-from-the-publisher-and-executive-editor.html (accessed 17 September 2023)

Suzor, N. P., Myers West, S., Quodling, A. and York, J. (2019) 'What do we mean when we talk about transparency? Toward meaningful transparency in commercial content moderation'. *International Journal of Communication*, 13(18): 1526–154. www.eprints.qut.edu.au/126386/11/126386p.pdf (accessed 6 October 2023)

Swaine, J. (2017) 'Donald Trump's team defends "alternative facts" after widespread protests', *Guardian*, 23 January. www.theguardian.com/us-news/2017/jan/22/donald-trump-kellyanne-conway-inauguration-alternative-facts (accessed 17 September 2023)

Thompson, E. P. (1963) *The Making of the English Working Class*. London: Victor Gollancz.

Tilley, B. P. (2020) '"I am the law and order candidate": a content analysis of Donald Trump's race-baiting dog whistles in the 2016 presidential campaign', *Psychology*, 11(12): 1941–74. DOI: https://doi.org/10.4236/psych.2020.1112123

Tingle, R. (2022) 'Poll shows support for rail strikes has INCREASED to 45 PER CENT after crippling walkout caused commuter hell but was embraced by others who got to spend week WFH', *Daily Mail Online*, 28 June. www.dailymail.co.uk/news/article-10960125/Poll-shows-support-rail-strikes-INCREASED-45-CENT.html (accessed 23 September 2023)

Trentini, M. (2022) 'Political attitudes, participation and union membership in the UK', *Industrial Relations Journal*, 53(1), 19–34. DOI: https://doi.org/10.1111/irj.12352

Turner, B. S. and Edmunds, J. (2002) 'The distaste of taste: Bourdieu, cultural capital and the Australian postwar elite', *Journal of Consumer Culture*, 2(2): 219–39. DOI: https://doi.org/10.1177/146954050200200204

Tyler, I. (2020) *Stigma: The Machinery of Inequality*. London: Zed Books.

Tyson, A., Funk, C., Kennedy, B. and Johnson, C. (2022) 'Majority in U.S. says public health benefits of COVID-19 restrictions worth the costs, even as large shares also see downsides', Pew Research Center, 15 September.

www.pewresearch.org/science/2021/09/15/majority-in-u-s-says-public-health-benefits-of-covid-19-restrictions-worth-the-costs-even-as-large-shares-also-see-downsides/ (accessed 23 September 2023)

Tyson, A. and Manium, S. (2016) 'Behind Trump's victory: divisions by race, gender, education', Pew Research Center, 9 November. www.pewresearch.org/short-reads/2016/11/09/behind-trumps-victory-divisions-by-race-gender-education/ (accessed 26 September 2023)

University of Glasgow (2021) 'UNIVERSITY OF GLASGOW PUBLISHES ACTION PLAN TO TACKLE RACISM AND RACIAL HARASSMENT ON CAMPUS', University News, 17 February. www.gla.ac.uk/news/archiveofnews/2021/february/headline_773866_en.html (accessed 23 September 2023)

Vaccari, C. and Valeriani, A. (2018) 'Digital political talk and political participation: comparing established and third wave democracies', *SAGE Open*, 8(2). DOI: https://doi.org/10.1177/2158244018784986

Vachon, T. E., Wallace, M. and Hyde, A. (2016) 'Union decline in a neoliberal age: globalization, financialization, European Integration, and union density in 18 affluent democracies', *Socius*, 2. DOI: https://doi.org/10.1177/2378023116656847

van der Veen, O. (2023) 'Political polarisation compared: creating the comparative political polarisation index', *European Political Science*, 22: 260–80. DOI: https://doi.org/10.1057/s41304-022-00400-x

Vanugopal, R. (2015) 'Neoliberalism as concept', *Economy and Society*, 44 (2): 165–87. DOI: https://doi.org/10.1080/03085147.2015.1013356

Virdee, S. (2014) *Racism, Class and the Racialized Outsider*. London: Palgrave Macmillan.

Virdee, S. (2023) 'The lines of descent of the present crisis', *The Sociological Review*, 71(2): 458–76. DOI: https://doi.org/10.1177/00380261221150341

Virdee, S. and McGeever, B. (2018) 'Racism, crisis, Brexit', *Ethnic and Racial Studies*, 41(10): 1802–19. DOI: https://doi.org/10.1080/01419870.2017.1361544

Wahl-Jorgensen, K., Berry, M., Garcia-Blanco, I., Bennett, L. and Cable, J. (2017) 'Rethinking balance and impartiality in journalism? How the BBC attempted and failed to change the paradigm', *Journalism*, 18(7): 781–800. DOI: https://doi.org/10.1177/1464884916648094

Wall, T. (2022) 'Industrial disputes in UK at highest in five years as inflation hits pay', *Guardian*, 2 April. www.theguardian.com/uk-news/2022/apr/02/strikes-in-uk-at-highest-in-five-years-as-pay-is-hit-by-inflation (accessed 23 September 2023)

Waterson, J. (2022) 'BBC preparing to go online-only over next decade, says director general', *Guardian*, 7 December. www.theguardian.com/media/2022/dec/07/bbc-will-go-online-only-by-2030s-says-director-general (accessed 6 October 2023)

Webster, F. and Robins, K. (1998) 'The iron cage of the information society', *Information, Communication & Society*, 1(1): 23–45. DOI: https://doi.org/10.1080/13691189809358952

Weigel, M. (2016) 'Political correctness: how the right invented a phantom enemy', *Guardian*, 30 November. www.theguardian.com/us-news/2016/nov/30/political-correctness-how-the-right-invented-phantom-enemy-donald-trump (accessed 15 September 2023)

Weldon, D. (2023) 'Jeremy Hunt's economic optimism will collide with voters' realities', *New Statesman*, 15 March. www.newstatesman.com/comment/2023/03/jeremy-hunt-economic-optimism-will-clash-voters-realities (accessed 7 October 2023)

Wellesley, L., Happer, C. and Froggatt, A. (2015) *Changing Climate, Changing Diets: Pathways to Lower Meat Consumption*. London: Chatham House.

Wheelwright, S. (2023) 'Why smaller, more private communities are thriving', *Medium*, 31 July. uxdesign.cc/small-is-the-new-big-in-social-1f2c9ab4ab43 (accessed 9 January 2024)

Whitmarsh, L. (2008) 'Are flood victims more concerned about climate change than other people? The role of direct experience in risk perception and behavioural response', *Journal of Risk Research*, 11(3): 351–74. DOI: https://doi.org/10.1080/13669870701552235

Whitmarsh, L. E., O'Neill, S. and Lorenzoni, I. (2013) 'Public engagement with climate change: what do we know and where do we go from here?', *International Journal of Media & Cultural Politics*, 9(1): 7–25. DOI: https://doi.org/10.1386/macp.9.1.7_1

Widmaier, W. W., Blyth, M. and Seabrooke, L. (2007) 'Exogenous shocks or endogenous constructions? The meanings of wars and crises', *International Studies Quarterly*, 51(4): 747–59. DOI: https://doi.org/10.1111/j.1468-2478.2007.00474.x

Wilkins, D. (2020) 'Biden presidency could be "more protectionist" than Trump, former U.S. ambassador says', *National Post*. https://nationalpost.com/news/world/biden-presidency-could-be-more-protectionist-than-trump-former-u-s-ambassador-says (accessed 23 October 2023)

Wilson, S. (2022) 'The working class is back', Yorkshire Bylines, 19 August. https://yorkshirebylines.co.uk/business/economy/the-working-class-is-back/ (accessed 5 June 2024)

Woodcock, A. (2021) 'Survey finds tumbling trust in Boris Johnson's handling of pandemic', *Independent*, 1 March. independent.co.uk/news/uk/politics/edelman-trust-barometer-coronavirus-pandemic-b1808812.html (accessed 19 September 2023)

World Health Organization (WHO) (2021) 'Climate change and health', 30 October. www.who.int/news-room/fact-sheets/detail/climate-change-and-health (accessed 7 October 2023)

Yang, S., Quan-Haase, A. and Rannenberg, K. (2017) 'The changing public sphere on Twitter: network structure, elites and topics of the #righttobeforgotten', *New Media & Society*, 19(12): 1983–2002. DOI: https://doi.org/10.1177/1461444816651409 (accessed 6 September 2023)

Yates, S. and Lockley, E. (2018) 'Social media and social class', *American Behavioral Scientist*, 62(9): 1291–1316. DOI: https://doi.org/10.1177/0002764218773821

Yerushalmy, J. (2022) 'Zero-Covid policy: why is China still having severe lockdowns?', *Guardian*, 29 November. www.theguardian.com/world/2022/nov/29/china-zero-covid-policy-what-is-it-and-why-lockdowns-quarantine-protests (accessed 7 October 2023)

York, J. (2021) *Silicon Values: The Future of Free Speech under Surveillance Capitalism*. London and New York: Verso Books.

YouGov (2022a) 'COVID-19 fears: YouGov COVID 19-tracker', 17 March. yougov.co.uk/topics/international/articles-reports/2020/03/17/fear-catching-covid-19 (accessed 7 October 2023)

YouGov (2022b) 'How well is Boris Johnson doing as Prime Minister?', YouGov Tracker, 29 August. yougov.co.uk/topics/politics/trackers/boris-johnson-approval-rating (accessed 19 September)

Zhang, X. and Dong, D. (2009) 'Ways of identifying the opinion leaders in virtual communities', *International Journal of Biometrics*, 3(7). DOI: https://doi.org/10.5539/ijbm.v3n7p21

Zelizer, B. (1993) 'Journalists as interpretive communities', *Critical Studies in Mass Communication*, 10(3): 219–37. DOI: https://doi.org/10.1080/15295039309366865

Zerback, T., Koch, T. and Krämer, B. (2015) 'Thinking of others: effects of implicit and explicit media cues on climate of opinion perceptions', *Journalism & Mass Communication Quarterly*, 92(2): 421–43. DOI: https://doi.org/10.1177/1077699015574481

Zhang, C. and Burn-Murdoch, J. (2020) 'By numbers: how the US voted in 2020', *Financial Times*, 7 November. https://www.ft.com/content/69f3206f-37a7-4561-bebf-5929e7df850d (accessed 26 September 2023)

Zhao, E., Wu, Q., Crimmins, E. M. et al. (2020) 'Media trust and infection mitigating behaviours during the COVID-19 pandemic in the USA', *British Medical Journal Global Health*, 5(10): e003323. DOI: https://doi.org/10.1136/bmjgh-2020-003323

Zuboff, S. (2019) *The Age of Surveillance Capitalism*. London: Profile Books.

Index

active audience research 56, 59, 76–7
Adam Smith Institute 135
algorithms 99, 100–1, 105, 147
Al Jaber, Sultan 137
Al Jazeera 83
Amazon Corporation 102
anti-immigration sentiments 35
anti-semitism 104, 109
anti-vaccine movement 10
Apple Corporation 102
Arendt, Hannah 37, 50
atomisation 37–8
austerity 27, 67, 127, 135, 145

Bad News for Refugees 88
Bakhtin, Mikhail 4
Bank of England 136
Baraka, Ajamu 48
Bauman, Zygmunt 37
BBC 42, 47, 64, 92, 102, 133, 137, 152–3
    attacks on 34–5, 38–9
    reporting on Covid by 124–5
    impact of neoliberalism on 29–30
Biden, Joe 40, 78, 80
Big Tech 102, 105–6, 118, 152
Bolsonaro, Jair 36
bots 110–11
botwatch 110
Bourdieu, Pierre 11–12, 16, 51, 91
boyd, danah 59, 81
Brand, Russell 20, 21
Brexit 7–8, 17, 29, 34–5, 39, 77–8, 80, 83, 93, 100, 110, 127, 146
Britain
    and Covid 1, 12–13, 46, 53–4, 98, 124–5

election (2017) 78
EU Referendum (2016) 7, 34, 35
    and Poll Tax 7
Bureau of Investigative Journalism 39, 40
Burley, Kay 92

Cambridge Analytica 100, 110, 147
Cameron, David 7
cancel culture 8, 114–15
CBBC (tv channel) 126
CBS (news channel) 39
Channel 4 (tv channel) 20, 21
Chatham House 14, 160
China 99, 103
    and Covid 123, 130
Chomsky, Noam 3, 25
class 59, 73–4, 78–90, 150
    see also middle class; professional-managerial class; working class
climate activism 82, 137–40, 146
climate change 20, 51, 79, 122–3, 129, 145–6
    as cause of deaths 134
    media reporting on 132–5
    research methodology with focus groups 160–3
    see also climate crisis
Climate Change Act (2008) 145
climate change sceptics 63–4
climate crisis 122–3, 133–5
Clinton, Bill 34
Clinton, Hillary 33, 40, 78, 80, 146
CNN (news channel) 39
'common sense' 9, 12, 26–7
Common Sense Media 151

Communicating Climate Change and Energy Security 159
communication circuits 6, 29, 97–8, 101–2
communications agencies 29
consent: manufacture of 3, 25, 101
Conservative Party 54, 89, 92, 126
conspiracy theories 34, 64, 146
COP (Conference of the Parties)
    COP 26 (2021) 137–8
    COP 28 (2023) 137–8
Corbyn, Jeremy 9–10, 38, 40–1, 82
cost-of-living crisis 20, 125–7, 135–6
COVID-19 pandemic 44–5, 53–4, 98, 123–5, 129–32
    attitudes to mitigation measures 69–70
    impact on ethnic groups 84
    lockdown 1, 13, 124–5
    media coverage of 129–32
    mortality rates 130, 134–5
    see also anti-vaccine movement
crime and punishment: attitudes to 54–5
crises 121–2, 129
    see also cost-of-living crisis; COVID-19; climate crisis; energy crisis
Cultural Studies 75
culture wars 8, 89

Daily Mail 87, 151
Daily Telegraph 34, 35, 125
data collection 99–100
Digger (magazine) 84
digital media
    management of 96–7, 152
    regulation of 99–100
digital technology 25–6
Discord (platform) 21, 63
Donald, Rosalind 122
Drake (rapper) 115

'echo chambers' 59–60
Edelman Trust 45
education 80–1
    culture of 79–82
Ehrenreich, Barbara and John 85–6
elites 4, 21, 119, 149
    attacks on 33, 34, 39, 45

Elliott, Rebecca 91
employment
    flexibility and gig economy 27–8
    and identity 28
energy crisis 125–6
ethnic groups 75, 83–4
    impact of Covid on 84
European Union 93, 99–100
Extinction Rebellion 132–3

Facebook 20, 58, 64, 85, 99, 100, 103, 105, 107, 116
'fake news' 10, 41–2, 148, 150–1
Farage, Nigel 34–5, 38, 39
Fauci, Anthony 46
Federal Trade Commission (FTC) 100
film industry: diversity in 89
Financial Times 48
Fisher, Mark 50
focus groups 15–16, 33, 50–2, 67, 88
    research methodology on 155–60, 165
food banks 126–7
Ford, Matthew and Andrew Hoskins
    Radical War 101
Fox News 34, 38, 39
Frankfurt School 75
Fraser, Nancy 28
free market economy *see* neoliberalism
Fukuyama, Francis 26

gatekeeping 25, 98, 103
Gdelt Project 133
General Data Protection Regulation (2018) 100
generation divide 51, 77–9, 80, 88–91, 150
    'boomers' and 'millenials' 77–8, 89, 91
Gerbaudo, Paulo 36, 47
Giddens, Anthony 24
Glasgow 84
Glasgow University Media Group 15, 92, 97, 154, 159
Glasgow University report (2019) 88–9
Global Financial Crisis (2008) 27, 31, 50, 67, 82, 86, 127, 136
Good Morning Britain (tv programme) 92–3
Google 99, 102

Gore, Al 145
Gove, Michael 42
Gramsci, Antonio 5, 26, 32, 50, 76
Guardian, The 83, 133

Habermas, Jürgen 11, 108
Hall, Stuart 4, 8, 24–5, 27, 50, 59, 75–7
   and 'maps of meaning' 76
Hamas attack on Israel (2023) 104
Harvey, David 10, 28, 30
Hautea, Samantha [et al.] 138, 139
health: as priority 53–4
hegemony 21, 26–7
Herman, Edward and Noam Chomsky 3, 25
Hezbollah 104
Higher Education (Freedom of Speech) Bill (2023) 8
Hoggart, Richard *The Uses of Literacy* 74–5, 95
Holocaust denial 109
Hopkins, Katie 115
Hunt, Jeremy 126, 136

identity and alignment 59–60, 94, 150
ideology 26–7, 49–53, 76
immigration and immigrants 34–5, 84, 88, 121
   attitudes to 68–9
   'migrant crisis' 121
   see also anti-immigration
Independent 133
Independent Food Aid Network 126–7
individual freedom 10, 27–8
individualisation 27, 37, 150
individualism 10–11, 27, 30
Infowars (website) 34
Instagram 20, 64, 102, 116, 138–9, 146
Institute of Economic Affairs (IEA) 135
instrumentarianism 99
Intergovernmental Panel on Climate Change (IPCC) 122, 133
   Fourth Assessment Report 145
internet 99, 102
interpersonal communities 49, 55–8, 73, 80–1
intersectionality 59

Ipsos MORI 78
Iraq war 29, 31
IRL (in real life) 68, 113, 143
Israel/Palestine 104, 109
Italy: and Covid 132

Jaspers, Eva 53
Johnson, Boris 35–6, 39, 42, 46, 89–90
Jorge, Ana 52
journalism and journalists 12–13, 24–5, 32, 39, 40, 42–3, 132, 148–9
   female journalists 117–18
   professional journalists 19–20, 21, 108
   and proximity 128–9
   and public interest 128
   social contract with public 2–3
justice system
   attitudes to 66, 161–2

King's College London Policy Institute 79
Kish, Claire 117
Klein, Naomi 122–3, 125
Kreiss, Daniel 3
Kuenssberg, Laura 53

Labour Party 90
Laffan, Brigid 121
Lancet, The 10, 130, 131
Lazarsfeld, Paul and Robert Merton 56
legal system: attitudes to 66
Leveson Inquiry 31, 38
Lippmann, Walter 3–4, 11, 25, 65–6, 143
Liu, Catherine 86
lived experience 1, 18, 49–50, 65–71, 128, 142
lobbying 14, 29, 103, 144
low-income groups 2, 31, 45, 83, 84–5
Luhmann, Niklas 24
Lynch, Mick 92–4

McVeigh, Rory 37
Madeley, Richard 92
mainstream culture 64–5, 101
mainstream media 20–1, 29–30, 38–9, 101, 120

Index

Manhattan Institute 26
mass culture 74–5
mass media 24, 75, 94
media 5–6, 24, 47
  decoding by 4, 76
  and disconnect from public 2, 30–1, 32, 38, 48
  engagement with 60–5, 69, 144
  as 'fourth estate' 24, 39
  influence of 40, 119, 146
  influence on behaviour of 9
  influences on 29–30, 32
  ownership of 29
  right-wing media 38
  use of imagery by 132
  see also digital media; journalism; mainstream media; mass media; press; social media
media culture 83–4, 121
media literacy 150–1
members of parliament: expenses scandal 31, 54
Merrin, William 30, 34, 63
  and 'me-dia' 63, 101
Merton, Robert 56
Meta (formerly Facebook) 9, 102
Microsoft 102
middle class 78, 88
Mills, Tom 92
misogyny 116–18
Modi, Narendra 36
Molder, Amanda [et al.] 138–9
moral values 54–5
Morley, David 59
  Nationwide Audience 76
Muggleton, Stephen 79
Murdoch, Rupert 38, 105
Musk, Elon 104

National Union of Rail, Maritime and Transport Workers (RMT) 92–3
neoliberalism 10, 16, 26–30, 32, 47–8, 78, 82, 97, 122, 127, 135
news avoidance 37–8, 63
New Scientist 79
New York Times 38, 39, 42
news outlets 15, 62–4, 151
newspapers *see* press
New Zealand massacre (2019) 99

O'Brien, James 93
O'Neill, Saffron 133
O'Reilly, Tim 25
Obama, Barack 34, 137, 138
Occupy movement 82
Office for Budget Responsibility 126
Office for National Statistics 130
Online Safety Bill (2022) 99
opinion leaders 16, 56–8
opinion polls 11–12, 51
  and Covid 130–1

Paris Agreement (2015) 145
platforms 6, 20–1, 59–60, 102
  and deplatforming 104
  legislation on right to moderate 102
polarisation 37
political parties: communication by 8
polls *see* opinion polls
populism 36
'poverty porn' (tv programmes) 87
press 6, 38, 146
  tabloids 82–3, 88
Private Finance Initiative (PFI) 27
private-public partnerships 27, 29
professional-managerial class 85–6, 88
Public Health England 84
public opinion 3, 11–17, 43–4
  management of 3–5, 41, 71–2, 88, 98, 101
  mis-management of 4–5, 23, 40, 93
  triangular relationship of 3–4
public relations agencies 29

Question Time (tv programme) 39, 92

racism 33–4, 78, 88–9
Rashford, Marcus 8–9
Rayner, Angela 87
Reddit 104, 106–7, 108, 110
  research methodology with focus groups 160, 164–5
Reich, Michael and Manuel Castells 86
remote working 81
Republican National Convention (GOP 2016) 33
research methodology 153–7
Resistance Through Rituals: Youth Subcultures in Post-War Britain 79

Reuters Institute Digital News Report (2021) 46–7
Reynolds, Matt 102
Roberts, Sarah 106
Rothwell, Jonathan and Pablo Diego-Rosell 80
Russia
  interference in Western elections by 110
  invasion of Ukraine by 125–6, 127

Sanders, Bernie 9–10, 38, 40, 78, 82
Savage, Mike 87
Sayer, Andrew 55
scientists: attitudes to 45–6
Scottish independence referendum (2014) 38
Simmel, Georg 24
single-issue political movements 28
Skeggs, Beverley and Simon Yuill 85
smoking: proposed bans on 144–5
Snapchat 64
social media 14–16, 20, 51–2, 57–8, 85, 94, 152
  censorship by 104
  content moderators of 6, 96–7, 104–10, 112–16, 152
  distortion of public opinion by 113–14
  intervention by content moderators of 109, 112–13
  and links to government 103–4
  monitoring by political parties of 8–9
  research methodology on content moderation 155–6, 163–5
  self-branding by users of 30
  self-censorship by users of 115–17
  self-identification by users of 63–4
  self-segregation by users of 59–60, 81–2
social movements 82
Soros, George 41–2
Spacey, Kevin 115
state, the
  interventions by 147
  links to social media companies 103–4
Stranger Things (tv programme) 115, 141
Strauss, Claudia 15, 35

strikes: public support for 93
students 31, 64, 80, 81, 88
Sturgeon, Nicola 118
Sun, The 92, 125, 146
Sunak, Rishi 54, 144–5
surveillance capitalism 6, 98–9, 100
Sweden: and Covid 123–4

Telegram (platform) 21, 63
television audiences 76–7
television industry: diversity in 89
television news broadcasting 24
Thatcher, Margaret 7
Thompson, Edward Palmer *The Making of the English Working Class* 75
Thunberg, Greta 21, 138–40
TikTok 21, 64, 138,139, 141, 146
trade unions 76
  media reporting on 92–3
  state attacks on 28
  see also Lynch, Mick
trolling 117
Trump, Donald 7, 17, 21, 36, 38, 44, 145, 148
  and 2016 election 33–4, 35, 39, 100, 146
  and Covid 45–6
  supporters of 78, 79–80
Trump's Media War 42
trust 148–9, 111
  collapse of 31, 43–4
  conceptualisation of 24
truth 42–3, 148–9
Twitter (later X) 8, 20, 36, 64, 84–5, 104, 116

UK Energy Research Centre (UKERC) 160
Ukraine: Russian invasion of 125–6, 127
United Arab Emirates 137–8
United Kingdom Independence Party (UKIP) 34
United States 105
  and Capitol riots (2016) 104
  college housing system 81
  and Covid 10, 45–6
  racism in 33–4, 78
  relations with Israel 104

universities: diversity in 89
user data: control of 99

value systems 53–5
Virdee, Satnam 75, 127
voting patterns 77–80
'vox pop' interviews 14

Wall Street Journal 48
wealth gap 127
'Web 2.0' 25, 102
welfare benefits 66
WhatsApp 9, 21, 84–5
women
    self-censorship by 117–18
    targets of abuse 116

working class 74–5, 86–90, 95
    white working class 75, 34
World Heath Organization 125, 134

Yates, Simon and Eleanor Lockley 84
York, Jillian *Silicon Values* 102–3
YouGov 13, 53, 78
young people 37–8, 51–2, 64, 78–9, 86, 89–90, 151
    and climate activism 82, 137–40, 146
YouTube 21

Zelizer, Barbie 108
Zuboff, Shoshana 6, 98–9, 100, 105
Zuckerbeg, Mark 100, 105

www.ingramcontent.com/pod-product-compliance
Ingram Content Group UK Ltd.
Pitfield, Milton Keynes, MK11 3LW, UK
UKHW020449060325
4871UKWH00046B/87